ACKNOWLEDGMENTS

Many scholars over the last two centuries have labored and contributed to the field of Egyptology. Most of them were not Egyptians. Their dedication, to unlock and to access ancient Egypt to modern eyes and thought, are greatly appreciated by this Egyptian writer.

My thanks to my wife, Faith, for her support and efforts, and to Sean Sexauer for his typing and computer assistance.

Historical Deception

The Untold Story Of
Ancient Egypt

Moustafa Gadalla

Bastet Publishing
Erie, Pa., U.S.A. / Cairo , Egypt

HISTORICAL DECEPTION

THE UNTOLD STORY OF ANCIENT EGYPT

BY MOUSTAFA GADALLA

Published by:

Bastet Publishing
Post Office Box 7234
Erie, PA. 16510, U.S.A.

First printing in the United States of America, 1996
Reprinted simultaneously in Egypt, 1996

Cataloging in Publication Data

Gadalla, Moustafa.
Historical deception : the untold story of ancient Egypt / Moustafa Gadalla.
p. cm.
Includes bibliographical references and index.
ISBN: 0-9652509-5-4 (pbk.)

1. Egypt--Antiquities. 2. Egypt--History--To 640 A.D. 3. Egypt--Civilization. 4. Egypt--Religion. 5. Egypt in the Bible. 6. Pharaohs. 7. Civilization, Western--Egyptian influences. I. Title. II. Title: The untold story of ancient Egypt.

DT60.G34 1996 932'.01
QBI96-20453
LCCN: 96-84763

TABLE OF CONTENTS

Part III. The Pharaohs and Their Buildings

Part V. The Daily Life

Epilogue

Preface

Why I Wrote This Book

When I was growing up in Egypt, I was taught to accept the Koran as the Book from God. Both the Koran and the Bible condemned ancient Egyptian beliefs and Pharaohs. My heart was torn between my history and my religion. A conflict between historical facts and religious convictions is very dangerous indeed. Because of such religious fear and intimidation, most fellow Egyptians do not appreciate their own ancient history, and as a result, they suffer from a self-imposed identity crisis. It is no wonder that the ancient Egyptian history is studied almost exclusively by non-Egyptians.

It was in 1969 that I read and was impressed by the story of the Emperor Without Clothes, by Hans Christian Anderson. It was the story of two con artists, who claimed to tailor very fine clothes which could only be seen by the honest and the competent. The fake tailors were able to persuade the high officials and even the Emperor to buy invisible clothes because who among them would want to admit dishonesty and incompetence. The Emperor led a public parade, so as to display his imaginary new clothes. Fear and intimidation caused the masses to ignore the truth about their Emperor, but it was a child who refused to be intimidated and cried out the truth, *"The Emperor has no clothes!"*

I chose to study the ancient Egyptian history, throughout my life. Most of the available books, however, seemed shallow and repetitive. It was John Anthony West's book, The Travelers' Key to Ancient Egypt, which clicked. West presented different views of ancient Egyptian practices and left it up to the reader to come to his/her own conclusions. The book was more of a fact-finding investigation and research than one man's opinion. Just like any good research, it posed more questions than it provided answers. He defined the causes of the common stereotyping of Ancient Egypt:

"The study of Egypt has in general suffered from a quite

> *unique form of double-barreled prejudice.*
>
> *[1] Religious scholars, whether Christian, Jewish, or Moslem, have been loathe to acknowledge Egypt as an important source of the most profound tenets of their respective creeds,*
>
> *[2] while rationalist scholars are equally loathe to acknowledge the existence of science and philosophy prior to the Greeks."*

This book led me to discover other books by other scholars who also had the courage to present the logical truth.

While most scholars tiptoed or stayed silent about the subject of the Bible and ancient Egypt, Ahmed Osman, in his books, Stranger in the Valley of the Kings, Moses: Pharaoh of Egypt, and The House of the Messiah, like a superb lawyer, presented all the evidence, pro and con, and unedited. He is an excellent researcher, who provided the source(s) for each point. He presented all the sides to each issue in an objective manner. Ahmed Osman is the child in H. C. Anderson's fairy tale, who told the truth, the whole truth, and nothing but the truth.

I have lived in the USA since 1971, with frequent and regular visits to my beloved land, for my body was molded from the Nile's mud, and my soul came from Horus, the God who is above. As I lived and continue to live in the USA, I discover that the more things change, the more they stay the same.

This book is an attempt to shed the truth on some aspects of ancient Egypt, and how it achieved eternity by influencing life everywhere and all times. It is a challenging effort, because of the double-barreled prejudice, as eloquently expressed by John Anthony West above.

The contents of this book are sample representations of various subjects. As Egyptians say, it is like *"a flower from each garden"*.

Some Standards Throughout This Book

We have gotten accustomed to repeating wrongly interpreted words and names, from the ancient Egyptian texts. Throughout this book, you will notice the following:

a- The ancient Egyptian word *'neter'*, and its feminine form *'netert'*, have been wrongly, and possibly intentionally, translated to *'god'* and *'goddess'*, by almost all scholars. There is no equivalent word in meaning to the word *'neter'*, in the English language. Honest translators should use the native word, if they cannot find its equivalent in their language.

The words *'god'* and *'goddess'* leave the impression that ancient Egyptians had a multitude of *'gods'*, which is absolutely untrue. Read more about the subject under 'Egyptian Religion' and 'Neterw, Angels of God'.

b- The names *'Twtankhamen'* and *'Twthomosis'* have been written by many scholars as *'Tutankamen'* and *'Tuthomosis'*. The second letter in their names is the consonant *'w'*, and not the vowel *'u'*. This has a significant impact, as shown in the chapter, 'Twthomosis III, The Warrior King'.

c- Fonting of quotations varies depending on the source of quotation. There are generally three types of fonting, ***one for the Bible and Talmud*, a second for ancient Egyptian records**, and *a third for Egyptologists and other scholars*.

How This Book Should Be Approached/Read

- Many myths have been retold for so long that they are generally accepted as truth. This book is intended to undo many of the false perceptions about the ancient Egyptians which have been absorbed into our minds, throughout our lives from history books, the Bible, movies, television,...etc.

- A reader of the subject matter will find as many views as there are books. With so many varied views, you may wonder which 'expert' or 'scholar' you want to believe, and why their views vary so much. It is the sad truth that most of the controversial issues could be resolved between the 'scholars' if they would take the trouble to consider the evidence presented by the opposition. In The Travelers' Key to Ancient Egypt, John Anthony West sums it up:

> *"Nobody likes being proved wrong, but in the case of the scholar or scientist, a sound theory that contradicts views held and pursued for a lifetime pulls the rug out from under his or her ego, and a familiar paradoxical situation develops. The people professionally engaged in discovering the 'truth' are those psychologically least*

capable of accepting the 'truth' if it happens to contradict what they already believe."

Because you are not an 'expert' in a particular field, it does not mean that you have to accept or be intimidated by other so-called 'experts'. Let logic, reason and unbias guide you toward the truth. As you wade through the various views, keep in mind Sir William Oster's words: *"The greater the ignorance, the greater the dogmatism!"*

- Take into account that our traditional information is based on texts and sources which survived systematic destruction and neglect over thousands of years. Therefore we should assume that their achievements were much greater than what the surviving records tell us.

- In our modern times, we are not supposed to take things at their face value. The same thought applies to ancient Egypt.

For ancient Egyptians, every so-called 'physical' fact of life had a symbolic meaning and at the same time every symbolic act of expression had a 'material' background, both were true and real.

Read this book with an open mind.

Moustafa Gadalla

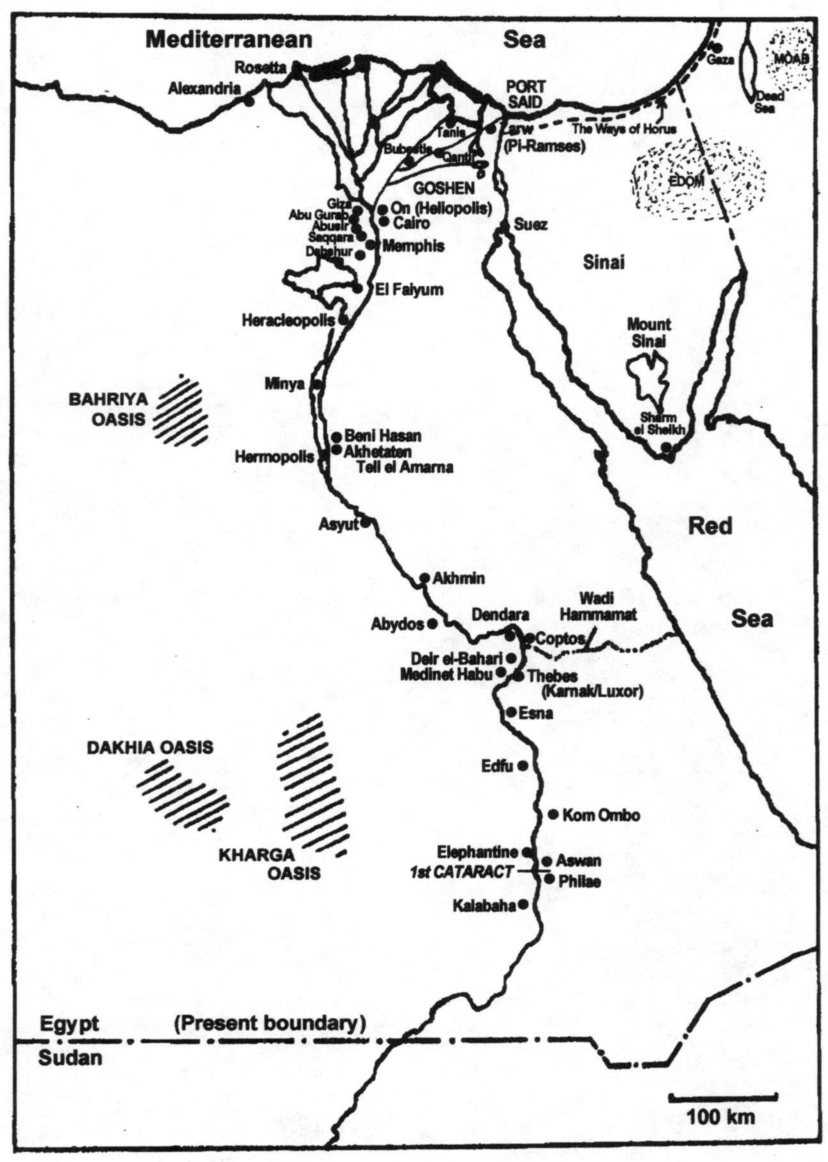

Mediterranean
Sea
Rosetta
Alexandria
PORT SAID
Gaza
MOAB
Dead Sea
Tanis
Larw
(Pi-Ramses)
The Ways of Horus
Bubastis
Qantir
EDOM
GOSHEN
Giza
Abu Gurab
Abusir
Saqqara
Dahshur
On (Heliopolis)
Cairo
Memphis
Suez
Sinai
El Faiyum
Heracleopolis
Mount Sinai
Minya
BAHRIYA OASIS
Sharm el Sheikh
Beni Hasan
Hermopolis
Akhetaten
Tell el Amarna
Asyut
Red
Akhmin
Wadi Hammamat
Sea
Abydos
Dendara
Coptos
Deir el-Bahari
Medinet Habu
Thebes
(Karnak/Luxor)
Esna
DAKHIA OASIS
Edfu
Kom Ombo
KHARGA OASIS
Elephantine
Aswan
1st CATARACT
Philae
Kalabaha
Egypt
(Present boundary)
Sudan
100 km

Part I

General Backgrounds

Chapter 1

The Land and People

The Archaic Period

Some time ago, earlier than 15,000 B.C., Egypt was not a desert country, but a subtropical grassland with scattered trees.

A dramatic change in the weather occurred between 15,000 and 10,000 B.C. which was probably brought about by the end of the last Ice Age. Major floods left their depositss throughout Egypt. As a result, one can easily find seashells in the Egyptian deserts.

The body of the Sphinx, at Giza, was subject to water erosion, at that very early time. (More on this topic is discussed in the chapter 'The Sphinx - Older than History'.)

After the flood waters receded, Egypt had a new look, similar to present conditions. A long and narrow strip of fertile land stretched along the Nile River, to what is now Cairo, and from there, the delta branched out to the sea. The rest of the land was desert. The Nile Valley in Egypt looked and still looks very much like a lotus with its long stem and triangular flower. The Egyptian climate was somewhat more moist in early times, but generally not very different than the present climate.

Origin of People

The origin of the Egyptians was undoubtedly from Asia; as is evidenced by the shape of the skull, which is that of a Caucasian race. The whole valley of the Nile, throughout Ethiopia, was peopled by Asiatic immigrants.

When the Asiatic newcomers arrived in Egypt, the original inhabitants, if any, were of insignificant number. Therefore, the change in the peculiarities of the Asiatic newcomers was proportionally slight as evidenced from the little variation in the shape of the skull from the Caucasian original.

Later, Egypt was conquered by others, but there were no significant changes. This is evidenced from the strong resemblance the Egyptians bear to their ancient predecessors. The conquerors of a country do not give an entirely new character to the original inhabitants. Since invaders, in most cases, make up a smaller portion of the population, the original race will continue to dominate the character of the rising generation. The newcomers will readily adopt existing customs which are suited to the peculiarities of the country they have been formed in. The habits of a small mass of settlers living in contact with them fade away more and more with each successive generation.

The Population

Herodotus affirmed that 20,000 populous cities existed in Egypt during the reign of Amasis. Diodorus calculated that there were 18,000 large villages and towns; and stated that, under Ptolemy Lagus, they amounted to more than 30,000. Josephus estimated the population during the reign of Vespasian, at 7.5 million in the valley of the Nile, in addition to the population of Alexandria, which was about 800,000.

Gloomy or Gay

• Ancient Egyptians have been incorrectly pronounced as a serious and gloomy people.

The interest shown by the Egyptians in their fate after death, and the elaborate preparations made by them for their burial, arose in part from their passionate interest in life itself.

Montaigne said, *"He who would teach men to die, would teach them to live"*.

• The Egyptians were therefore a gay, happy people, with a lively sense of humor. This is demonstrated in their skill in the art of caricature. There are many humorous scenes in the paintings. For example, a group of people at a party have lost their balance as a result of drinking, while others are shown vomiting. There are many scenes of game playing, dancing, juggling, etc. A cat is shown serving a mouse. Numerous stories were told about life in the harem with a great deal of saucy remarks and suggestive innuendoes. Advice is given to husbands who want to cover up their adulterous affairs: Bite into an onion on the way home. The wife will be convinced that no kissing would be going on with breath like that.

- Egyptians took the maximum advantage of any opportunity for a good time. The day-to-day life of the Egyptians was livened by a large number of festivities, most of them religious in nature. One can sense the liveliness, of their participation in these activities, on the walls of the temples. Historians gave their accounts of these gay people. Herodotus described the festive atmosphere of a "religious" occasion, when all participated, men and women, poor and rich. He told us about their singing, dancing, chanting, applauding, eating, drinking, ...etc.

The ancient festivities have survived under new names. Ironically, the festivals of the Moslem Sophists, in the countryside of Egypt, closely resemble the ancient celebrations.

General Characteristics

- In a short phrase, Herodotus told us of them: *"Of all the nations of the world, Egyptians were the healthiest, happiest and most religious".*

- They were also (and still are) fundamentally pragmatic and down to earth.

- The Egyptians were particularly remarkable for their great love of their country, which is also inherited by their successors. They considered themselves to be under the protection of God, the center of the world. They even call Egypt the "world" itself.

- No Egyptian was allowed to live an idle life. Everyone had to have an identification card which was issued from the local magistrate. Such a personal identification card had to include the occupation of the person.

- Gratitude is a distinguished Egyptian trait, ancient and present.

- They were very organized and as a result, government was invented thousands of years ago. In their daily existence, people often communicated with one another by letter. All government business was put in writing. The Egyptians kept economic and labor records on papyri. These written communications followed a particular form, models of which have survived until today.

- Their *code of conduct*, as gathered from survived papyri, was simple and straight-forward. Here is some of the advice:

  - *Don't be proud of your own learning, but take counsel with all, for it is possible to learn from all.*
  - *Treat a wise man with respect, but correct your equal when he maintains a wrong opinion.*
  - *Don't be proud of earthly goods or riches, for they come to you from God without your help.*
  - *Don't repeat slanders.*
  - *Deliver messages accurately.*
  - *Be content.*
  - *Be industrious, an idle man is not honorable.*
  - *Do not enter uninvited into the house of another.*
  - *Do not look around in the house of another. If you see anything, be silent about it, and don't relate it to others.*
  - *Speak not too much, for men are deaf to the man of many words.*
  - *Guard your speech, for "a man's ruin lies in his tongue".*
  - *Do not overeat.*
  - *Don't eat bread while another person is present unless you share the bread with him.*
  - *He who is rich this year, may become a pauper next year.*
  - *Be respectful, and do not sit down while another stands, who is older than you, or who holds a higher office than yours.*

As you proceed through this book, you will learn more about their theology, Pharaohs, buildings, their encounters with the Israelites, as well as other aspects of their daily life.

Chapter 2

Languages, Now and Then

Languages Now

• Our main access to the ancient Egyptian history is restricted by our knowledge of their languages. The Rosetta stone is our only key to read, pronounce and understand hieroglyphs. It consists of fourteen lines of Egyptian hieroglyphics (shown above); thirty-two lines of Egyptian Demotic, and fifty-four lines of ancient Greek. There were no dictionaries, language learning books, etc., to guide us. What if the fourteen lines of hieroglyphs, on the Rosetta stone, were replaced with English words. Would those fourteen lines have been sufficient to read, write, and understand the English language?!

More about the Rosetta stone later.

• The English language is the most frequently used language of communication in the world, although not because it is a *'good'* language. On the contrary, the language is as difficult if not more difficult than the hieroglyphs. English is, however, the language of the powerful during this time in history, and therefore it is the most important international language of communication.

• No one can ever pronounce a word in the English language without phonetics. The sound of the basic five vowels are never consistent. There are additional compound vowels such as *'oo'*, *'ou'*, *'ei'*, *'ie'*, *'au'*, *'eu'*, *'ea'* and *'y'*. There are different sounds to the consonant letters of the alphabet and to add to the confusion, some of them are often silent. The consonant letter *'s'* sounds as an *'s'* in many words, but it could sound as a *'z'* in *'has'*, as an *'sh'* in *'sure'*, or as *'zh'* in *'confusion'*. The combination *'gh'* in the middle of a word is never pronounced. And on and on.

• Furthermore, how do we expect other cultures, in this or a different era to:

√ Know that the word *'spirit'* has several completely unrelated meanings.
√ Know that the word *'race'* has different meanings if it is a car *'race'* or human *'race'*.
√ Know that the word *'bear'* has a meaning as a verb and a totally unrelated different meaning as a noun.
√ Know what a *half-sister* is? The top or the bottom half? Or is it the right or the left half?

• It is therefore a myth to think that ancient languages have evolved and improved to easier systems. Every language has many rules, and the modern languages are as confusing if not more confusing than the ancient languages.

Symbolism and Languages

• A symbol is something that represents something else by association or resemblance. Most, if not all, symbols have private meaning known only to a group of people at a certain time in history. Symbols need only represent something meaningful to a particular intended audience. Symbolism is present in everything we do in life. It is subtle like breathing, we are unaware of it most of the time.

Even for people who speak the same language and live at the same time in history, many symbols will differ from one place to another. A popular sitcom in the USA may be found to be boring in England, and vice versa.

It is therefore unwise to label the ancient writing as confusing or superstitious. Their symbolism then is as unique as our symbolism now.

Interpreting the Egyptian Languages

• The problem of translations for us is compounded by the symbolic language employed by the Egyptians. It is therefore up to modern scholars to penetrate the symbolism and interpret it as well as they are able to. What results from such efforts is, to a very considerable extent, determined by the attitudes of the scholars involved in the work. Those who believe that the ancient Egyptians were basically barbarians will come up with one kind of interpretation, while those, who are convinced that the Egyptians were enlightened people, will make of the same text a totally different interpretation.

• When you read translations of ancient Egyptian texts, do not be irritated by those mysterious gaps in the middle of a particularly interesting passage. It may be, that part of the manuscript is missing, or that, after trying hard to arrive at the meaning, the translator has had to give up rather than commit himself to a doubtful reading.

From the above it is clear that we should be careful when we try to learn about other cultures through their languages, and most importantly we should have an open mind and not to be bound by pre-conceived notions.

The Rosetta Stone

• After Egypt became an Arab colony in the late sixth century B.C. the language of ancient Egypt was declared dead. The inscriptions on the monuments and documents of ancient Egypt were a total mystery until the Frenchman Champollion discovered the key to the ancient language in 1822. The young Frenchman studied many languages, old and new, so as to help him understand the ancient Egyptian languages. His discovery was made possible because of a black granite commemorative tablet which was discovered in 1799, in Rosetta, during Napoleon's expedition in Egypt.

• The tablet was inscribed in 196 B.C. during the reign of Ptolemy V Epiphanes (205-180 B.C.). It measures about 3' 9" x 2' 4 1/2" x 11' on the inscribed side. The texts inscribed upon it consist of fourteen lines of Egyptian hieroglyphics, thirty-two lines of Egyptian Demotic, and fifty-four lines of ancient Greek.

- In spite of the damaged condition of the tablet (no single line on it is complete), enough remained of the Greek to understand the subject matter on the tablet. The Greek text provided the invaluable information, which indicated that the hieroglyphs and Demotic were reproductions of the same text.

- Champollion was able to match the hieroglyphs to the Greek once he realized that the two cartouches on the tablet, contained glyphs that read phonetically Ptolemaios and Cleopatra. These two names became the keys to solving the mystery of the hieroglyphics.

- Champollion followed up his discovery of the two names by intense study. By 1822, he was able to decipher names, inscriptions and short sentences.

- From the few words on the Rosetta stone, Champollion and other Egyptologists began to learn not only that the hieroglyph signs have phonetic equivalent, but also how the language was structured, in rules of grammar and particular syntax.

- It was largely Coptic (the language of the Egyptian Christians) that enabled modern scholars to achieve our present knowledge of the hieroglyphs. Scholars used the sounds of Coptic words (basically ancient Egyptian words written in the Greek alphabet) to estimate the sounds of the unwritten ancient Egyptian vowels. So, to simplify matters scholars agreed to a certain way of pronunciation, but by no means is it the true sound. Therefore, the sounds made by the vowels you see in translated Egyptian texts are an approximation.

The Structure of the Ancient Egyptian Language

- In spite of its complexity, the Egyptian language is one of the best and easiest to be read in the world.

• The ancient Egyptians expressed their ideas in writing, more than seven thousand years ago, by means of a large number of picture signs which are commonly called hieroglyphics. The word *'hieroglyph'* has its origin in the Greek and means *'holy script'* (Hieros = holy, Glyphein = impress).

• Most parts of speech are present in the ancient Egyptian language. There were nouns, pronouns, verbs, adjectives, adverbs, prepositions, and so forth. There were rules regarding word order, as well as endings that determined gender (masculine and feminine, but no neuter) and number (singular, dual, and plural). The Egyptians often used particles to impose certain nuances on a clause or a word. Their main negative particle usually stood at the beginning of a sentence, and that place was also reserved for their mark of interrogation.

• As in all Semitic styles of writings, hieroglyphic writing was limited to the consonants of the words. For them, vowels had a secondary position. In all these languages, the meaning of the word is generally contained in the consonants, while the vowels are added, as a rule, only to indicate the grammatical forms.
So, because vowel sounds were not included in the written language, changes that might have helped to identify, for example, different parts of speech, are not often visible to the modern reader. Therefore, a regular verb may be interpreted in some instances as a noun, a participle, an infinitive, or another part of speech. In such cases, the context or a syntactical feature would provide aid in translation. Sometimes a consonantal ending or a determinative helps in distinguishing among the possibilities.

• The ancient Egyptians

ankh gem nu pa sha

were the first to discover an alphabet of 24 letters. They also introduced, in addition to the 24 letters (phonetic signs), more than 700 further signs called *'syllabic'*.

In addition to these phonetic and syllabic signs, a great number of determinative

man woman water

signs were also used because no short vowels existed in the hieroglyphic system. For example, if we were to translate into English the two signs D and R, these could read either door or deer. To differentiate them, the representation of a door or a deer was added, after the word. The hieroglyphic writing was a highly developed system by which everything, even grammatical forms, could be expressed.

• It is impossible to say when the Egyptians first began to add determinatives to their words, but they must have been the product of pre-dynastic times. However, they occur less frequently in the texts of the earlier than of the later dynasties.

• The specific sentence patterns that the Egyptians followed are unique. Their sentences (or independent clauses) could contain verbs or omit them. A verbal sentence usually had the following pattern: (1) verb, (2) subject, (3) direct object, (4) indirect object, (5) adverb, (6) prepositional phrase.

• The exact pronunciation of a great many words must always remain unknown, to us, but by comparing forms which are common both to Egyptian and Coptic, a tolerably correct idea of the pronunciation may be obtained.

Hieroglyphic Script

• The hieroglyphic form of writing, like many things in ancient Egypt, was the result of profound knowledge of a cosmic nature.

• Inscriptions from the earliest dynasties show that hieroglyphic characters were used as pictures, ideographs and phonetics side by side, which indicates that these distinctions must have been invented in pre-Dynastic times.

• Hieroglyphic characters may be written in columns or in horizontal lines, which are sometimes to be read from left to right and sometimes from right to left. There was no fixed rule about the direction in which the characters should be written, but the heads always turned towards the beginning of the sentence.

The orientation of the characters could be affected by a multitude of factors: such as the type of material written on, the position of the text in relation to figures or other texts, or the nature of the inscription. In certain cases, texts were deliberately written backwards. There are also examples of inscriptions that make sense only when read from bottom to top!

- Hieroglyph writing was in use until about 400 A.D.

Hieratic Script

- Little by little the hieroglyphics lost much of their pictorial character and degenerated into a series of signs which went to form the cursive writing called hieratic. It was used extensively by the priests in copying literary works during all the dynastic periods.

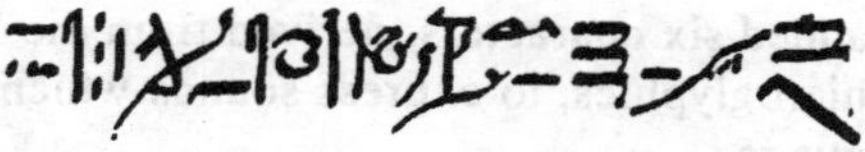

- The difference between hieroglyphic and hieratic writings is similar to our type and handwriting.

- Hieratic is usually written in horizontal lines which are to be read from right to left, but in some papyri dating from the Twelfth Dynasty, the texts are arranged in short columns.

- Hieratic writing was in use from about 5100 B.C. to about 250 A.D.

Demotic Script

- By the middle of the seventh century B.C., the phase of the language called Demotic came into use primarily for texts dealing with non-literary material, but it quickly spread into other areas and can be found in literary and religious texts also. Both the script and the structure of Demotic derive from Late Egyptian. Funerary texts were often written in Demotic, but other religious and monumental inscriptions continued to be expressed in the classical language, and written in hieroglyphs.

- Demotic writing was in use from 100 A.D. to about 640 A.D.

The Coptic Language/Script

ⲟⲩⲧ ϧⲉⲛ ⲑⲏ ⲉⲧⲉ ⲑⲱϥ ⲙ̀ⲃⲁⲕⲓ

- Coptic was developed in the first century A.D. and used until A.D. 640.

- The ancient language continued to be spoken by the Copts, the Egyptian Christians.

- Coptic is written with the letters of the Greek alphabet, to which were added six characters, derived from the Demotic forms of ancient Egyptian hieroglyphics, to express sounds which were peculiar to the Egyptian language.

The Phoenician Language

- Many scholars are of the opinion that the Phoenicians, from whom the Greeks borrowed their alphabet, derived theirs in turn from the ancient Egyptians.

- All the signs of hieroglyphs are pictures of <u>Egyptian</u> animals and birds and therefore it was of an Egyptian <u>origin and not imported or influenced by other cultures.</u>

- The Phoenicians adopted 22 signs of the numerous Egyptian signs to form their own language.

Part II

Theological Beliefs

Chapter 3

The Egyptian Religion

John Anthony West, in his book, The Traveler's Key to Ancient Egypt, wrote:

> *"Her entire civilization was based upon religion and religion entered into every aspect of it, including her system of weights and measures. Every action, no matter how mundane, was in some sense a religious act: plowing, sowing, reaping, brewing, building ships, waging wars, playing games - all were viewed as earthly symbols for divine activities."*

General

- Egyptian religion, though it may possess some strange features, is neither as inconsistent nor inexplicable as was once supposed. It is actually a good deal easier to explain to a total stranger than, say, the Roman Catholicism's creed and rituals.

- The entire Egyptian doctrine was based on the manner in which the spiritual generates and interacts with the physical. The study of physical realities is the essence of physical science; the study of spiritual realities is the essence of sacred science. The latter is expressed in myth, symbolism, harmony, and proportion.

- It is important to realize that for Egyptians, every *'physical'* fact of life had a symbolic meaning. At the same time, every symbolic act of expression had a *'material'* background.

- The ancient Egyptians noticed, at an early stage of their history, an analogy between life and the daily cycles of the sun:

Sunrise	Shining	Sunset	Sunrise	Another cycle
↕	↕	↕	↕	↕
Birth	Life	Death	Resurrection & Rebirth	Another cycle

• Temples were not built for public worship. They were shrines for the neterw, who represented various aspects of the One God. There was no prescribed or organized system of worship as per our *'modern'* understanding. Good deeds, not lip service, were the method of worship.

The Principles of Egyptian Religion

Religion by definition is any system of belief, worship, and conduct, which often involves a code of ethics and philosophy. The main elements of the Egyptian religion, as existed since its earliest history, consisted of:

1- God, the Divine Origin
2- Creation of the Universe
3- Creation of man and his role
4- The Canons
5- The After-life

1- God, The Divine Origin

• Egyptian religion is, in the strictest sense, monotheistic (one God). The Egyptians regarded the universe as a conscious act of creation by the One Great God. The fundamental doctrine was the unity of the Deity. <u>This One God was never represented</u>. It is the functions and attributes of his domain that were represented. Once a reference was made to his functions/attributes, he became a distinguishable agent; reflecting this particular function/attribute, and its influence on the world. His various functions and attributes as the Creator, Wise, Healer, Everlasting, and the like, were called the neterw (pronounced net-er-oo, singular: neter in the masculine form and netert in the feminine form). As such, an Egyptian neter/netert was not a *'god/goddess'* but the personification of a specific function/attribute of the One God.

Furthermore, each of his functions/attributes were sub-divided further into various sub-functions and duties. Egyptians dealt with them separately; and for non-Egyptians they appeared to be distinct gods.

- Most people think that the above is too complicated and too cumbersome. It is not. Most of the present day religions believe in angels whose functions are to perform specific and various functions in the Kingdom of God. Their functions are similar to the functions of the Egyptian neterw.

- These Godly attributes, represented by the neterw, either worked individually or in triads. The third neter resulted from the other two neterw. In every city one of these combinations was the triad of that location. The first members were not always of the first order of neterw, and an attribute of the deity might be combined with some abstract idea to form a result, the third member of the triad.

The trinity of the Christian belief is similar to the Egyptian idea of triads.

- In order to simplify and convey these abstract notions of God's attributes, some fixed representations were invented. As a result, the figures of Ptah, Osiris, Amun, Mut, etc., became the signs of such attributes/functions.

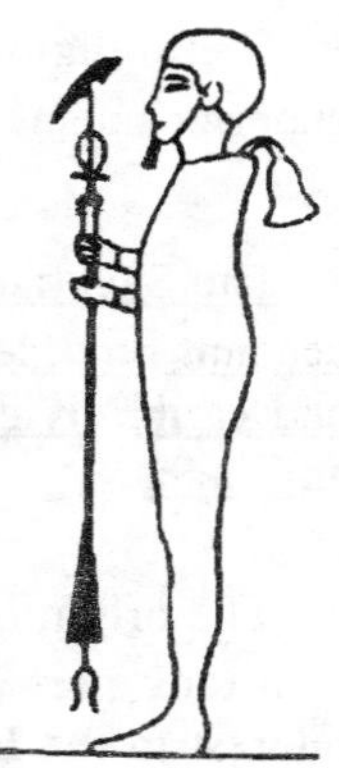

These figures were intended merely to fix the attention or represent some legendary tale or abstract idea, and were not intended to be looked upon as real personages. There was no prescribed form for a neter/netert, and the Egyptians believed that a neter/netert could take on any shape a person desired, since the object of a form was only to fix the attention or represent an abstract idea.

- People everywhere and at all times use a variety of objects in their worship to focus the attention or represent some legendary tale or abstract idea with items such as a cross, an ark, statues, paintings, ...etc.

- **There was no animal worship.** The animal-headed neterw, "monsters" and other "strange creatures" were symbolic expressions of a deep spiritual understanding. This view is also shared by the Hermetic, Masonic orders and the Renaissance Neoplatonists.

• Animals were considered as embodiments of certain specific divine principles and functions. A dog, for example, is the best representation and embodiment of *'loyalty'*. A vulture, which is the fiercest mother on earth, is the embodiment of *'protective motherhood'*.

It was their superior knowledge of animals and appreciation of their role in the universe that made them consider animals for the embodiment of the divine principles and functions.

2- Creation of the Universe

The creation of the universe and of man have complementary and intertwining themes. Each creation will be discussed separately, starting with the creation of the universe.

• Their religious ideas were expressed by myth and symbolism, which are superior means for expressing metaphysical concepts.

• The Egyptian creation myths, regarding the universe, are similar to the account provided in the opening chapter of Genesis: God creates heaven and earth, divides the waters, creates the light, and gives life to animals and man.

• The origin of the world and the nature of the neterw who took part in its creation were subjects of constant interest to the Egyptians. The Egyptian cosmology was divided into four separate but complementary teachings, each with its center of worship. These teachings are to be viewed as detailed versions of the various stages outlined in the opening chapter of Genesis. The four Egyptian separate teachings at the four centers were sponsored by four different neterw. The main neterw of creation are *Re of Heliopolis*, *Ptah of Memphis*, and *Amon of Thebes*. The fourth, namely *Thoth of Hermopolis*, provided an account of creation as a result of the word-analogous to the opening of the Gospel according to St. John.

Thoth

According to the Heliopolitan tradition, the world began as a watery chaos called *Nun*, from which the sun-neter *Atum* came out on a mound. He then begat the deities *Shu* (air) and *Tefnut* (moisture), who in turn produced *Geb* (earth) and *Nut* (sky). *Geb* and *Nut* then produced *Osiris*, *Isis*, *Seth*, and *Nephthys*. The created nine neterw formed the divine ennead. In later texts, the ennead (i.e. company of nine) was often regarded as a single divine entity.

As a result of this system, the commonly accepted conception of the universe is represented as a figure of Shu, standing and supporting with his hands, the out-stretched body of Nut, with Geb lying at his feet.

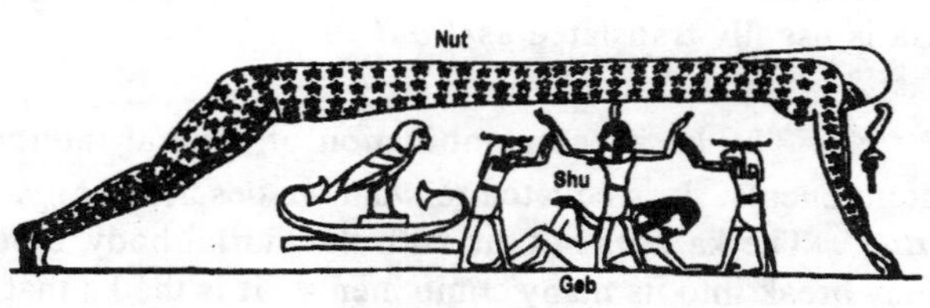

Creation of the Universe

These neterw were the personifications of the characteristic elements of creation where earth emerged out of chaos.

• The Osirion or tomb of Osiris, at Abydos has, at various times, been thought to represent the mythical ancient Egyptian Island of Creation emerging from the primeval waters.
Read more about it under the chapter *'Osiris, the Holy Spirit'*.

3- Creation of Man & His Role

• According to the Egyptian theology, though all creation is spiritual in origin, man is born mortal but contains within himself the seed of the divine. His purpose in this life is to nourish that seed, and his reward, if successful, is eternal life, where he will reunite with his divine origin. Nourishing plants in the soil is analogous to nourishing the spirit on earth by doing good deeds.

Spiritual Elements of Man

According to the Egyptians' theology, the inner man consists of several spiritual elements. The Egyptians dealt with these elements, in the same manner as our modern chemistry deals with the chemical elements and compounds of oxygen, hydrogen, carbon, ...etc. The major spiritual elements are:

- **Ba** The ba is immortal. When the ba departs, the body dies. The ba is represented as a human-headed bird, which is the opposite of the normal depiction of neterw as human bodies with animal heads. The ba may be shown as a stork, or as a falcon. The stork is known for its migrating and homing instinct. Ba is usually translated as *'soul'*.

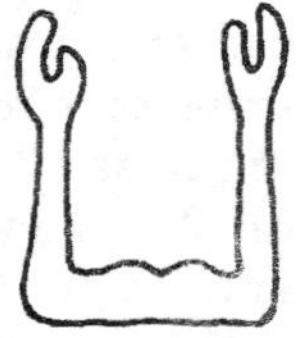

- **Ka** The ka is the combination of several intertwined components. It is equated to what we describe as *'personality'*. The ka does not die with the mortal body, though it may break into its many components. It is the ka that reincarnates, by seeking another physical vehicle in order to continue the work of self-perfection.

  - The ka is portrayed as a pair of arms outstretched towards heaven.
  - Immortality is achieved when a man perfects his deeds and, as a result, is able to unite his ka to his ba, his ultimate goal.

- **Khaibit** The khaibit seems to correspond with our notion of the ghost.

- **Khu** Khu is a higher spiritual element. It is a shining, and luminous component. Khus are also heavenly beings living with the neterw. Each khu may then be equivalent to the guardian angel.

- **Ab** Ab was the heart, which corresponded to conscience.

- **Sekhem** Sekhem was the personification of the inner strength of a man.

4- The Canons

A canon by definition is a collection of books officially accepted by a religious body as genuine. As such, the Bible is the Christian canon. The Bible was formulated as a result of the church selection, from many previous writings some time ago. Their final choice resulted in our common Bible which contains thirty-nine (39) different books in the Old Testament and twenty-seven (27) writings in the New Testament.

Ancient Egyptians also had several sacred writings and teachings, but they were never incorporated into a singular canon. Egyptians had never discarded any view no matter what. Some of the writings were contradictory, but that did not matter, because it was not anybody's business to select and choose for the people. Each view was like a key to the truth and the various views were like keys resembling the pattern of the lock. As such, they decided to respect and retain all views.

There was never a single religious authority who had the power or the desire to choose some writings and incorporate them into one canon, as the case with the Bible, except during Akhenaton's reign which was an aberration.

It is a fact that no two people in any religion can interpret all the aspects of their religion in the same way. Each interpretation is as different as each person's fingerprint. The ancient Egyptians recognized this fact, and as such, religion to them was a truly personal matter. This is actually the TRUE FREEDOM OF RELIGION.

- The essence of the Egyptian religion is based on metaphysical beliefs. The whole universe is an intentional creation. Man was created to accomplish a specific role within the grand cosmic scheme. Man, who is born of flesh, has the potential to become spirit. The Egyptian canons described in detail the stages of the transformation process from man's earthly carnal to the pure spiritual.

- To achieve the ultimate goal of reuniting with the divine origin, one must conduct oneself throughout life on earth in a manner consistent with the forty-two ethical commandments, which are expressed in the terms of the Negative Confession in Chapter CXXV of the Book of the Coming Forth by Day (commonly known as the Book of the Dead). More about it later in the chapter under 'The After-Life'.

Additionally, the expected conduct and the ideas of responsibility and retribution were expressed in several literary compositions which are usually termed as wisdom texts. Among them are the thirty chapters of The Teaching of Amenemope, which contain collections of poetic phrases of moral content and advice. These teachings found their way into the Old Testament's Book of Proverbs. Read more about it under the chapters 'Amenhotep III' and 'Literature'.

- Most funerary and religious writings derive from the earlier Unas

Funerary (pyramid) texts. Each book explores the same basic theme, of life/death/rebirth, from a different angle. These compositions are known as: The Book of the Coming Forth by Day (commonly known as The Book of the Dead), The Book of What Is In the Duat (or Underworld), The Book of the Gates, The Book of Caverns, The Litany of Re, The Book of Aker, The Book of Day and The Book of Night.

Each of these texts emphasizes specific aspects of the Egyptian doctrine of life/death/rebirth. The Book of the Caverns has a psychological focus; and its theme of punishment and reward is paramount. The Book of the Gates has a spiritual focus. The Book of What Is In the Duat has a magical/alchemical focus. The Book of Day and The Book of Night emphasize the cosmological and the astronomical aspects.

- The Book of the Coming Forth by Day, wrongly translated and commonly known as The Egyptian Book of the Dead, consists of over a hundred chapters of varying lengths, which were mostly derived from the Unas funerary texts. This book is to be found, in its complete form, only on papyrus scrolls that were wrapped in the mummy swathings of the deceased and buried with him.

- Other related literary writings include legendary tales (such as the Isis/Osiris/Horus Legend), wisdom and meditation literature and hymns to the neterw. Read more about it under the chapters 'Osiris' and 'Literature'.

5- The After-life

- In a book of instructions, an Egyptian King advised his son, the prince, to attain the highest qualities, because upon his death he will see his whole lifetime in a single instant and his performance on earth will be reviewed and evaluated, by the judges. In recent years, numerous books addressed the near-death experiences of many people. In this phenomenon, it is reported that seeing the person's whole life span in an instant, is a recurrent theme for all persons with near-death experiences. Death is not the end, but rather it is a transitional state. Such an experience matches exactly the Egyptians' belief of the transformation process, which starts with the Day of Judgment where the life of the person is evaluated.

- The soul of the deceased is led to the hall of Judgment of the Double-Ma-at. She is "double" because the scale balances only when there is an

The Forty-two Judges

equality of opposing forces. Ma-at's symbol is the ostrich feather, representing judgment or truth. Her feather is customarily mounted on the scales.
Read more about Ma-at under the chapter 'Justice System'.

- The heart, as a metaphor for conscience, is weighed against the feather of truth to determine the fate of the deceased.

- Anubis, as *"opener of the way"*, guides the soul to the scales and weighs his heart.

- The seated Osiris presides in the hall of Justice. The jury consists of forty-two judges [equated to the forty-two nomes (governate) of ancient Egypt]. Each judge has a specific jurisdiction over a specific sin or fault.

The spirit of the deceased denies committing each sin/fault before its assigned judge, by reciting the forty-two negative confessions (analogous to the famed **Ten Commandments**). These negative confessions come from The Book of the Coming Forth by Day (commonly known as The Book of the Dead). Here is a translation of some of them. Some of them may seem repetitive, but this was probably caused by not being able to translate the exact intent of the original language.

I have not done iniquity
I have not robbed with violence
I have not done violence
I have not committed theft
I have not slain man or woman
I have not acted deceitfully
I have not stolen the things which belong unto God
I have not uttered falsehood
I have not uttered evil words

I have attacked no man
I have not defiled the wife of a man
I have not committed any sin against purity
I have not struck fear into anyone
I have not been a man of anger
I have not made myself deaf to the words of right and truth
I have not stirred up strife
I have abused no man
I have not judged hastily
I have not fouled water
I have not behaved with insolence
I have not sought for distinctions

• The ibis-headed Thoth, scribe of the neterw, records the verdict as Anubis weighs the heart against the feather of truth.

The outcome of the judgment will determine the fate of the person.

• Awaiting the verdict, is Ammit, Eater of the Dead. This protean cross-breed is most commonly depicted as part crocodile, part hippopotamus and part lion. Ammit represents the world of pure materialism. The person that lived simply as matter, died as matter. This resulted in Ammit eating it. There was no exact Egyptian equivalent to the idea of *Hell* as a place of eternal punishment.

• The imperfect soul will be reborn again in a new physical vehicle (body) in order to provide the soul an opportunity for further development on earth. This cycle continues until the soul is perfected by fulfilling the forty-two Commandments, during his life on earth.

• The Egyptians seemed to hinder the reincarnation process by the mummification process. By maintaining the conditions of the physical vehicle, the soul was able to continue its existence in the unknown world of the Duat. As such, the soul was eventually capable of working towards its own resurrection, and thence, excluding the necessity of another physical reincarnation.

• The perfected soul will go through the process of transformation, and as the Egyptian writing describes it, ***"becomes a star and joins the company of Re, and sails with him across the sky in his boat of millions of years"***.

Chapter 4

Neterw
The Angels of God

General

• In the last chapter we talked about the neterw as the personifications of universal principles, functions and attributes of the one great and supreme God. The neterw who were called *'gods'* by some, were endorsed and incorporated into Christianity under a new name, *'angels'*.

The Song of Moses in Deuteronomy (32:43), as found in a cave at Qumran, near the Dead Sea, mentions the word *'gods'* in the plural: ***"Rejoice, O heavens, with him; and do obeisance to him, ye gods."*** When the passage is quoted in the New Testament (Hebrews, 1:6), the word *'gods'* is substituted with *'angels of God'*.

• The term *'angels'*, according to the Metaphysical Bible Dictionary, refers to those who *"guard and guide and direct the natural forces of mind and body, which have in them the future of the whole man."*

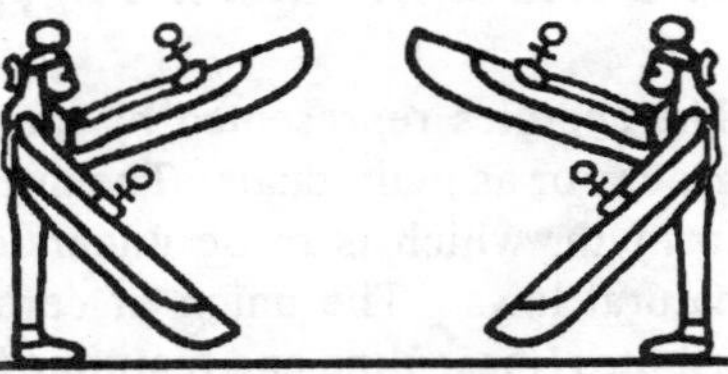

• Angels, or neterw, are living energies. In the wisdom teaching of various cultures, these Causal Powers are called by many names including Agents, Angels, Conscious Thought Forms, Creative Energies, Devas, Fathers, Fountains, Gates, Governors, Hands of God, Lords, and Shining Ones.

• Edwin C. Steinbrecher, an astrologer, metaphysician, and author of The Inner Guide Meditation, says that angels are *"living energies that contain ideas and information, specific patterns of instinctual behavior and thought. They are the energies which somehow attach themselves, without our conscious awareness, to everything we meet in the world we call real. [They] are the life energies that pour out of each of us unceasingly night and day . . . influencing everyone in our lives and causing us to be influenced in return."*

• Just like the Egyptian's neterw, each angel has been given a name and specific function(s).

• And just as each neter of Egypt did not always take the same form and shape, so is the case for each angel. As your projection on them changes, so will their appearance. Sometimes, they are so blocked by the ego that you can only see their dim, hazy outlines. Many have seen angels change from a shining light to a form resembling a human being, then into a symbol (cube, triangle, etc.), and back to human features.

• Upon careful examination, the concept of the Egyptian neterw was accepted by ancient and modern societies, who merely chose new names to express Egyptian ideas.

The Triads of Ancient Egypt

The energies represented by the various neterw may function together in groups or as individuals. The interaction between the neterw are expressed in myth, which is to be understood as the dramatization of cosmic and natural laws. The union of certain pairs of complementary energies/attributes (masculine and feminine forms) resulted in a third energy/attribute.

Some of the major Egyptian triads are:

Amon - Mut - Khonsu
***Osiris* - Isis - Horus**
Ptah - Sekhmet - Nefertum

This is not an odd concept and it was copied in the trinity of the Christian faith.

The following chapters will present a few of the neterw of Egypt.

Chapter 5

Re

You Light Up My Life

General

• Re means either sun or light. The Egyptians were called *'cattle of Re'*, a parallel to the Christian *'sheep'*.

• Re personifies the primeval, cosmic, creative force. He is the solar principle responsible for all creation. All the Egyptian neterw,who took part in the creation process, are aspects of Re. There are seventy-five forms or aspects of Re. The texts attribute to them the same qualities of Re, such as: self-created, all-powerful, supreme, One.

Re is often incorporated into the names of other neterw such as in Amen-Re of Thebes, Re-Atum, etc.

• The chief shrine of Re was located at *'On'*, now a suberb of eastern Cairo. The Greeks called it Heliopolis (city of the sun). At Heliopolis Re was worshipped in his form of Atum, or Re-Atum, designating the evening sun, which is the sun at the end of the creative process.

The Eye of Re (Utchat)

• The most distinctive Egyptian symbol is the eye, which plays many complex and subtle roles. The right eye is called the Eye of Re, symbolizing the sun. The left is called the Eye of Thoth, symbolizing the moon. Both eyes together are the Two Eyes of Horus the Elder. The physical eye is to man what the sun is to Re. The eye is the part of the body able to perceive the light, and is therefore a symbol for the spiritual ability. This is equated to the Gospels, *"those with eyes to see"*.

The Litany of Re

The composition of this Litany can be found at the entrance to some of the ancient tombs. In it, the king addresses the seventy-five forms of Re by their names.

Each recited name represents a specific aspect/attribute of Re. These names are not just labels. In ancient Egypt, a name was like a short resume or synopsis of the qualities of the neter/person/principle/animal. Here is an excerpt from the Litany, translated by the Egyptologist Piankoff:

> "Homage to thee, Re, supreme power, Lord of the Caverns, with hidden forms, he who goes to rest into the mysteries when he transforms (himself) into Deba of The One Who Joined Together! Homage to thee, Re, supreme power, this Becoming One who folds his wings, he who goes to rest in the Netherworld, and transforms (himself) into He Who Comes Out of His Own Members! Homage to thee, Re, supreme power, Exalted Earth, who gives birth to his neterw, he who protects what is in him, He who transforms (himself) into He at the Head of His Cavern!"

Our Modern Experience With Re

There are hundreds of people who, in their near-death experiences, met God and came back to tell us about it. The description of their experiences are all very similar, for after separating from their bodies, they went through a dark tunnel and were met at its end with glorious Light (Re). Here is the personal description of one of them, when he saw the Light:

> *"As I reached the source of the Light, I could see in. I cannot begin to describe in human terms the feelings I had over what I saw. It was a giant infinite world of calm, and love, and energy, and beauty. It was as though human life was unimportant compared to this. And yet it urged the importance of life at the same time it solicited death as a means to a different and better life. It was all being, all beauty, all meaning for all existence. <u>It was all the energy of the Universe forever in one place.</u>"*

Re, You Light up our Lives.

Chapter 6

Amen

The Hidden One

General

• His name has been repeated by many, millions of times, for thousands of years, in ancient Egypt and throughout the rest of the world. His name is still being repeated nowadays, by people of all faiths, without even realizing it. For the faithful of Judaism, Christianity and Islam end their prayers by saying *"Amen"*.

• Since there are no written short vowels in the ancient Egyptian language, his name may be written and pronounced as Amen, Amon, or Amun. All three are one and the same. Amen's name means *'Hidden'*. For he is everywhere, but you cannot see him.

• Amen is the delicate breath of the living. He provides the spirit which animates the living earth and all creatures.

• **The Leyden Papyrus**, (now in the Leyden Museum in Holland), which is dated to ca. 300 B.C., describes Amen in the section called **Stanza 600** as follows:

> Sia (Knowledge) is his heart,
> Hu (The Word) is his lips,
> His ka is everything that exists by virtue of his tongue.
> His ba (soul) is Shu, the air, his heart is Tefnut, the fire,
> He is Horus of the double horizon who is in the sky.
> His right Eye is the day, his left is the night.
> He is everybody's guide in all directions.
> His body is Nun ...
> >> He gives birth to everything that is and causes all that exists to live.

- Another section, in the **Leyden Papyrus**, is called **Stanza 60**, which states that Amen governs the earth and that his power extends to the edge of the universe. He has no definition, but he is the reason why the universe exists.

- When Amen is combined with Re, they form Amen-Re. He is hawk-headed and wears the solar disk surrounded by the cobra.

When Amen combines with Min, as Min-Amen, he is shown with an erect phallus, with the flail cocked over his upraised arm. Min-Amen symbolizes the creative urge manifested as the universal sexuality. In the Greek mythology, Min-Amen and his flail is equated to Zeus and his thunderbolt.

The Age of Aries

- During the Old Kingdom, Montu, symboled as the bull, was worshipped at Thebes because it was the Age of Taurus. Around 2000 B.C., Taurus gave way to the Age of Aries, whose symbol is the ram. Ancient Egyptians were responsive to cosmic changes, and therefore as the zodiac signs changed, Amen rose to eminence with his ram-headed symbol.

Some people invented, without any evidence whatsoever, a priestly power struggle at around 2000 B.C. and the result was the victory of Amen's priests. There is absolutely no evidence of priestly warfare during the history of ancient Egypt except with the 'apparent' exception of Akhenaton. His story will be told in later chapters.

- Additional confirmation of the ram-headed Amen and its symbolism of the Age of Aries, is found in the Triple Shrine of Amen/Mut/Khonsu, at the Karnak Temple. On the left wall he is pictured as a ram, traveling across the heavens on his barge. This representation, together with the references in many texts, to Amen as **"a ram in the sky"**, support the astronomical/astrological interpretation.

- The great temples of Karnak and Luxor, in Thebes, with their acres of carved reliefs, are all dedicated to Amen.

Mut, The Holy Mother

Mut is the companion of Amen at Thebes. The name '**Mut**' is connected linguistically with the many similar-sounding words for *'mother'*. She is another personification of the one Great God whose other forms include Hathor, Sekhmet, Isis, and Nut.

Mut is usually depicted as a woman wearing a vulture headdress, sometimes she is shown with the body of the vulture so artfully forming her own head that it passes for a headdress. The choice of the vulture for this particular feminine role is possibly because:

1- The vulture is supposed to be particularly zealous in caring for its young.

2- Legends were told that the vulture had no male species. The female vulture impregnated herself by exposing herself to the winds (i.e. gods). The vulture is therefore a symbol of virgin birth.

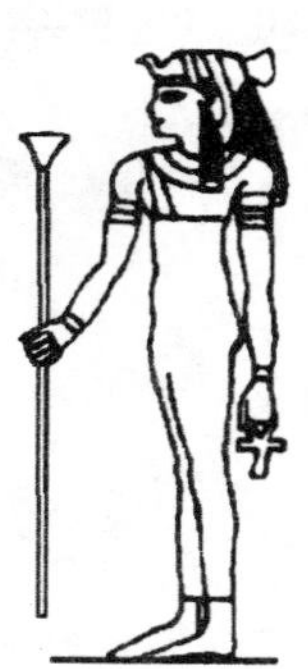

Sometimes Mut, this zealous mother, is shown with feathered, outstretched winged arms, which matches our common expression: (See page 44)

Festivals

Among the many festivals held at Thebes are the Apet Feast and the Feast of the Valley. The Apet Feast celebrated the two kilometer journey of Amen from his sanctuary at Karnak Temple to the temple of Luxor and back again. The statue of Amen traveled partly on land, carried in a model boat on the shoulders of the priests, and partly in a real boat on the river, while crowds of spectators gathered on the banks. Scenes from an Apet Feast, celebrated during the reign of Twtankhamen, decorate the walls of a colonnade in the Luxor temple, and give a lively impression of the occasion.

Queen Hatshepsut also commemorated this event in the 'Red Chapel', at the temple of Amen at Karnak.

It is ironic that the present-day Moslems, of Luxor, perform the same ancient festivities, starting at the Abu-el-Haggay mosque located at Luxor Temple.

The boat of **The Hidden One** (invisible to all) still tours Thebes, as it always did.

This is another confirmation that the more things change, the more they stay the same.

Chapter 7

Khnum

The Molder

- Khnum, in Egyptian, means "**molder**". Khnum is usually shown as a ram-headed deity working at his potter's wheel, fashioning men and all living creatures out of clay. This Egyptian concept is reminiscent of the biblical account of God fashioning Adam from clay.

- The ram head of Khnum is a representation of the zodiac sign of Aries. The onset of the Arian Age occured around 2000 B.C.
Read more about the Arian Age under the chapter "*Amen, The Hidden One*".

- Khnum is the Divine Craftsman performing the plans of Ptah, the Divine Architect.

- Esna was dedicated to Khnum, where his Temple is located.

- The mighty pharaohs of Egypt dwelt in mud-brick palaces. The impermanent body, formed of clay by Khnum, called for an equally impermanent abode, for everybody including the mighty pharaohs. The palaces of the kings have returned to the earth just as the body of man, at the end of life, returns to earth.

Chapter 8

Osiris

The Holy Spirit

Osiris The Divine

- Osiris has the most interesting features of the Egyptian theology. He came to earth for the benefit of mankind, with the title of **"manifester of good and truth"**. His death by the evil one was followed by his burial and resurrection, and then becoming the judge of the dead. He had been revered throughout Egypt, long before its recorded history.

- Osiris is a Greek interpretation of the Egyptian **Ausar**, the meaning of which is unclear. Osiris was equivalent to Pluto and with Dionysos in the Greek mythology.

- Osiris manifests the divine in mortal form. He represents the physical creation and its cycles of death and renewal. He is the great neter of a future state.

Despite his mythical death and dismemberment, Osiris carried the living seed of eternity (Horus) within him. As such, Osiris represents the mortal man carrying within himself the capacity and power of spiritual salvation. All dead persons were equated to Osiris.

- As a lunar deity, Osiris was related to the number seven, and its multiples, which relate to physical lunar cycles.

Osiris was also a solar deity, because it was Re (the sun) who, after descending beneath the earth, illuminates the moon. Such an astronomical fact was recognized by the Egyptians since its earliest history.

- Osiris was to every Egyptian the great judge of the dead, and as such he presided over the procedures of the Day of Judgment. Read more about it under the chapter 'The Egyptian Religion'.

• Osiris is usually represented as a mummified, bearded human body wearing the white crown of the north. He carries **1-** the shepherd's crook, being the shepherd of mankind, **2-** the flail symbolizing the ability to separate wheat from chaff, and **3-** the scepter of supremacy.

He is often associated with the djed pillar, symbol of the backbone or support of creation.

Since Osiris has numerous roles, he could be shown wearing a variety of headdresses and costumes and is shown in a wide variety of ceremonial poses and gestures.

The Osiris Legend (Isis/Osiris/Horus)

• It is an incredible fact that there is not a single complete Egyptian record of the Osiris legend, probably because it was so common to all Egyptians.

Our knowledge of this legend comes from several versions which were written by the Greek and Roman writers of classical antiquity. These writers relied on second or third-hand information, and possibly added their own personal flavors to appeal to their own readers at home. It is therefore impossible to determine which portions of the story are true and which are fabrications.

The common version of the story of Osiris, was that Osiris married Isis, and Set married Nephthys. Osiris became King of Egypt, at which time the Egyptians were a totally uncivilized people.

Osiris taught Egyptians the arts of agriculture and irrigation. He showed them how to build houses and gave them laws and education and even the skill of writing, using the hieroglyphic script which was invented by Thoth.

Isis supported her husband in every way. Both Osiris and Isis were adored by their subjects. But their evil brother Set hated Osiris and was jealous of his popularity. Set managed to pick a fight with Osiris, murdered him, and cut his body into fourteen pieces, which he scattered all over Egypt. Osiris's faithful wife Isis found every part of her husband's body, except the phallus, which had been swallowed by a fish. She assembled his body, making the first Egyptian mummy.

At the time of his death, Osiris and Isis had no children, but by mystical means, Osiris was resurrected for one night and slept with Isis. As a result, Isis conceived a son. He was called Horus and was raised secretly in the marshes of the Delta to protect him from his evil uncle.

After Osiris' death, Set seized the throne of Egypt and ruled as a tyrant.

As soon as Horus had grown to manhood, he challenged his evil uncle, Set, for the right to the throne. After many battles and challenges, Horus eventually overcame Set, avenged the murder of his father, and regained the throne of Egypt. Horus became a role model, the type of perfect Pharaoh. Subsequently, all other rulers used the name Horus as one of their official titles, throughout the Egyptian history.

The Pharaohs identified themselves with Horus as a living king and with the soul of Osiris as a dead king.

During the battle, Set snatched away the eye of Horus, and threw it into the celestial ocean. Thoth recovered the eye which was later called the **Udjat-Eye**. It was identified with the moon and became a very popular symbol of protection. It was this Eye which Horus used to revive his sleeping father. Osiris was resurrected as a soul to rule the Netherworld. Osiris became for the Egyptians the spirit of the past, the neter of the Dead and a hope for resurrection and after-life.

Another version of the story indicates that as soon as she heard of this tragedy, Isis set out to search for the fragments of her husband's body, embalmed them with the help of the neter Anubis, and buried them wherever they were found. According to this version of the story, the head of Osiris was buried at Abydos. The heart was buried on the island of Philae, near Aswan. The phallus was thrown into the Nile and was swallowed by a fish. For this reason the eating of fish was forbidden to the priests.

Another tradition says that Anubis and Isis assembled the embalmed fragments and buried them all at Abydos.

In the oldest versions of the story, which are found in the Unas Funerary (Pyramid) Texts, and date from the Fifth Dynasty, it is simply stated that Set murdered Osiris in Abydos and left his body lying on the bank of the canal. It was later found by Isis and Nephthtys, embalmed by Anubis, and buried at Abydos.

Abydos, The Pilgrimage Place

• Abydos (Abtu in Egyptian) was the major place for the worship of Osiris. Both Abydos and Saqqara were the major funerary sites from the earliest dynasties on record, and perhaps even earlier.

• The funerary remains at Abydos have provided scholars with much of what is known of those remote pre-Dynastic times.

• As a consequence of the murder and dismemberment of Osiris, various Egyptian cities claimed the honor of being the burial place of parts of his body. Abydos claimed to be the burial place of the head of Osiris and as such became the well-known place of pilgrimage in honor of Osiris.

• In addition to the extensive funerary remains at Abydos, there is the Temple of Osiris, which was built by King Seti I (1306-1290 B.C.) and completed by his son Ramses II. The Temple was built next to the mysterious and massive Oseirion (supposedly the tomb of Osiris himself).

Below is an overview of the Oseirion and the Temple of Osiris.

The Oseirion (Tomb of Osiris!)

• Nothing is clearly known about the function of this structure.

• The Oseirion building is very similar to the Valley Temple of Chephren south of the Sphinx at Giza. Both have the same massive simplicity, the mighty square granite pillars and the total absence of inscriptions and carvings.

• The Oseirion structure, or Tomb of Osiris, is located much below the foundation of Seti's Temple of Osiris and is partially submerged underneath the ground water table. The Oseirion's foundations are cut many feet below the present level of the water table, which has risen some twenty feet since New Kingdom times.

• The entire Oseirion is built into an artificial mound. This fact together with the watery foundations may possibly suggest that the building is more of a representation of the creation myths (the primeval mound emerging from the waters) rather than as the tomb of Osiris.

• Because Seti I inscribed his name on some parts of the building, some scholars were quick to attribute the building of the Oseirion to Seti I. The Oseirion is extremely different from any other building in the New Kingdom. There is a huge difference between its massive, bare, and brutal simplicity as compared to the elegant and sophisticated main temple with its acres of exquisite carvings. The Oseirion constitutes extreme contrast in architecture, style and design to Seti's temple.

• The tremendous difference in elevation between the Oseirion and Seti's Temple, as well as the dramatic difference in style between the two, suggested to many scholars that the Oseirion is a much older building.

• The evidence at the Oseirion and other funerary remains at Abydos is consistent with the evidence at Giza and elsewhere, regarding the greater antiquity of the Egyptian civilization.

Refer to the chapters 'The First Pharaoh of Egypt' and 'Sphinx, Older Than History'.

Temple of Osiris

• The Seti Temple differs from all other Egyptian religious shrines in two important aspects:

1. The temple is L-shaped.
2. Instead of being dedicated to just one principal neter (and that neter's consort and son), it has seven sanctuaries. They are for the three creator neterw

of Memphis *(Ptah)*, Heliopolis *(Re-Horachty)*, Thebes *(Amon)* as well as the Osirian triad *(Osiris, Isis and Horus)* and the seventh sanctuary for *Seti I*.

- The Temple has forty-two steps, representing the forty-two assessors of the Duat, where Osiris presides in the final judgment day.

- The Osiris chapel at Abydos has an overview of the various forms and functions of Osiris as symbolized by different headdresses, emblems and gestures.

- The walls of this Temple do not show any part of the Osiris Legend that reached us through early Greek and Roman historians, or even a different Osiris Legend.

- The quality of the relief work at the temple is superb.

Re & Osiris (Cycle of Life & Death)

Re and Osiris are the two neterw who personify the cycle of life and death. Re, who is the cosmic principle of energy, moves toward death, and Osiris, the dead neter, represents the process of rebirth. The dead person in death is Osiris. But he will come to life again, and be identified with Re. The creation is continuous: it is a flow of life progressing towards death. But out of death a new Re is to be born, sprouting new life.

Chapter 9

Isis

The Virgin Mother

The Virgin Mother

• Many elements of the Isis myth and the story of the Virgin Mary are very similar, for both were able to conceive without the male impregnation. Horus was conceived and born after the death of Isis's husband, and as such she was revered as the Virgin Mother.

• Isis is the power responsible for the creation of all living creatures.

• Isis is the Greek translation of the Egyptian '**Aset**'. Aset, in Egyptian, means *'throne'*.

• She is portrayed wearing the vulture headdress, the crescent and disk, with a pair of horns surrounding the disk. Sometimes she is shown in purely human form.

• Isis was related to the star Sirius, whose annual appearance ushered in the Nile's inundation and the Egyptian New Year. (Read more about it under the chapter 'Egyptian Calendar'.)

• Since Isis had many names and forms, she was equated in the Greek mythology with Persephone, Ceres and Athene.

• Her Temple is located on Philae. This Temple was begun under the Ptolemies and finished under the Romans. It was built on a site which was used previously, and its Egyptian name, meaning "**Island of the Time of Re**", suggests an extremely remote antiquity.

At Philae, Isis was revered in a fashion similar to the reverence accorded to Mary, mother of Jesus, at a later time in history.

Divine Love

• Many are frightened by the relationship of Isis and Osiris as a married couple and also as brother and sister.
Within a larger cosmology, this relationship can be seen as an instinctive form of devotion and love. It was, and still is, common in Egypt, for a husband/wife to call each other sister/brother as a sign of love and devotion, and not because they are biologically brother and sister. (Also see the chapter, '*Love, Egyptian Style*'.)

• Any woman who truly loves her husband is considered to be like Isis, and has the power of awakening him into greater life, as Horus. Father S.J. Vann likened the awakening of Christ by Mary Magdalene, as he emerged from his tomb, to Isis awakening Osiris from the dead.
The comparison between the two cases is illuminated in the "**Lament for Osiris**" in which Isis and her sister Nephthys bewailed their brother Osiris' death and pleaded with him to come back to life. The text for this duet was derived from a much older lamentation.

• "**Lament for Osiris**" was described by Andrew Lang to *"have the power to stir our deepest emotions"*:

Sing we Osiris dead,
Lament the fallen head:
The light has left the world, the world is gray.
Athwart the starry skies
The web of darkness flies,
And Isis weeps Osiris passed away.
Your tears, ye stars, ye fires, ye rivers shed,
Weep, children of the Nile, weep for your lord is dead!

Softly we tread, our measured footsteps falling
Within the sanctuary sevenfold;
Soft on the dead that liveth are we calling:
'Return, Osiris, from thy Kingdom cold!
Return to them that worship thee of old.

Within the court divine
The sevenfold sacred shrine
We pass, while echoes of the temple walls
Repeat the long lament
The sound of sorrow sent
Far up within the imperishable halls,
Where, each in other's arms, the sisters weep,
Isis and Nephthys o'er his unawakening sleep.

Softly we tread, our measured footsteps falling
Within the sanctuary sevenfold;
Soft on the dead that liveth are we calling:
'Return, Osiris, from thy kingdom cold!
Return to them that worship thee of old.'

O dweller in the west,
Lover and lordliest,
Thy love, thy sister Isis, calls thee home!
Come from thy chamber dun,
Thou master of the sun,
Thy Shadowy chamber far below the foam!
With weary wings and spent
Through all the firmament,
Through all the horror-haunted ways of hell,
I seek thee near and far,
From star to wandering star,
Free with the dead that in Amenti dwell.
I search the height, the deep, the lands, the skies,
Rise from the dead and live, our lord Osiris, rise!

Chapter 10

Horus

The Highest

The Highest (Number 10)

• His name means '*he who is above*'. He was the outcome of the heavenly marriage between Isis and the holy ghost of Osiris. The reverence of Osiris/Isis/Horus was the focal point of the Egyptian theology.

• Horus is the Greek rendering of the Egyptian '**Heru**'.

• Horus is the personification of the goal of all initiated teachings. As the son of Isis and Osiris, he is the tenth neter of Heliopolis. Ten is the highest number of the original unity. At ten, Horus is a new One; he is the return to the source.

In the Osiris Legendary, he is the fifth member (after Osiris, Set, Isis and Nephthys).

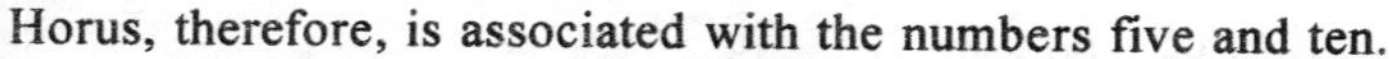

Horus, therefore, is associated with the numbers five and ten.

It is no coincidence that the Greek philosopher Pythagoras and his followers, had subsequently adopted the sacred numbers of five and ten.

• Horus was worshipped in many forms. The most common five forms of Horus are Harpocrates, Horsiesis, Harmachis, Haroeris, and Horus Behdety.

Harpocrates is the Greek rendering for **Heru-p-khart** (meaning Horus the Child). He is often shown as an infant being suckled by Isis, which is identical to the later Christian representation of Madonna and her child.

- Horsiesis is the Greek translation for **Hor-sa-Aset** (meaning Horus, Son of Isis). This is the representation of Horus in the Osiris/Isis/Horus Legendary.

- Harmachis is the Greek rendering of **Horachty** (meaning Horus on the Horizon). This name was used for the Great Sphinx of Giza.

- Haroeris was the Greek for **Heru-ur** (meaning Horus the Elder or Horus the Great). In this form he is the cosmic version of Horus, son of Osiris and Isis, representing the principle of return in the creation process, as realized in mankind.

- Horus Behdety is Horus who avenged the death of his father, and flew up to heaven, in the form of a winged disk. The Edfu temple is dedicated to Horus Behdety who is depicted as a hawk-headed neter.

- Apollo, in the Greek mythology, corresponds to Horus Behdety.

Horus Behdety

The Sons of Horus

The four sons of Horus were in charge of the protection and furtherance of the viscera, contained in the canopic jars of the deceased. The sons were:

Amset (human-headed) protects the liver.

Duamutef (jackal/dog-headed) protects the stomach.

Hapi (baboon-headed) protects the lungs.

Qebsennuf (hawk-headed) protects the intestines.

Read more about the canopic jars and the four sons under the chapter 'Tombs'.

Chapter 11

Set/Satan

The Power of Opposition

General

- Reactions to Satan range from terror to contempt to worship.

- The human tendency has always been to look for a scapegoat, preferably non-human, on whose shoulders can be loaded the blame for evil, violence, pain and misfortune.

- The Manual of Discipline, which is one of the Dead Sea Scrolls, says that God created two great spirits, one of truth and one of contrariety, the latter being the Angel of Darkness.

- Satan, as the Angel of Darkness, therefore, represents the power of opposition. The name Satan means *'adversary'* in Hebrew, and originally meant simply an opponent, and not necessarily a supernatural one.

- The name Satan was derived from the ancient Egyptian name of **Set** (referred to as Seth in Greek.)

- For ancient Egyptians, the initial act of creation caused the division of the original unity. This breaking up created multiplicity, which resulted in the various elements of the world. This break-up, by its nature, is an opposition of the original unity.

Set represents this power of opposition. Opposition is always at work preventing peace, harmony and order. Therefore, Set and his accomplices represent the forces of darkness, chaos, ...etc. The texts contain curses upon Set and his accomplices.

However, without opposition there can be no creation. As such, Set is an important neter, because opposition is an essential aspect of creation.

- Unlike Christian theologians, the question of the nature and existence of evil gave the Egyptians no trouble at all. In the court of the Pavilion at the Mortuary Temple of Ramses III on the west bank of Thebes, on the north wall the king is shown making an offering to a defaced figure of Set. To make offerings to Set is, in effect, to "give the Devil his due." As mentioned above, Set represents the necessary power of opposition, and not the biblical concept of evil. So, the Egyptian king regularly and ritually paid dutiful respect to the divine principle of opposition.

- Set is depicted as a human figure with the head of an unidentified animal. Set is also depicted as an animal with a forked tail.

- Set is associated with the wilderness/wastes and their animals, such as the immense coiled serpent, the black pig, and the ass. Each animal symbolizes a different aspect of the carnal world.

- The Greeks identified Set with Typhon, in their mythology.

- Set's main temple, in ancient Egypt, is located at Tanis.

- Apopis is the Greek rendering of Apop, the immense coiled serpent. Apop is a form of Set. Funerary texts contain many curses upon Apopis and his accomplices. The similarity between Apop, Set's wicked serpent, and the biblical Satan and the serpent in the Garden of Eden is striking.

Set Worship in Ancient Times

- From an early time in Egyptian history, Set was regarded as a neter of Upper Egypt. He was also associated with the area of the Eastern Delta, near the start of the Sinai desert and the road to Asia. This area was the ancient Egyptian fourteenth nome (province), and was called Sethrotic, after him.

- From the end of the Sixth Dynasty, (during the twenty-second century

B.C.), Set became discredited as a result of the development of the myth that he had been responsible for the assassination of Osiris. He then became associated with Evil and was the source of the later name Satan. As a result, his worship stopped.

• However, after another four centuries, Nehesy, a king of the Thirteenth Dynasty, reestablished the worship of '**Seth, Lord of Avaris**' as the chief deity of the fourteenth nome. Nehesy (c. 1715 B.C.) is known from several monuments, as the first king with the title: **Beloved of Seth, Lord of Avaris**.

• Seth later became the principal god of the Hyksos (c. 1663-1550 B.C.), but he was already well established in Avaris before the rise of the Hyksos rule.

Satan and The Bible

Jehovah (Yaweh) and Satan

• The root ideas of Satanism go far back beyond the 19th century B.C. to the Gnostic sects. They saw the world about them as profoundly evil, as the real hell, and life on earth as a sentence served in a prison. If the world is evil, then the power which made it and rules it must be evil too. Some of the Gnostics identified this evil power as the God of the Jews, who is described as creating the world, in the book of Genesis, and whose behavior in the Old Testament they found impossible to reconcile with Christian principles. The good God, they said, lives far away in some distant heaven and we on earth are in bondage to the evil Jehovah.

• The god of the Jews, Jehovah, was at first only one of numerous gods. After the *'miraculous'* crossing of the Red Sea, Moses and the Israelites sang his praises: *'Who is like thee, O Lord, among the gods?'*

• The picture of Yahweh (Jehovah) as one god among many gradually gave way to the belief that he was the only God, who had created the universe and everything in it. If he had created everything, then on the face of it he must have created evil.

• In Jewish and Christian theory the Devil never attained the status of an independent god but was always subject to God's control. Later, Jewish writers increasingly revised the older picture of Jehovah, separating out the good and evil elements in his earlier character and attributing actions which they felt to be evil, not to God but to other supernatural powers.

An example of such revisions is the story of David and the census. The Old Testament tells us that Yahweh (Jehovah) ordered David to complete a population census and then, after it was done, Jehovah punished them with a plague that killed 70,000 men. But when the story is retold in (I Chronicles chapter 21) it is Satan who suggests the census. Incidentally, this is the first and only use of Satan as a proper name in the Old Testament.

Satan and The Garden of Eden

• Satan began his career as a useful official of the heavenly court, but we were told later that he had become the master of evil and the enemy of God. Two stories were told to explain how this change had happened, those of the fall of Lucifer and the fall of the Watchers.

• Taking the form of the serpent, Satan deliberately encouraged in Adam and Eve the same arrogance which had caused his own downfall.

The ancient serpent, who is called the Devil, Satan, and the deceiver of the whole world, was thrown down to earth, and his angels were thrown down with him. ***"And I heard a loud voice in heaven saying, ... the accuser of our brethren has been thrown down, who accuses them day and night before our God ... But woe to you, O earth and sea, for the devil has come down to you in great wrath, because he knows that his time is short!"***

• Christian writers accepted that the Devil's successful temptation of Adam and Eve had brought death into the world and made him very powerful. It was the Devil who offered Jesus ***'all the kingdoms of the world and the glory of them'*** (Matthew, chapter 4), with the clear implication that the gift is his to make. In St. John's Gospel (12.31), the Devil is called ***'the ruler of this world'***, and St Paul calls him ***'the god of this world'*** (2 Corinthians 4.4).

When the Old Testament was translated into Greek *'the satan'* became **diabolos**, *'the accuser'*, with the implication of false accusation or slander, and this is the origin from which the word *'devil'* is derived.

Part III

The Pharaohs and Their Buildings

Chapter 12

The Pharaoh

Our Holy Father

General

• Holy means *"spiritually pure, commanding adoration and reverence"*.

Father means *"a beloved leader"*.

• A lot of religious people like to present to us the distorted image of the Pharaoh as a harsh tyrant who would bend justice according to his caprices and who would indulge in extremes of useless cruelty in judging offenders. This notion is incorrect because having the *"inalienable right"* to administer justice all by himself, was never the case.

• In the first place, his function was fundamentally religious. He was a priest-king. There are still a few priest-kings in the world, including the British monarch who is both the head of the state as well as the head of the Church of England.

The Pharaoh was a representative of the people in a far more profound sense than that implied by the modern use of the phrase. He was very much like a popular Catholic Pope.

• The Egyptians paid the most marked respect to their monarch, as the father of his people. He was obeyed with courteous submission. They believed that he had been blessed by the deities themselves, based on his extensive religious training. They entertained a strong feeling of gratitude for the services done by him to the state; and he was honored and remembered by the people after his death.

The Holy Father

• To us, an absolute monarch ruling with the wholehearted support of his subjects is almost inconceivable. Understanding this unique aspect of ancient Egypt can be simplified if the Egyptian Pharaoh is to be looked at, in our modern eyes, as a kind of a popular pope.

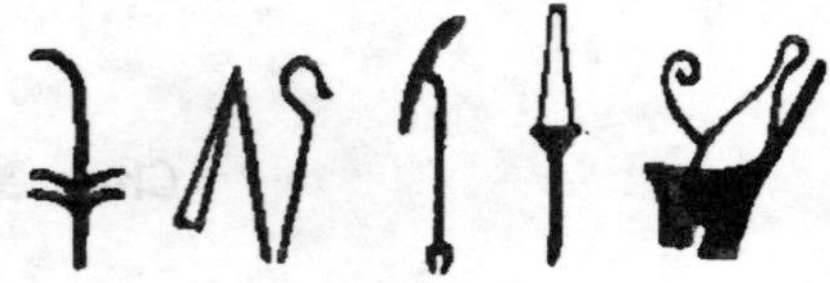

• Explaining some terms of the 'symbolic' language could clarify why the king was called **"Our Lord"**, or **"Our Master"**. It could also clarify what they really meant when they said, *'We worship you'*, or *'I am your slave'*. All these words are expressions of respect and affection. Modern day Egyptians use the same expressions in their daily life. *'I am your slave'*, could mean that *'I am at your service'*, or *'I love you passionately'*. *'My Lord'* or *'My Master'*, could be used to address a child or a spouse as an expression of love and tenderness, etc. Read more about symbolism in language under chapters 'Languages Now and Then' and 'The History of the Bible'.

• The Pharaohs were not bragging in any personal sense when they dedicated their great monuments to the neterw, declaring **"I, Ramesses (or Twthmosis, or Amenhotep), built this monument for my father, Amon. Never has the like of it been seen before,"** that *'I'* was, in the spiritual sense, quite objective and impersonal.

The king's declaration is not different than when Christ declared in the Gospels, ***"I am the way, the truth and the life."***

• Despite the repeated charges of vanity against the Pharaohs, it is worth remembering that their abodes while on earth were never made of stone, but of mud-brick, the same material used by the humblest peasants. These absolute monarchs could have built stone palaces for themselves. But the impermanent body, formed of clay by Khnum, the ram-headed neter, called for an equally impermanent abode on this earth. The palaces of the kings have long since returned to the earth from which they were raised.

• The king represented the divine in mankind. His name, Phrah (Pharaoh), signified **'the sun'**. From the early Fifth Dynasty (2465-2323 B.C.), every king was called **'Son of Re'**, in commemoration of the relationship between Re and the king. The title **'Son of Re'** continued to be used by all ancient Egyptian kings and was transformed by some writers to **'Son of God'**.

The Divine (Virgin) Birth

In ancient Egypt, divine birth was looked upon as an aspect of royal birth. Although the child was regarded spiritually as the son of the deity, this did not exclude the human father or the sexual relationship between the parents. In symbolic terms, the spirit of the deity (the Holy Spirit) used the physical body of the king to produce the child. In Christian belief, however, no human father is involved: the mother is a virgin, and the child is conceived by the Holy Spirit without any sexual relationship.

The holy birth of the king is documented in scenes as well as texts found in many places, such as on the north wall of the central colonnade of Queen Hatshepsut's mortuary temple at Deir el Bahari, as well as at the Luxor Temple. In the Luxor Temple, at the Birth Chamber, as called by classical Egyptologists, we find the scene of the spiritual conception and birth of the king. The reliefs on the west wall depict a scene with many similarities to the familiar Christian's Immaculate Conception. The king was a royal, conscientious man, with divine potential. The Egyptian king is therefore considered to be the son of God, the son of the neterw, the divine principles.

The Power Behind the Throne

- The line of royal descent in Egypt was through the eldest daughter. Whoever she married, became the Pharaoh.

It was not mere influence that the eldest daughter possessed, it was a right acknowledged by law, both in private and public life. Egyptians, from their earliest history, knew that unless women were treated with respect, and had the opportunity to exercise an influence over society, the standard of manners and morals of the people would suffer.

- Several women, who were the legal heirs, did not marry and subsequently became rulers themselves.

Coronation

- The coronation of the king was an imposing ceremony. It was one of the principal subjects represented in the court of the temples. It is represented, for example, at Medinet Habu at the west bank of Thebes. Here are some of the highlights.

First comes the king, carried in his shrine or canopy, and seated on a throne. Behind him stand two figures of Truth and Justice, with outspread wings. His sons bear the shrine. Others follow, of whom there are two scribes and eight attendants of the military class.

The king officiates as priest before the statue of Amen-Re. He presents libations and incense before the altar, which is loaded with flowers, and other suitable offerings. The queen stands as a witness of the ceremony; and before her, a scribe reads from an unfolded scroll.

The king is shown in his headdress which incorporates the Horus falcon so adroitly it seems part of a natural design. One can see that the Horus falcon is doing far more than merely protecting the king; the king has assimilated the spiritual qualities, as personified by the falcon into his own head, or consciousness.

- Another ceremony, represented in the temples, was the blessing given by the neterw on the king, at the moment of his assuming the reign of government. They laid their hands upon him; and presented him with the symbol of life. They promised that his reign should be long and glorious, and that he should enjoy tranquility and victory over the dark forces.

The Anointed King (Messiah)

One of the principal ceremonies connected with the coronation was the anointing of the king, and his receiving the emblems of majesty from the neterw.

The king was not anointed with oil, but with the fat of the crocodile. This is the original source of the word *'Messiah'*. **MeSSeH** was the word for crocodile, in ancient Egypt. The image of two crocodiles formed the title of the king, which was given to him at the time of his coronation. The letter *'s'* in Egyptian is equivalent to *'sh'* in Hebrew and Aramaic. It is therefore evident that the biblical word ***Messiah*** originated from **mesheeh**, the ancient Egyptian word signifying the ritual of anointing the king.

The Bible claims that the Jews had adopted the same ratification process for the sacred offices of priests. The Jewish ceremony includes pouring oil upon the head of the high priest after he had put on his entire dress, with the mitre and crown. Anointing of the Egyptian priests and kings commenced after they were attired in their full robes, with the cap and crown upon their head.

Their Training

• In their young age, princes were brought up in a disciplined environment. Most of the kings had military training, and during the glorious days of Egyptian history, the younger princes generally adopted the same profession. Many held offices also in the royal household, such as fan-bearers on the right of their father, royal scribes, superintendents of the granaries, or of the land, and treasurers of the king. Some of them were also generals of the cavalry, archers, or admirals of the fleet.

• The princes were taught about morals and ethics. A book of instructions, (c. 2100 B.C.), was found, written by one of the rulers for his son, Prince Merikare, detailing the proper duties and attitudes of a good and conscientious king. The advice was both spiritual and practical. The king counseled justice and impartiality as the best long-run policies from a practical and political point of view. He also emphasized the spiritual development of the Pharaoh-to-be. Merikare was assured that only this kind of conduct would be agreeable to the judges at the Day of Final Judgment when one **"sees the whole life's span in a single instant."** They were taught of the awesome responsibility of governing and the consequences of not living up to it.

• Horus, the son of Isis and Osiris, was held forth as the role model for all princes, and as the type of royal virtue that they should aspire to. Princes were distinguished by a badge hanging from the side of the head, which enclosed, or represented, the lock of hair symbolic of a *'son'*, in imitation of the youthful Horus. Growing up with such discipline helped to prepare them for their spiritual, as well as practical duties of governing.

- They were also instructed in all aspects of the religion, and the various offices of a pontiff. They learned all that relates to the neterw, the service of the temple, the laws of the country, and the duties of a king.

- Another clue to the responsibility of the high office, can also be appreciated when we review other available evidence. For example, when the vizier, or supreme magistrate, was appointed, he was read the following exhortation:

> **"The height of the divine abomination would be to show bias. These, then, are your instructions: you shall treat those you do not know exactly as you would treat those you do know, and those who live near you just as you would those who live far away ... Beware, because you will keep this post only so long as you stay within its prerogatives!"**

Regulating The Monarchs

The Pharaoh's conduct and mode of life were regulated by prescribed rules, so as to protect the community from the caprices of an absolute monarch. Laws were laid down in the sacred books, for the order and nature of his occupations. He was forbidden to commit excesses; even the kind and quality of his food were prescribed with precision. He was constantly reminded of his duties, both in public and in private.

Even if the king had the means of defying prescribed rules, the voice of the people could punish him at his death, by the disgrace of excluding his body from burial in his own tomb. These laws were set forth as a precaution. They were seldom enforced. The indulgence of the Egyptians to their king gave him no excuse for tyranny or injustice. It was no difficult task for a king to be popular; the Egyptians were prone to look upon him with affection and respect. The public knew of their crown prince while he was growing up. His personality and character were not a surprise to them once he ascended the throne.

He easily secured for himself that good will which was due from children to a parent. The whole nation cared for the welfare of the king as they did for their own wives and children. Diodorus credits the duration of the Egyptian civilization to this form of government, which not only lasted a long time, but enjoyed the greatest prosperity.

When The King Dies

• After the Pharaoh died, love and respect for him continued. Diodorus said:

> *"What can convey a greater testimony of sincerity, than the cordial acknowledgment of a benefit, when the person who conferred it no longer lives to witness the honor done to his memory?"*

• On the death of every Egyptian king, a general mourning period of seventy days was observed throughout the country. The temples were closed and no sacrifices were offered. No feasts or festivals were celebrated during the mourning period.

• During these seventy days, the funeral was prepared, and on the last day the body was placed in state near the entrance of the tomb. The pontiffs first praised his character, enumerating all his noble actions, and their merits. The assembled people responded favorably, except if his life had been stained with vice or injustice. Then they showed their dissent by loud murmurs: Some instances are recorded of Egyptian monarchs having been deprived of the honor of the customary public funeral because of public opposition. The historian Diodorus further stated:

> *"The effect of this was that succeeding kings, fearing so disgraceful a censure after death, and the eternal stigma attached to it, studied by their virtuous conduct to deserve the good opinion of their subjects; and it could not fail to be a great incentive to virtue, independent of the feelings arising from a wish to deserve the gratitude of men, and the fear of forfeiting the favor of the neterw."*

• The custom of refusing funeral rites to a king was later adopted by the Jews, as shown by the speech of the biblical Samuel, on leaving his post of judge, *"Whom have I defrauded?"*

• The Egyptians, however, did not go to extremes by degrading the dead as the Jews sometimes did to those whom they rejected. The body of a bad Egyptian, though excluded from the burial at the necropolis, was not refused his right to be buried somewhere else.

• At their tombs, the Pharaohs are depicted in the prime of their life.

They are shown with an expression of the inner peace of enlightenment. They generally do not show any human emotion. Anything to do with the king's personal history and his individual personality are omitted from his tomb.

The Heb-Sed Festival (Time of Renewal)

• The most important festival from the point of view of the kingship was the Sed (Heb-Sed), at which the authority of the king was renewed. Normally this mysterious Sed-festival took place after the king had ruled thirty years, and was repeated thereafter, at three year intervals. Sometimes, however, it was held earlier than the thirtieth year, perhaps on the thirtieth anniversary of the king's becoming crown prince. It was usually held at Memphis. Among the various acts performed in the course of the festival were the double coronation of the king as ruler of Upper and Lower Egypt, a ritual dance and the running of four courses by the king. Additionally, the king visited the chapels of Horus and Seth, and was presented with four arrows so that he might discharge them against his enemies at the four cardinal points of the compass.

Several Titles and Several Names

• It was common practice, during these times, for the Egyptians to have several names, some of which were kept secret. Twtankhamen, for instance, had five — the one by which he is commonly known and, in addition, Ka-Nekhet Twtmes (his Horus name), Nefer-Hebo Gereh-Tawi (Nebti), Re-neb Ka-w Schetep Neteru (Golden Horus) and Neb Kheparu-Re (Nesubet). Each name or title had a specific meaning, reason and function.

It was also the custom to use pet names as well as abbreviated forms for the longer and more complex names.

• The power of the name, and its role in ancient thought, is one of the least understood aspects of the ancient Egyptians. The name was not, as per our modern-day thinking, a mere label. The name of a neter, person, animal, or principle, represented a resume or synopsis of the qualities of that object or person.

• As a result of the Pharaohs using multiple titles and names, it becomes difficult to identify the kings of the earliest dynasties because of the fragmentary nature of the evidence.

At War

• Egypt was not interested in an empire, and certainly not in military occupation. Egypt was only interested in neutralizing the hostile elements that threatened to disrupt her own security. The Pharaohs of the New Kingdom utilized diplomacy and marriage to foreign princesses, and used force only when all else failed.

• The wars of the twentieth century of bombing and burning would have been considered unthinkable barbaric actions. War, for the ancient Egyptians, followed rules as strict as a chess game and had specific rituals. They were truly the civilized people.

• A war had a profound religious significance. It symbolized the forces of order controlling chaos and the light triumphing over darkness.
The typical scene on the temple's outer wall, shows the King, the royal principle, controlling the power of darkness in order to ensure the order in the temple.

• The famous war scenes of Ramses II, at Kadesh, are a good example of the concept of war in ancient Egypt. Ramses is shown both betrayed and abandoned by his own troops. This theme of betrayal and abandonment also occurs in other military friezes by other kings, which is a strong indication that we are dealing with symbolism, not a historical event. The "enemy" is always the power of darkness and chaos. The king is the spiritual principle. Betrayal and abandonment are the unchangeable consequences of reliance on earthly supports.

The Battle of Kadesh is the personal drama of the individual royal man (the king in each of us) single-handedly subduing the inner forces of chaos and darkness.

- The war scenes are present in many other places so as to symbolize the never-ending battle between Good and Evil. In many cases there is no historical basis for such war scenes even though a precise date is given. Such is the case for the war scenes on the Temple Pylon of the Mortuary Temple of Ramses III, at Medinet Habu.

Chapter 13

The First Pharaoh of Egypt

Menes Is Not It

• The Pharaoh Menes (c. 3050 B.C.) is reputed to have unified northern and southern Egypt and began the civilization that lasted for more than three thousand years.

• Menes, however, was neither the first Pharaoh of Egypt nor the first or the last one to unify northern and southern Egypt.

• We know for a fact that the union of the two lands of Egypt re-occurred, after Menes' reign, in the twentieth, sixteenth and eighth centuries B.C., and there is no reason to doubt that unification took place several times throughout history, prior to Menes.

Narmer (c. 3100 B.C.)

• Many historians have told us that the ancient Egyptian civilization is much older than Menes. Their accounts are stated below.

Pre-Dynastic Egypt

• The Greek and Roman writers of antiquity, basing their accounts on information received either first or second-hand from Egyptian sources, claimed a far greater antiquity for the Egyptian civilization than that currently established by Egyptologists. These Egyptian sources called for antiquity ranging from 24,000 and 36,000 years during which Egypt was civilized.

• Even though the above reports were current in those Late Kingdom and Ptolemaic days, most modern scholars continue ignoring them because they lack physical evidence to support an antiquity of this order. Since such remote antiquity is hard to handle, they ascribe these legendary millennia to the Egyptian imagination. It is, however, difficult to provide convincing archaeological evidence that is older than 5,000 or 7,000 years, or longer periods because nothing can logically survive such long periods. As such, we should continue to mention the different sources of information, and not to arbitrarily choose to ignore or accept them. Circumstantial evidence, from varied historical sources, can be as strong or even stronger than physical archaeological evidence. Here are some of these sources:

- Herodotus reported that he was informed by Egyptian priests that the sun had twice set where it now rose, and twice risen where it now set. Egyptologist Schwaller de Lubicz explained the statement to mean that it may be a reference to the progressional cycles of the equinox. The progression results in the rising against a different sign of the Zodiac approximately every two thousand years. This would mean that the Egyptians counted their history back for at least a cycle and a half, some 36,000 years. This is in a general agreement with other accounts and evidential findings.

- Later, in the chapter '*Sphinx - Older Than History*', several corroborative pieces of evidence will confirm this very remote antiquity.

- The Greco-Egyptian historian Manetho (3rd century B.C.), under the early Ptolemies, wrote the only substantive history of Egypt to come down to us. He gathered his information from Egyptian records. A few pre-dynastic inscribed tablets and papyri have been found, but all were incomplete because of their remote age. Manetho acknowledged greater antiquity of the Egyptian history. However, because of the overwhelming task, he chose Menes as a starting point, about 3000 years earlier.

- In Plato's Timaeus, Solon quoted the Egyptian priest who told him of the Atlantis legend and that Egypt was already civilized many thousands of years earlier.

The First Pharaoh

According to the ancient traditions, Osiris was the first Pharaoh of Egypt.

But, was Osiris a historical or a fictional character? The answer could be a little bit of both. The human nature tends to glorify old beloved leaders. In the U.S.A., for example, there is the tendency to glorify the "ingenuity" of the founding fathers. They are the "wise men", the "visionaries", ...etc. One must suspect that a few centuries from now, Americans will have these people elevated to a status equivalent to the Egyptian Ennead (The company of nine responsible for the creation of the universe).
Therefore, it is possible that Osiris was a real person who was martyred and glorified over the millennia to sainthood and was thereafter deified.

It is clear, however, that someone held the position of First Pharaoh of Egypt a long time before Menes did.

Dynastic Ancient Egypt

- Manetho started with Menes and then divided the entire chronicle of events into thirty-one dynasties, from the unification event of Egypt under Menes, to the conquest of Alexander the Great in 332 B.C. Manetho's list of kings and their years of rule have been preserved in the writings of early Christian record keepers. Modern historians selectively use such records, and accept the numbering of Manetho's dynasties, which seems to follow very ancient practice. They also continue to use the Greek versions of the pharaohs' names.

- The thirty-one dynasties, of Manetho, have been further grouped by modern historians into larger time-spans, so as to coincide with distinct cultural pattern periods, separated by unknown periods of political upheaval. Sometimes these periods are further sub-divided.

- Estimated dates for the dynasties are given below. Those before the Twenty-sixth Dynasty are approximations. The dates of individual kings, queens and other individuals mentioned in the text will be found throughout the book, in conjunction with each subject.

Neolithic Period	before 5000 B.C.
Pre-dynastic Period	c. 5000-3300 B.C.
Protodynastic Period	c. 3300-3050 B.C.

Dynasty	Dates	
I	3050 B.C. - 2890 B.C.	Early Dynastic Period
II	2890 B.C. - 2649 B.C.	
III	2649 B.C. - 2575 B.C.	
IV	2575 B.C. - 2465 B.C.	Old Kingdom
V	2465 B.C. - 2323 B.C.	
VI	2323 B.C. - 2150 B.C.	
VII-X - 1st Intermediate Period	2150 B.C. - 2040 B.C.	
XI	2040 B.C. - 1991 B.C.	Middle Kingdom
XII	1991 B.C. - 1783 B.C.	
XIII-XVII - 2nd Intermediate Period	1783 B.C. - 1550 B.C.	
XVIII	1550 B.C. - 1307 B.C.	New Kingdom
XIX	1307 B.C. - 1196 B.C.	
XX	1196 B.C. - 1070 B.C.	
XXI (Tanis)	1070 B.C. - 712 B.C.	Third Intermediate Period
XXII (Libyan)	945 B.C. - 712 B.C.	
XXIII (Nubia & Thebes)	878 B.C. - 712 B.C.	
XXIV (Sais)	740 B.C. - 712 B.C.	
XXV (Nubia & Thebes)	712 B.C. - 657 B.C.	Late Kingdom
XXVI (Sais)	664 B.C. - 525 B.C.	
XXVII (Persian)	525 B.C. - 404 B.C.	
XXVIII (Sais)	404 B.C. - 399 B.C.	
XXIX	399 B.C. - 380 B.C.	
XXX	380 B.C. - 343 B.C.	
Second Persian Period	343 B.C. - 332 B.C.	
Macedonian Kings	332 B.C. - 304 B.C.	Greco-Roman Period
Ptolemic Dynasty	323 B.C. - 30 B.C.	
Roman Emperors	30 B.C. - 323 A.D.	
Byzantine Emperors	323 A.D. - 642 A.D.	

Chapter 14

Numbers Are Not Just Numbers

General

• The use of numbers, in ancient Egypt, was always based upon an implicit and consistent symbolism. The Egyptian concept of number symbolism was subsequently popularized in the West by and through the Greek philosopher Pythagoras.

• The dimensions and number of architectural features, in Egyptian buildings, were consistently based on their number symbolism.

• The Leyden Papyrus (now in the Leyden Museum in Holland) confirms that number symbolism has been practiced in Egypt, at least since the Old Kingdom. The Leyden Papyrus consists of an extended composition describing the principle aspects of the ancient creation myths. The system of numeration, in this Papyrus, identifies the principle/aspect of creation and matches each one with its implicit symbolic number. Some of the numbers and their symbolic significance will be listed later in this chapter.

• The ancient name for the Karnak Temple complex is **Apet-sut**, which means '**Enumerator of the Places**'. The design and enumeration, in this temple, is consistent with the number symbolism of the physical creation of the universe.

Some Numbers & Their Significance

One: is the One, the original unity.

Two: is the result of the first act of creation, i.e. the split of the One into two.

Three, Thirty & Three hundred: have to do with the triple nature of the One. The third proceeded from the union of the two. There are several triads in the ancient Egyptian theology, and there is also the familiar Trinity of Christianity.

Four: is the number of the cardinal points. Horus has four sons who are associated to the four canopic jars which contained the viscera of the mummified person.

Five: is associated with Horus, as mentioned earlier in the chapter 'Horus, the Highest'. Five is also the number of points on the stars that decorate the ceilings of the tombs.

Six: is the number of directions (four cardinal points plus up and down) and as such signifies volume, space and time.

Timekeeping all over the world is based upon the number six and its multiples. (Read more about it under the chapter 'Egyptian Calendar'.)

6, 60, 600: have to do with volume, space and time.

Seven: is the number of process, growth, and the undying cyclical aspects of the universe. Osiris is associated with number seven and its multiples. Read more about it under 'Osiris, the Holy Spirit'.

Eight: is the number of the four pairs of primordial deities, called Night, Obscurity, Secret and Eternity. The neter **Thoth** was called **'Master of the City of Eight'**.

Nine: The **'Company of Neterw'** forms an **Ennead**, or group of nine. The Great Ennead brought the Universe into being and sustained it.

Ten: is the highest number of the original unity. The tenth of such a unity was Horus. There are ten chapels at the Horus Temple of Edfu representing his association with this sacred number.

Eleven: is often associated with Hathor. There are eleven Hathor columns at Deir-el-Bahari.

Nineteen: The classic Egyptian grid upon which all reliefs and human figures are laid out is based on nineteen squares.

Forty: is associated with the embalmment process and other aspects. This number is frequently used in ancient Egypt and the Bible.

Seventy: is associated with the mummification process and other aspects.

One Hundred Ten: signified the symbolic and not the actual age of wisdom.

Examples of Number Symbolism in Buildings

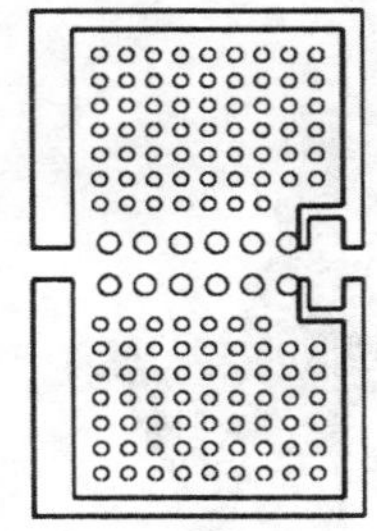

• The Hypostyle Hall of the Karnak temple consists of seven rows of nine columns each, on either side of the double row of the six higher columns in the center. This theme of six, seven, and nine is only found at the Karnak temple. The Hypostyle Hall is a representation of the papyrus thicket of Creation.

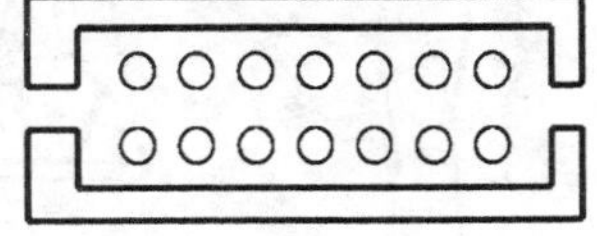

• The Colonnade of Amenhotep III, at Luxor Temple consists of a double row of seven smooth papyrus columns. The significance of the number seven and the papyrus thicket of creation were mentioned above.

• The floor plan of the so-called *"King's chamber"*, at the Great Pyramid, is a 2 x 1 rectangle, 34' 4 " x 17' 2" (10.5 x 5.2 m; 20 x 10 Egyptian cubits). The height of the King's Chamber is 19' 2" (5.8 m). This measure is equal to one half the length of the diagonal of the floor.
The diagonal of a 2:1 rectangle is very significant. In a religious sense, when the one became two, the result (diagonal) is the universe. The diagonal symbolizes the functions of creation itself. The diagonal of the 2:1 rectangle is the square root of five. The modern formula for the proportion called the golden section or Phi is 1/2 (1 + square root of 5).

Read more about it in the chapters 'The Mystery of the Pyramids' and 'Science and Technology'.

Chapter 15

Temples

General

• It is difficult to view the Egyptian temples with any measure of objectivity, considering all the negative views, including the biblical account of the Exodus, which have been drummed into our heads from childhood.

• An Egyptian temple was not a place of public worship. It was the shrine for the neter, who represented some specific aspect of the One God. Only the priesthood had access to the inner sanctuaries, where the sacred rites and ceremonies were performed. In some instances, only the King himself or his authorized substitute had permission to enter.

• The purpose and/or significance of the inscriptions on the walls of the temples, are unknown to us. As these temples are now open to the public, thousands of years later, understanding these private inscriptions is an illusive task.

• Much of our knowledge about Egypt comes from temples which were reconstructed or built during the Ptolemies' rule of Egypt. The Ptolemies ruled Egypt and kept it independent through three centuries of turmoil, often murdering each other to acquire the throne.

• Ptolemic temples, however, have a different style than the original Egyptian style. Some peculiarities of the Ptolemic style include the following:

- The sculpture in these temples is quite elaborate but not very inspiring.
- Women may appear beautiful, but in a coarse and vulgar way, which is different than the graceful Egyptian style.

• The religious practice of the common people, if any, is unknown to us. However, we know that they participated in the many great festivals and celebrations held in honor of the various deities, which took place within the outer courtyards of the chief temples.

Layout of the Temples

• The choice of location and design peculiarities of a temple were not based on economical considerations, but rather on a deeper knowledge, of which we are still unaware.

• Great temples were not built quickly, or by one king alone. Such temples were built over the years, by successive kings.

• In general, the Egyptian temple was surrounded by a massive wall of mud-brick. This wall isolated the temple from its surroundings which, symbolically, represented the forces of chaos. Metaphorically, the mud resulted from the union of heaven and earth. The brick wall itself was therefore set in wavy courses to symbolize the primeval waters, representing the first stage of creation.

The exterior walls of the temple resembled a fortress, so as to defend it against all forms of evil. The temple was entered through two pylons, beyond which lay an open court. This court sometimes had colonnades along the sides and an altar in the middle. Next, along the temple-axis, came the hypostyle, a pillared hall often surrounded by small rooms which are used for the storage of temple equipment and for other secondary functions. Finally, there was the sanctuary, which was a dark room containing the shrine, where the figure of the neter was placed. The sanctuary's doors were shut and sealed all year long, and were open only for the great festivals. The sanctuary was called the "Great Seat". Outside the walls of the temple were the residences of the priestly staff, the workshops, storerooms, and other ancillary structures.

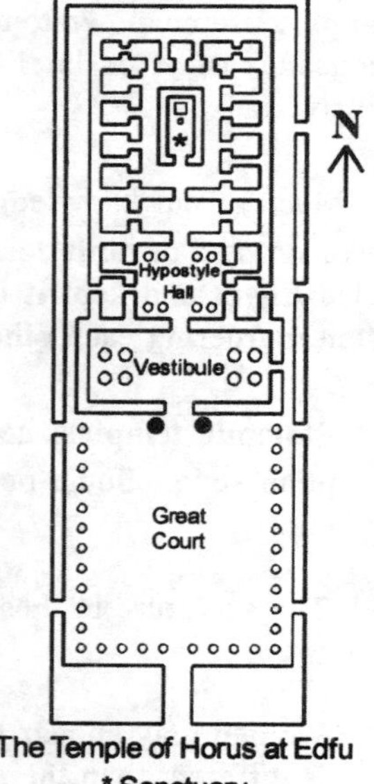

The Temple of Horus at Edfu
* Sanctuary

• Three major temples have some distinctive variation from the general layout described above. They are:

1- The Luxor Temple which has four axes, not just one axis. The axes represent the major parts of the figure of a man. The functions of the various parts of the body were seen as manifestations of cosmic functions, and as such the man is the embodiment of the laws of creation.

2- The Temple of Osiris, at Abydos, which has two major peculiarities.
   a) It is L-shaped.
   b) It has seven sanctuaries, and not the usual one sanctuary for just one principle neter (and that neter's consort and son).

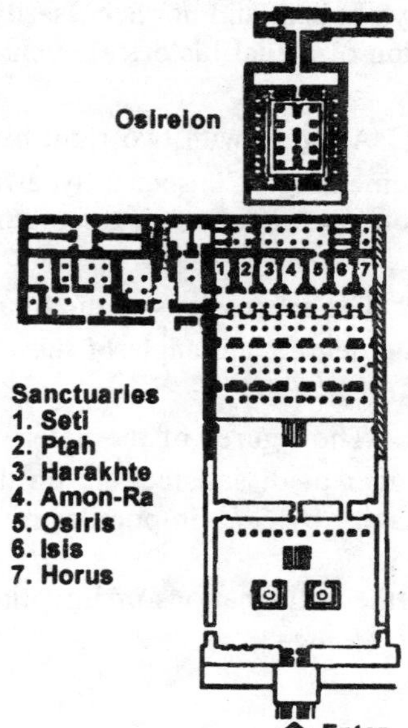

3- The Temple at Kom Ombo is dedicated to two separate divine triads, namely Sobek and Haroeris.

• The design of the temple usually started from the sanctuary, which is the focal point. Accordingly, the floor of the temple descended and the roofs ascended, outwardly towards the temple's pylons.

Symbolism on the Walls

As mentioned earlier, symbolism is in everything we do in life. It is like breathing, we are not aware of it most of the time. Accordingly, the inscriptions and illustrations, on these walls, have private meanings known only to certain people, who lived and worked there, thousands of years ago.

The following are observations of some wall scenes:

- The scene on the outer walls of the temple and the walls of the outer courtyard, show the battle of the forces of light, represented by the king, subduing the forces of darkness, represented by the foreign enemies.

The same scene is repeated, at temples throughout the country, which signifies its symbolism and not necessarily a representation of actual historical events.

- A figure with two right hands signifies an active role such as offering something. Consequently, a figure with two left hands signifies a passive role such as receiving something.

- The expressions of the figures changes from hour to hour depending on the degree and angle of the light throughout the day.

- The figures of the neterw <u>never</u> show an expression of contempt or anger or dissatisfaction, on their faces, unlike the threats and angry behavior by God, in popular religious books.

Other explanations of Egyptian symbolism will be discussed in the chapter 'Tombs'.

Temple Organization

- The temple priesthood consisted of various grades, such as the chief priests, or pontiffs; the king's priest; the prophets; sacred and royal scribes; and other support staff such as dressers, or keepers of the sacred robes; the bearers of the shrines, banners, and other holy emblems; draftsmen; masons; and embalmers. Various other officers were in charge of the processions and other religious ceremonies.

- The temple was a self-contained holy city that combined the functions of the medieval cathedral with the functions of all the guilds. The elaborate temple services required a variety of offerings. These provisions came from nearby workshops and kitchens.

Temple Rituals

• The Egyptian temple had its own distinctive rituals. There is nothing so alien as another culture's rituals. A Catholic person, for example, has trouble understanding an Orthodox Jewish service, and vice versa.

Offerings at the altar

• The most prominent aspect of the Egyptian rituals was the presentation of material offerings: bread, beer, rolls of linen, meat, fowl, and other goods. The offerings symbolized the man's success in transforming raw matters into finished products-bread, beer, linen, etc. - as offerings to the neterw. The offerings are made to the neterw who originally transformed the chaos of the primeval waters into the orderly world of creation.

• The Egyptian view was that all mundane activities were resonant of the cosmic process of transforming raw matters into perfected creations.

• Ceremonies were performed throughout the day. There were two main services, in the morning and evening.

• Offerings were prepared at dawn in the kitchens and bakeries. The priests, meanwhile, purified themselves in the waters of the sacred lake outside the temple. The priests entered the temple and performed further purification in the temple's outer corridors. They then led a long procession of offering-bearers, incense bearers, and a chorus of singers chanting hymns of praise. The procession proceeded deeper into the temple, as a priest opened the successive doors one by one, up to the sealed sanctuary. The offerings were then laid out on tables and altars.

• The high priest then entered the sanctuary, which included a model of the holy boat of the sun and a little shrine of granite or basalt. The shrine contained the image of the neter. The priest held the effigy of the neter, and then prayed towards each of the four cardinal directions. The platter of symbolic offerings was then presented.

A short while later, other offerings were made to the subsidiary deities of the temple.

- The effigy was then washed and dressed again, in brand new fine linen. It was then anointed with precious ointment and placed back in the shrine.

- The rituals, of washing and dressing the effigy of the neter, were based upon and coordinated with the movements of the stars in heaven. Because these movements were the result of the divine cosmic law, the rituals showed that Egypt was always attuned to the eternally unfolding rhythms of the universe.

- The priest then sprinkled the shrine with holy water and gave offerings of sacred resins and salts to the neter. He then veiled the effigy again, sealed the shrine, and retraced his way back out of the temple.

- A relatively short service was observed at noon. The evening service was longer. It was, however, the morning celebration that manifested the victorious spirit of light and which best represents Egyptian ritual.

Processions and Festivals (Public Participation)

- This was the form in which the general public participated in activities related to the temple. These celebrations were frequent in the New Kingdom. There were about sixty of these celebrations a year and some of them lasted for several weeks.

- Some of these celebrations commemorated events in the solar and lunar cycles. Others were celebrations for agricultural and Nile events or related to the king. Some, such as the resurrection of Osiris, were celebrated all over Egypt. (Read more about this particular celebration under the chapter, 'Easter and Ancient Egypt'.) Other celebrations were strictly local events.

Chapter 16

Monument Appropriation

General

• The act of monument appropriation in ancient Egypt has been misunderstood by many. The Karnak Temple is an interesting site for the study of such a phenomena. From the Middle Kingdom on, almost every king left some mark of his presence at Karnak. In some cases, a later king had removed the name of the earlier king responsible for the original building, and chiseled in his own. Some conclude then that the later king willfully "appropriated" the work of the earlier. Yet, the matter is not that simple and is more interesting than that. These appropriations are selective and not arbitrary. Only certain names in certain places have been removed. This can only be deliberate, even though the reasons and basis for such selectivity are not yet understood.

• One can find temples which were torn down over and over again. Other temples were never torn down, but were carefully cared for, repaired and added to, periodically.

• There is the typical standard explanation that they did it for economic or for egotistical reasons. Such simplistic answers also ignore the fact that the powerful Pharaohs of the New Kingdom were in total command of unlimited riches. They did not need to save a few pennies, and they never lacked the authority to destroy others' work, if that was their intention. Most importantly, these simplistic answers don't account for the major question regarding the still unknown specified rules for the selectivity of appropriation.

• The famed Egyptologist, Schwaller de Lubicz, was able, in his research, to show that there was a rational system in the dismantling and rebuilding processes. Certain blocks from an old temple were placed beneath the columns of a new temple, as if it was the seed to nourish a new plant.

In his view, the temple had its natural, organic lifetime, and when the temple had completed its predestined cycle it was torn down, or revised, or added to. Even though he could not show exactly what these cycles were or how they were determined, he found much interesting evidence to support his idea, throughout Egypt.

Many other scholars have accepted that the re-deployment of blocks was deliberate, and that the purpose of this re-deployment was to regenerate the new temple.

- Thus, when a king dismantled the work of a predecessor, that action was completely legitimized and had its own sacred meaning. Every king would understand that if he was acting out of egotism, his own monuments would suffer the same mistreatment after his death.

- The works of the *'Great Criminal Akhenaton'* were razed to the ground. His case does not apply to monument appropriation. His story will be told in later chapters.

We shall review three interesting cases of monument appropriation.

1- The Case of Ramses II

Ramses II, the greatest builder of all Egypt, was also the greatest "appropriator." The "appropriations" of Rameses pose many questions. Sometimes, Rameses cut the names of his predecessors out and inserted his own, but in other instances he did not. Sometimes he completed work begun by a previous king and gave that king appropriate credit. In many instances, when he did "appropriate" a temple, he also left many of the prior cartouches untouched and plainly visible. Yet in other cases, he altered all the cartouches.

Rameses ruled for sixty-seven years. He was the greatest builder in Egypt's history since the pyramid age. No subsequent kings appropriated or re-appropriated any projects of Rameses. Why not? Nobody knows!

2- Twthomosis I Obelisk

- One of two obelisks, at the Karnak Temple, was erected by Twthomosis

I, the father of Hatshepsut. No one touched this obelisk for four hundred years, though the kings during those four centuries did a lot of usurping and dismantling. After all this time, two kings left the original inscription in place and merely added their own on either side of the obelisk. They were Ramses IV and Ramses VI. No explanation!

3- The Case of Twthomosis III and Hatshepsut

• There is, to say the least, no love lost between these two Pharaohs. (Read more about it under the chapter 'Twthomosis III, The Warrior King'.)

• The other obelisk at the Karnak Temple is the Obelisk of Hatshepsut (1490-1468 B.C.). This is the second tallest standing obelisk after the Egyptian made *"Lateran Obelisk"*, now standing in Rome. When Twthomosis III (1490-1436 B.C.) came to power, one of his acts was to erect a high wall around Hatshepsut's obelisk that hid only its lower two-thirds and left its top third visible for miles.

• The common simplistic explanation for such an action is that it was cheaper to hide the bottom two-thirds of its height than removing it. But building a wall around an obelisk leaving the top 15 feet (4.6 m) visible for 50 miles (80 km) does not make sense. Twthomosis, the mighty king, could certainly have pulled down an obelisk in the blink of an eye if he wanted to. There has to be a better explanation for this wall. It is possible that this action was a part of the same campaign to undo the queen's works in a selective way, for reasons that to this day are unknown to us.

• In certain instances, the queen's name has been left intact in full view of one and all. In other instances, it has been erased from hidden inaccessible shrines. It is the selectivity of the damage that has baffled and fascinated the scholars for centuries.

• At Deir el-Bahari, two images of Hatshepsut are left intact. Also in the Hathor sanctuary, one can see Hatshepsut and Twthomosis III kneeling; she is holding an offering of milk and he is holding one of wine. There is no defacement here.

• At Deir el-Bahari also, there is a figure of Hatshepsut's great architect, Senmut, who some theorized had an affair with Hatshepsut. Both figures of Hatshepsut and Senmut are left intact!

- Many years ago, the famed Egyptologist E. A. Wallis Budge remarked, *"The wonder is not that [Twthomosis III] destroyed so much, but that he did not destroy more."*

The Answer Is No Answer

The mystery of monument appropriation is acknowledged by all scholars who have studied the matter. The Ramses, Hatshepsut, and other cases, await explanations.

This chapter may leave us with more questions than answers. It simply means that we have no answer at this time. To try and fabricate answers will only display one's own ignorance. Einstein was quoted to say *"The greatest experience we can have is the mysterious."*

Chapter 17

Tombs

General

• Since the majority of ancient Egyptian findings are tombs, this may lead many of us to conclude that the ancient Egyptians were obsessed with death. If one considers the fact that an estimated 150 to 200 million people died in Upper Egypt alone between the times of the Old Kingdom and the Roman Rule, one should conclude that a few hundred tombs along a strip of desert 450 miles long, is actually a small number by comparison.

• The death of a person is analogous to the sun setting at the end of the day. Therefore, all burials in ancient Egypt took place on the west bank of the Nile to conform with the symbolism of the setting sun.
Only Akhenaton reversed the ancient tradition. However, he was never buried in Egypt (Read more about it under 'Akhenaton and Moses' and 'The Exodus, The Bitter Divorce'.)

• After the sun sets every day, it travels into the netherland. Similarly, the death of a person is a journey into another dimension, a place of endless possibilities. As we sleep each night, we experience a kind of a shadow version of life. Afterlife was considered to be this type of a shadow life.

• The basic principles of the ancient Egyptian tomb represent the actual voyage of the spirit as it leaves the body. The design of the royal ancient Egyptian tomb corresponds to the standard near-death experience. Similarities include:

- Being sucked up in a long tunnel (**The tombs have a tunnel**)

- Meeting angels who function as guides or companions to the person, through the tunnel, on their journey to unite with a bright Light [**The Egyptian tunnel is decorated with different neterw (angels of God)**

guiding the deceased person through the voyage until transformation is completed and unification with Re (the Light) occurs.]

- Seeing their whole life reviewed (**Judgment Day scene is depicted on the walls.)**

• The tombs of the kings are spiritual in their entirety. They represent stages of transformation in symbolic and metaphorical form, of the soul in its journey to resurrection and/or reincarnation.

• The decorations in the royal tombs are taken from a number of separate but complementary compositions.

The familiar scenes of daily life activities are never seen in the tomb or mortuary temple of the king, but on the walls of the causeway leading to them.

• The scenes of daily activities are portrayed in the tombs of nobles and high officials. The scenes provide graphic representation, of all manner of Egyptian activities: hunting, fishing, agriculture, warfare, law courts, and all kinds of arts and crafts. All these worldly activities have spiritual meaning.

• Portraying these daily life activities in the presence of the neterw or with their assistance signifies their spiritual intent. The agricultural scenes are similar to the symbolism of Christ referring to the sower of the seed. It was spiritual and never meant to be agricultural advice.

• One may wonder: why was the master of the tomb not shown, performing his real duties instead of these farming and hunting scenes?

A few scholars respond with a simplistic but unsatisfactory answer to this question: artists were selecting scenes from a standardized stock of set themes representing their vision of paradise. If these scenes are intended to portray paradise, one wonders why are many of the best pleasures of this life not shown?!! Therefore, there must be a deeper meaning to all these scenes.

• Despite the repetition of daily life scenes, no two tombs are identical. The theme may be the same but there is always a variation.

• One must continue to be reminded that these tombs were never built as public monuments. Additionally, the Egyptians intended not to share some of their afterlife knowledge, as evidenced by their endlessly reiterated allusions to *'mystery'* and *'hidden knowledge'*.

We are trespassing onto their final resting place, in search of answers.

Viewing The Tombs

In viewing the tombs, it is worth repeating the point that for ancient Egyptians, every 'physical' aspect of life had a symbolic meaning. But also, every symbolic act of expression had a 'material' background.
Symbolism in ancient Egypt is not weird, but it is as unique as symbolism in any other place, at any other time.

Here are the evaluations of some wall scenes:

• An active right hand symbolizes giving. An active left hand signifies receiving. When the symbolic role of the king is wholly active, he is shown with two right hands. When his role is wholly passive, such as when he is receiving the gift of life from the neterw, he has two left hands.

• A queen sniffing at the lotus is a recurrent theme. The perfume of the lotus is its spiritualized essence, similar to the "odor of sanctity" in the Christian doctrine. The lotus is very common in Egyptian symbology. The four sons of Horus are shown coming out from a lotus flower. Also Nefertum, son of Ptah, the Creative Fire, is born of the lotus.

• The typical sowing and reaping scene parallels the biblical parable ***"Whatsoever a man soweth, that shall he also reap"***.

• The scene of rams treading seed into the ground can be equated to the biblical seed on "fertile ground".

Osiris/Horus is portrayed as the "Perfect Shepherd". The hieroglyph for a neter is a human figure dressed in the shepherd's long robe, and seated in the classic shepherd's pose as he tends his flock.

• The wine-making process of growing, harvesting, pressing and fermenting is a metaphor for spiritual processes, which can be equated to the biblical wine symbolism.

• The state of the world of primeval vegetal creation is portrayed on walls by showing a person sailing through the marshes and papyrus thickets. The wildlife is exquisite.

Marsh scenes are a recurrent theme, with no two ever quite alike. They typically include detailed representations of the various Nile fish which scientists can easily identify.

• The familiar scene of duck hunting in the marshes shows the man hunting and his wife aiding him.

This is in reference to the well-known Osiris/Isis/Horus myth. As the young Horus, born of Osiris, he is subduing the forces or spirits of the primordial chaotic swamp by hunting the wild spirits represented by the ducks and other birds. As per the legendary tale, Isis is aiding him in the swamp.

• The bird-netting scene and the various species of birds depicted on walls have some specific significance. In general, these wild birds represent "wild" spiritual elements that must be trapped, caged, sometimes tamed, or offered to the neterw in sacrifice. A modern similarity in symbolism is found in Mozart's Masonic opera, The Magic Flute, where Papageno is the free spirit whose specialty is to trap wild birds.

• Fishing scenes are plentiful in tombs. In Egyptian texts, Horus assumes the form of a fisherman and his four sons also fish with him. Christ used a similar symbolism by making his disciples fishers of men.

• The hunting scenes symbolize the man taming the wild aspects of nature which participated in the primordial hostility of chaos.

Funerary Rites

• The existence of funeral rites in any society reflects the belief that something essential survives man's physical death, and that the mode of burial in some way influences existence in that spiritual region.

• The Book of the Coming Forth By Day (wrongly translated as the Book of the Dead) is a literary composition, and is found in its complete form on papyrus scrolls that were bound in the mummy wrapping of the deceased, and were buried with him. This book consists of over a hundred chapters of varying lengths, most or all ultimately derived from the earliest Unas Funerary Texts (commonly known as Pyramid Texts). (More about such texts under the chapter 'Mystery of the Pyramids').

• The Book of The Coming Forth By Day includes the "Negative Confession," (Read more about them under 'The Egyptian Religion') which are occasionally shown in the tomb paintings. The royal tombs make little reference to this book, but more references are made to The Book of What Is In the Duat (or Underworld), The Book of the Gates, The Book of Caverns, The Litany of Re, The Book of Aker, The Book of Day and The Book of Night. Each text explores the same basic theme of the transformation of the soul in the region of the Duat after death, from a different angle.

• During the soul transformation process, the Egyptians used terms such as soul, shadow, and spirit with each having its own identity and its own function. The meanings of such terms are unclear. Even our modern languages cannot give us a clear definition of these terms. The reference to Horn of the West, Gate of the Western Horizon, etc. are metaphors that have no clear meaning to us. This leaves us with infinite subtleties which are impossible to figure out.

The Mummification

• Funerary rites are present in almost all societies. Mummification, however, was only practiced in a few societies, with Egypt being the most prominent. It took many centuries for mummification to become such a predominant practice in ancient Egypt.

• In pre-dynastic times, the deceased were placed in shallow graves, in the fetal position. Burial in the desert conditions resulted in natural mummification. Once they started the new practice of constructing formal tombs for burial, some form of artificial mummification was needed. Mummification was highly developed, by Old Kingdom times. It became very elaborate by the late New Kingdom. It then required some seventy days to complete the process, and only kings and the nobility could afford this kind of attention. Many of the best preserved royal mummies date from the New Kingdom. Less complex mummification versions were performed on ordinary citizens.

• John Anthony West described in his book, The Travelers' Key to Ancient Egypt, the process of a royal mummification as follows: *"(1) The brain extracted through the nostrils. (2) Removal of the viscera through an incision in the flank. (3) Sterilization of body cavity and viscera. (4) Viscera cleaned, treated, dehydrated, anointed, and coated with molten resin. (5) Body packed temporarily with natron (a naturally occurring mixture of carbonate, bicarbonate, chloride and sulphate of sodium, an effective dehydrating and preserving agent). (6) Body packed in natron for forty days. (7) Temporary packing materials removed. (8) Subcutaneous packing of limbs with sand, clay or other earthy material. (9) Body packed with resin-soaked linens, and fragrances such as myrrh and cinnamon. (10) Anointing with unguents. (11) Final treating and anointing of the body surfaces. (12) Elaborate wrapping in fine linen gauze, with innumerable amulets, magic symbols, and jewelry included in the wrapping."*

• Some hold the simplistic view that the elaborate Egyptian texts represent merely a material conception of the afterlife, and as such, mummification is the result of such thinking. It is their view that as long as the physical body (mummy) exists, then its soul can enjoy the material benefits in a kind of celestial welfare state. There are some scholars, however, who hold more meaningful views, among them Piankoff, Daumas, and Schwaller de Lubicz, who believe that there must be some symbolic and/or actual reason for the elaborate process of mummification. The significance of mummification was never stated in the Egyptian texts.

- The mummy was placed in one of several nested wooden coffins. These were in turn placed in a stone sarcophagus.

- The viscera of the deceased were placed in four individual containers called canopic jars. The jars were usually made of alabaster, limestone, pottery or faience. Canopic jars may have had a separate funeral of their own in the early times. It was therefore possible that the function of the early "double burials" at Abydos and at Saqqara were devised to keep the mummy and the viscera physically as well as symbolically separate. (Read more about double burial under the chapter 'The Mystery of the Pyramids'.)

Later the jars were placed in the tomb chamber near the mummy. The jars became more elaborate over time, with lids shaped after the heads of the four sons of Horus, who were in charge of the protection and/or progression of the viscera. Each of the four sons was himself under the protection of a netert, and each was associated with one of the cardinal points.

Canopic Jars

Horus Sons	Head Shape	Netert	Contents of Jar	Direction of Head
Duamutef	jackal/dog	Neith	stomach	north
Qebsennuf	hawk	Selkit	intestines	south
Hapi	baboon	Nephthys	lungs	east
Amset	man	Isis	liver	west

The detailed arrangements of the canopic jars reflects an understanding of the great cosmic process. Each respective organ is embodied in a respective netert, which commands a *'direction'*, or sector of the cosmic cycle of creation.

The Funerary Boats

It was a common practice from the earliest times to construct nicely shaped stone lined pits to store the hulls of the boats which had an important role in Egyptian funerary symbolism. The many personifications of the sun were often portrayed traveling across the day or night sky in boats, and the goal of the exalted dead was to become a star and join the company of Re in his **"Boat of Millions of Years."**

Chapter 18

The Mystery of the Pyramids

We were taught in schools that the pyramids are nothing but tombs which were built by tyrant Pharaohs, and that slaves were used to haul these big stones up temporary ramps, in the construction of these pyramids. These commonly held views are without any evidence. Some of the "common knowledge" about the pyramids was based on:

◊ What someone told Herodotus (c. 500 B.C.) about the pyramids which were already 2,000 years old at that time. No one had access to and/or knowledge of the pyramids' interiors at that time.

◊ A total of three empty and unmolested coffers, which were found inside the nine major pyramids, a few hundred years ago, after forced entry was made into them.

When one examines the facts, especially as one visits the pyramids, one will find that the commonly held beliefs about the pyramids are so incredibly illogical that you may doubt yourself.

Please note the evidence highlighted with a bar in the margins. This evidence will prove the inadequacy of the existing, yet unfounded formulated theories.

How Many Pyramids Are There?

There are ten large pyramids within 50 miles of each other, and they are located in Giza, Saqqara, Dahshur and Meidum.

Were the Pyramids Tombs?

Only one pyramid, which is Zoser's Step Pyramid at Saqqara, is a tomb, as proven by its complete burial chambers. The nine remaining pyramids are not tombs. These nine pyramids contain a total of fourteen chambers and just three empty sarcophagi.

These nine pyramids do not make any reference to any Pharaoh. They have been attributed to specific Pharaohs, based only on the surrounding pyramid complexes, which repeatedly refer to them. But there is very little direct evidence linking these Pharaohs to the pyramids themselves.

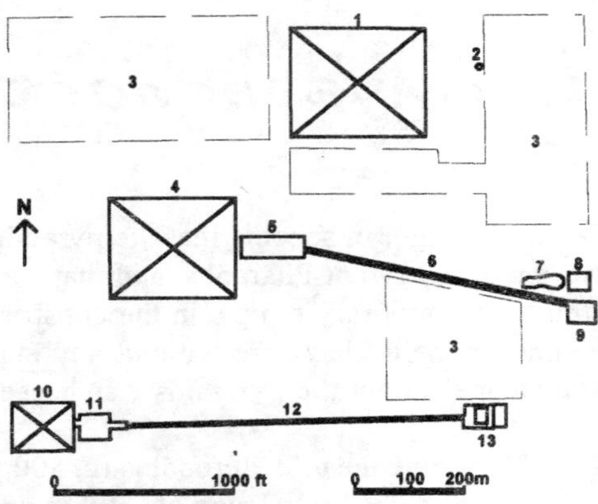

Giza Plateau
1 Great Pyramid of Cheops (Khufu). 2 Tomb of Hetepheres. 3 Mastaba Fields. 4 Pyramid of Chephren (Khafre). 5 Mortuary Temple of Chephren. 6 Causeway to Valley Temple. 7 Great Sphinx. 8 Temple of the Sphinx. 9 Valley Temple of Chephren. 10 Pyramid of Mycerinus (Menkaure). 11 Mortuary Temple of Mycerinus. 12 Mycerinus causeway. 13 Valley Temple of Mycerinus.

The "common" story continues to be taught in schools, stating that the pyramids are about 5,000 years old. There are some scholars who challenge this, and place the building of the pyramids at around 10,000 B.C. These views should not be dismissed, because the "common view" itself is not well supported.

Early Historical Accounts of the Great Pyramid

- Herodotus told us that his sources told him that Cheops' body was placed in a chamber deep below the pyramid, that the chamber was fed with water via a canal from the Nile and that the water turned the tomb into an underground island. This description sounds more like the Oserion Structure at Abydos, which is an island tomb, more or less. (Read more about it under the chapter, 'The Sphinx, Older Than History'.)

Modern excavations and explorations never found such a chamber, and if it ever existed it would have been found almost another one hundred feet below the level of the existing unfinished chamber, which is already one hundred feet into the bedrock below the base of the pyramid. This will put it two hundred feet below the bedrock.

- NO early historians ever mentioned any hidden chambers or passages.

The Physical Evidence Inside the Great Pyramid

Let us review the main components of the *Great Pyramid of Giza*:

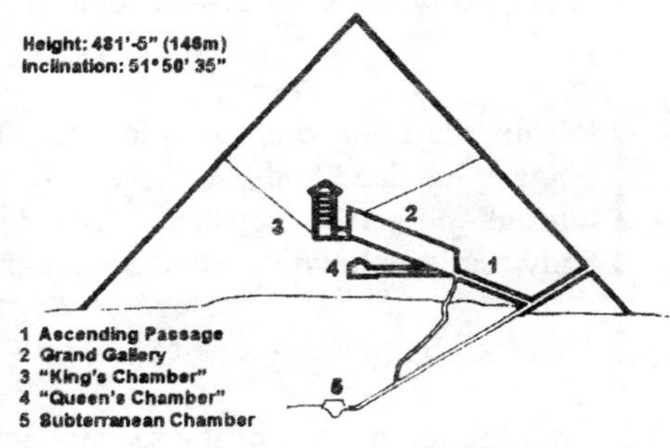

1. **Ascending Passage:** After passing through the entrance, this passage rises at an angle of 26 degrees for a distance of 129 feet (39m). The passage is too low to stand up in and one must go through it hunched over.

   The unnecessary smallness of this passage is contrary to all Egyptian tombs, where ample passages or shafts are provided for the manipulation of the sarcophagus. The Great Pyramid and all other pyramids of Giza, Dahshur and Meidum are distinctively lacking in such space arrangements.

   At the end of the ascending passage, there are two passages, one continues horizontally and ends at the "Queen's Chamber" while the other one is the famous Grand Gallery which leads us to the "King's Chamber".

2. **Grand Gallery:** Like all internal passages, its angle of ascension is 26 degrees. It is 157 feet (48m) long, 29 feet (8.5m) high and 62 inches (1.6m) wide at the bottom and 41 inches (1m) wide at the top..

   Egyptian tombs always contained figures of neterw, offerings or inscriptions, which are all noticeably absent here as well as the other eight pyramids.

   Once inside the gallery, especially at its top, one can envision this gallery open to the sky, acting as an astronomical observatory.

3. **"King's Chamber":** The passageway leading from the top end of the Grand Gallery to the "King's Chamber", contains distinctive features. The passageway is too narrow for the lidless sarcophagus that is now in the "King's Chamber", to pass through it. This means that

the coffer was placed in the chamber, as the pyramid was being built. The passage leads to a side room which consists of a short constricted passageway for several feet, and then opens into the "King's Chamber".

If this chamber was used for the dead Pharaoh's, they must have dragged his dead body up these difficult passages so as to squeeze him through the narrow constrictions to his final resting place! Does anybody really believe that could have happened?!

There are no inscriptions of Cheop's name anywhere in the pyramid.

Even though the top of the sarcophagus is grooved to accommodate a lid, no lid, or remains of a lid, have been found in any of the pyramid passages or chambers, in spite of careful research.

The "King's Chamber" got its name from the Arabs, since their men were usually buried in tombs with a flat roof and their women in rooms with a gabled roof. So, in the Great Pyramid, the flat-roofed granite chamber was called the "King's Chamber" while the gabled, limestone chamber was called the "Queen's Chamber".

4. **"Queen's Chamber":** The horizontal passage, from the top of the ascending passage to this chamber, is 127 feet (39 m) long. At the end of this passage, the floor drops suddenly two feet. No explanation was given by any scholar as to the purpose of such a drop.

   The totally empty chamber convinced all scholars that nobody was ever buried, in this chamber.

What Are The So-Called "Pyramid Texts"?

Before answering this question, some background information is in order. King Zoser's Step Pyramid was built at Saqqara, about 2630 B.C., and contains inscriptions, offering rooms, and most of the funerary features found in both earlier and later tombs.

The later great pyramids of Giza, Dahshur, and Meidum were built during the Fourth Dynasty (2575-2465 B.C.), and they have no inscriptions whatsoever, and in every other aspect, differ from other earlier and later tombs, simply because they are not tombs.

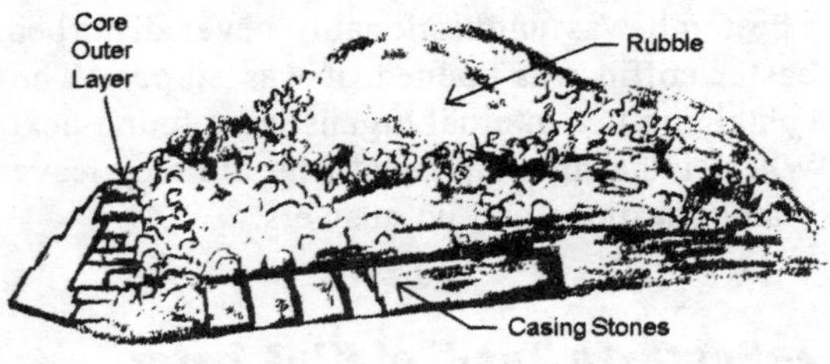

One hundred years later, at the end of the Fifth Dynasty, King Unas built a small and ungenuine pyramid at Saqqara. (Saqqara was the burial ground of Northern Egypt.) It was nothing more than a heap of rubble, built up to support the outer layers of the core, which in turn, supported the casing stones. The earliest Egyptian funerary texts are found in its underground burial chamber and its ancillary rooms. It is these funerary texts, carved on the walls, that are called the '**Pyramid Texts**'.

They should have been called the '**Unas Funerary Texts**', because the superstructure is actually a heap of rubble, and not a pyramid structure.

Nobody is sure about the use of these texts. No one knows when these texts were composed, but everyone who has studied them agrees that for the most part, they date from much earlier times.

The **Unas Funerary Texts** form the basis for all subsequent funerary literature in Egypt, such as, The Book of the Coming Forth by Day (known, mistakenly, as The Book of the Dead), The Book of What Is In the Duat (or Underworld), The Book of the Gates, The Book of Caverns, The Litany of Re, The Book of Aker, The Book of Day, and The Book of Night.

What is a Double Burial?

This ancient mysterious custom may shed some light on the subject of the pyramids. It appears that the early dynastic kings have had two *'tombs'*, one in the north at Saqqara, and another in the south at Abydos. What is even odder is that, in many of them, no actual evidence of burial has been found in either one!!

Here are some interesting cases:

1- Queen Hetepheres (Cheops' Mother) Tomb

In 1925, the only undisturbed Old Kingdom tomb ever found was discovered at Giza Plateau. In it was found the alabaster sarcophagus and the funerary furniture of Queen Hetepheres (Cheops' mother and Snefru's wife).

The tomb was unquestionably never disturbed. However, when the alabaster coffin was opened, it was empty. The canopic jars of the queen containing her internal organs were found next to the empty sarcophagus. Where is her mummy? and why did they leave an empty coffin? Many questions and no answers.

2- Southern Tomb of King Zoser

The Southern Tomb is a remarkable set of chambers, located 700 feet from the Zoser Pyramid, in a pit, at a deep subterranean level. These chambers are lined with blue tiles similar to the burial chambers of the Zoser Step Pyramid. These unmolested empty rooms are too small to hold the body. Some have guessed that it may have been intended to hold Zoser's canopic jars. What is the purpose of this empty tomb, located 700 feet from the actual burial tomb of Zoser? No explanation.

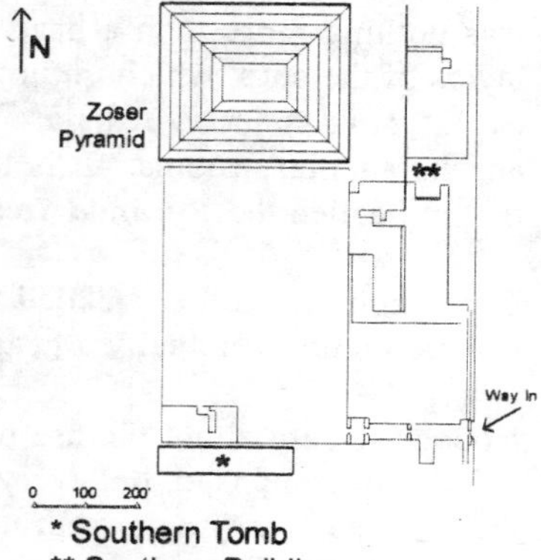

* Southern Tomb
** Southern Building

3- Snefru's Pyramids

Snefru (Cheops father) seems to have had two, possibly even three, large pyramids, at Dahshur and Meidum. One could not expect him to be buried in all of them!

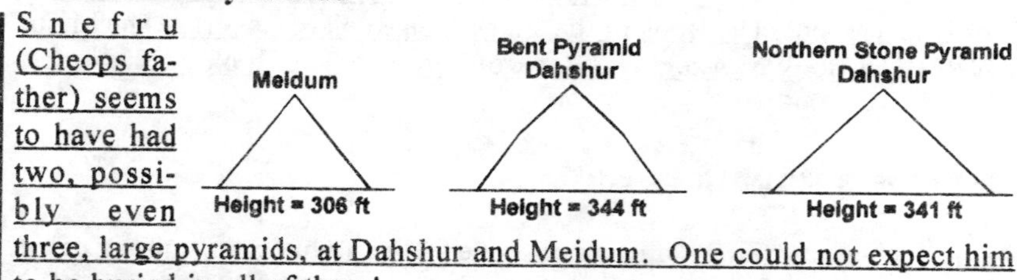

- The undisturbed and empty sarcophagi of Queen Hetepheres, the southern chamber of King Zoser, the empty lidless sarcophagi of Cheops and Chephren, all these and many similar cases present a difficult question. Something other than a mummy was intended to be ritually entombed in these empty sarcophagi.

- Most scholars, however, tend to escape difficult questions and provide us with unreasonably simplistic (almost stupid) answers which do not add up.

• Some scholars have explained this double burial custom as a political move, designed to maintain unity between the north and south, by having the king buried in both.

• Other scholars, however, believe that the division into north and south was spiritually symbolic, and not political. These separate "tombs" may have intended to represent the solar principle in the north and the lunar principle in the south.

How About the Only Pyramid as a Tomb?

The Step Pyramid at Saqqara, has the only burial chamber, of all the ten large pyramids. The burial chamber of the Step Pyramid contains inscriptions, offering rooms, and most of the other funerary features found in both earlier and later tombs. The arrangement of the corridors and chambers inside the Step Pyramid are very different from what you see at Giza, Dahshur and Meidum.

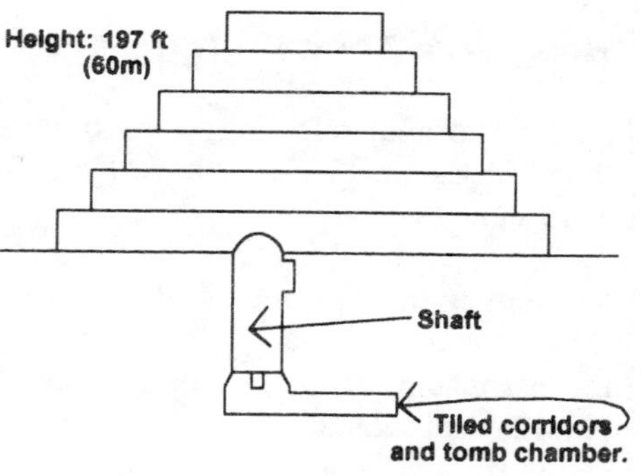

Who Built the Pyramids?

• Almost no historical information exists about the builders of the pyramids. The alleged "tyranny of Cheops" cited by Herodotus, was generally accepted, and even elaborated upon, by non-factual writers. Rational scholars challenged the notion of slave labor, since managing such huge numbers of disgruntled slaves, gathered in one small area, would have been a difficult task and potentially explosive.

• Slavery, in Egypt, was a small, captive minority living in a large and populous country. A very large work force must have been mobilized to produce the pyramids. Upon rational reflection, it is reasonable to suppose that they labored willingly. This is not hard to comprehend once the notion of the pyramid being a tomb is dismissed.

Additionally, slaves had more rights in ancient Egypt than African-Americans did before the Civil Rights Act. Slaves also had more rights than the present day illegal migrant workers in the United States.

- Herodotus reported that his Egyptian guide told him that Cheops' predecessor, Snefru, was a good king. Yet the two mighty pyramids of Dahshur (and possibly the "collapsed" pyramid of Meidum) attributed to Snefru required more than three times the stones and labor required for the Great Pyramid itself. The longest estimate of Snefru's reign is twenty-four years, which is about the same period estimated for Cheops' reign. This is a major contradiction in Herodotus' account of the "tyrant" and "good" kings.

How Were They Built?

Nothing official referring to the building of the pyramids has ever been found in Egypt. We only have Herodotus' account of how the pyramids were built.

Remember that Herodotus was hearing a tale handed down by word of mouth for two thousand years. His account is straightforward but full of inconsistencies and foolishness. Herodotus' and other views will be discussed, with related points of interest throughout this book. Here are excerpts from Herodotus' account:

> *"The work went on in three-month shifts, a hundred thousand men to a shift. It took ten years of this oppressive slave labor to build the track along which the blocks were hauled—a work in my opinion, of hardly less magnitude than the pyramid itself: for it is five furlongs (3300 ft = 5/8 mile) in length, sixty feet wide, forty-eight feet high at its highest point, and constructed of polished stone blocks decorated with carvings of animals."*
>
> *"To build the pyramid itself took twenty years."*
>
> *"The method employed was to build it in steps, or, as some call them, tiers or terraces. When the base was complete, the blocks for the first tier above it were lifted from ground level by contrivances made of short timbers; on this first tier was another, which raised the blocks a stage higher, then yet another which raised them yet higher still.*

Each tier or story had its set of levers, or it may be that they used the same one, which, being easy to carry, they shifted up from stage to stage as seen as its load was dropped into place. Both methods are mentioned, so I give them both here."

- The stone ramp mentioned by Herodotus, being forty-eight feet high, is the causeway between the mortuary temple and the valley temple, for each of Chephren and Mycerinus. The actual track (ramp) which was probably used to haul the blocks from the Nile to the foot of the Cheops pyramid was a temporary affair made of mud-brick. Aerial photographs, of the Giza Plateau, show remains of similar ramps to other smaller pyramids.

- Most scholars estimate Cheops' reign at no more than twenty-five years, and don't agree with Herodotus' account of fifty years.

- No one was able to reproduce the lifting device mentioned by Herodotus.

- Many scholars dismiss any existence of Herodotus' lifting device. They want to believe that the only way to build the pyramid is by increasing both the height and length of a temporary ramp, as it was raised to the successive levels of the pyramid.

By not having an open mind, these scholars made it difficult for themselves to come up with answers to many questions.

The Staggering Calculations

The Danish civil engineer, P. Garde-Hanson's calculations showed that a ramp built all the way to the top of the pyramid would require 17.5 million cubic yards of material (seven times the amount needed for the pyramid itself) and a work force of 240,000 to build it within Cheops' reign.

Garde-Hanson estimated that if there were a ramp built to the top of the pyramid, a work force of 300,000 would require a further eight years to dismantle the ramp at the completion of the pyramid. Logically this huge amount of rubbish should still be visible somewhere in the vicinity - and it is not.

Garde-Hanson then theorized that maybe they built a ramp that reached halfway up the pyramid. At such a level, about ninety percent of the material needed for the pyramid would have been used, by using only half the material needed for the ramp.

Additionally, Garde-Hanson proposed a mysterious lifting device of some kind, which is, of course, still an unresolved question.

Garde-Hanson had gone into certain practical aspects which were ignored by others. Try to visualize the staggering figures as you visit the pyramid: 4,000 year-round quarrymen producing 330 blocks per day. During inundation season, 4,000 blocks per day are transported to the Nile, ferried across, hauled up the ramp to the Giza plateau, and set into place in the core –a rate of 6.67 blocks per minute! Imagine 6.67 blocks every 60 seconds!!!

The Forgotten Casing Stones

- The pyramid was dressed with 115,000 casing stones, 5.5 acres of them on each face of the pyramid. Each weighed more than ten tons apiece. A tolerance of .01 inch was the maximum allowed between these stones, so that a paper cannot fit between them.

- No one knows if the casing stones were set in place from the top down, as Herodotus claims, or from the bottom up.

- Were the casing stones set in place first and then had the core masonry filled in behind them? No one knows.

- Were the stones dressed and polished before setting them in place or after? And if before, then setting these huge sharp-edged blocks in place, without banging or chipping them, must have been a major task by itself.

The Forgotten Snefru Pyramids

If the two main pyramids at Dahshur are to be attributed to Snefru, and possibly a third pyramid at Meidum, it means that he, in the course of his reign of twenty-four years, was responsible for the quarrying, transport, and dressing of some nine million tons of stone - **more than three times the quantity of the Great Pyramid.** Even trying to calculate the logistics of such work, in modern terms, is overwhelming.

The Possible Answers

Given the lack of satisfactory answers to the problems of pyramid construction, it is no wonder that any number of unorthodox methods have been suggested, such as:

1. The Egyptians knew some method for reversing the force of gravity.

2. They were able to utilize sound waves to do mechanical work.

3. They were able to transport the blocks by water and floated them into place, since even the biggest block once afloat could be handled with very little effort.

   The problem, of course, is showing how the water could have been brought uphill from the Nile to the Giza plateau.

4. In states of heightened consciousness, men can perform unthinkable physical acts. There is medical evidence to support this condition. Eastern mystical literature contains many reports of specially skilled people achieving such a state.

5. It is not illogical to suggest that the Egyptians understood and utilized techniques of mechanical balance unknown to us. They were able to manipulate these large stones with complete understanding of mechanical principles which required only small tools.

   In short, they were big men (brain wise) with small machines.

In conclusion, there is no definite answer. There are many theories, but most of them reflect our failure to admit the superiority of those ancient people. Our egotistical notions lead us to simple answers for difficult questions. As long as we are so conceited about our "modern technology and capabilities" which really amounts to smaller men and bigger machines, the problem of how the pyramids were built will probably remain open. Not until the spirit that motivated these ancient people can be comprehended by us, will we ever be able to figure out the answers.

What Were the Pyramids For?

Here are some possible uses for the Great Pyramid of Cheops:

1. Arab legends spoke of the pyramid gallery as an observatory. Fully 80% of the night sky would have been observable from the Grand Gallery.

2. The wonderfully long polished inner corridors of the pyramids originally served some astronomical function.

3. The lidless sarcophagus, in the so-called "King's Chamber", is a sort of three-dimensional yardstick, and was designed to embody different key units of the Egyptian system of volumes.

4. The Great Pyramid, in particular, acts as an enormous sundial. Its shadow to the north, and its reflected sunlight to the south, annually marked solstices (longest and shortest days in the year), and equinoxes (days of equal day/night) with very high level of accuracy.

5. Egyptians, since the very beginning of recorded history, knew the exact dimensions of the earth, and their ancient systems of measurements were based upon that knowledge.

   The Great Pyramid is, in some sense, a model of the earth, or contained within it, are elements that relate to the dimensions of the earth, such as:

   a. It's apex represents the pole, and the perimeter represents the equator. This is the reason that the ratio of the perimeter to the height is equal to (2 x Pi).

   b. The Great Pyramid represents the northern hemisphere, to a scale of 1:43,200. This scale for the northern hemisphere represent one half 86,400. There are 86,400 seconds in 24 hours for both the northern and southern hemispheres.

c. The very small discrepancies (of several inches over the 754-foot length of the base) were deliberate. They were meant to reflect an ingenious means of incorporating into the pyramid the "discrepancies" of the earth itself, which is the flattening of the earth's globe at the poles.

d. The golden section, or Phi, was incorporated into the pyramids. It is this ratio that is the "key to structure of the cosmos" acknowledged later by the Greeks. Read more about it in the chapter, 'Numbers Are Not Just Numbers'.

6. The pyramid symbolizes the creative principle of nature and also illustrates the principles of geometry, mathematics, astronomy, and astrology. The interior of the building may have served as a temple of initiation where men rose towards God and God descended toward man.

The specific scientific, or other functions of the other pyramids remain to be discovered.

What is Pyramid Power?

- Many researchers found that there was some property in the pyramidal shape that made it responsible for extraordinary powers. They experimented with various items, by placing each item in the equivalent position of the "King's Chamber", within a scaled model of a correctly oriented pyramid. They found out that highly perishable materials were preserved, blunt old-fashioned carbon steel razor blades regained their sharp edges after an overnight stay, etc. Many concluded that the pyramidal shape itself was responsible: which somehow changed the physical, chemical, and biological processes that might take place within that shape. This experimentation led to the phenomenon known as "Pyramid Power".

We know from physics that when a beam of light goes through a prism, the beam will split into its constituents and produce a rainbow. Only the shape of a prism can do it and one could have called it "Prism Power" because of its special effect. Similarly the shape of the pyramid has special powers. Therefore, pyramid power should not be viewed as an unproven fantasy.

• The physical effects of color are known to affect us. Certain color schemes have pacifying and others stimulating effects. If colors affect us physically, it is not illogical to propose that shapes and forms might also affect us in some way.

• Science has finally recognized that the earth is a living body, with "channels" transferring magnetic, electromagnetic and other subtle currents from the soils of the earth. The surface of the earth is subjected to a whole range of invisible but detectable forms of wave energy. Science is finally confirming what researchers have long insisted, which is that ancient monuments such as the pyramids and other temples of Europe and elsewhere were deliberately constructed, at sites where these subtle energies converge.

What Now?

We have ended this chapter with more questions than answers. It is like a mirage, as soon as we think we found an answer, we find the horizon is even more expansive.

> **The answers to our questions are probably in front of our noses, but we cannot see them. As long as we examine, evaluate, and judge the ancient Egyptians through our present way of thinking, the answers will be elusive and the pyramids will continue to mystify us.**

Chapter 19

The Sphinx
Older Than History

• One can never forget the first glimpse of the Sphinx. It is a common experience among its viewers, to be "struck" by its presence. It is a masterpiece of artistic composition with nothing like it on earth. The fusion of the body of the lion with the head of a man resulted in a seemingly singular natural being.

• All scholars agree that the Sphinx is a solar symbol. The Sphinx consists of the body of the lion symbolizing the power, in its physical form and the head of man, symbolizing intelligence and consciousness. The significance of the Sphinx is an ongoing debate.

• One cannot help but admire this marvelous statue and the nicety of proportion of its head. The mastery of the sculptor is evident in his ability to preserve the exact proportion and balance of every part, (nose, eyes, ears, ...etc.), in a face of such colossal size.

But when was the Sphinx built? And who built it? Many believe the answers are somewhere between 2520-2494 B.C., during the reign of Khafre (Chephren). But these commonly held beliefs are wrong. Let us study the evidence...

The Physical Evidence

1- The Sphinx

The original site, where the Sphinx is located, was a gently sloping plane with an outcrop of harder rock. The head of the Sphinx was carved out of this outcrop.

To form the body of the Sphinx, the stone has been quarried away from all around the soon-to-be body. The quarried stone was used to build the two temples east and south of the Sphinx.

The main features of the Sphinx are comprised of different geological conditions.

A- The head of the Sphinx was made of a hard strata which is resistant to the effects of the natural elements. The present damage to the face was caused by soldiers who used the Sphinx as an artillery target in the eighteenth century.

B- The body of the Sphinx was made of a softer limestone strata which in turn consists of alternate harder and softer layers. These alternate layers are visible on site as weathered corrugation, which is about two feet deep into the bedrock.

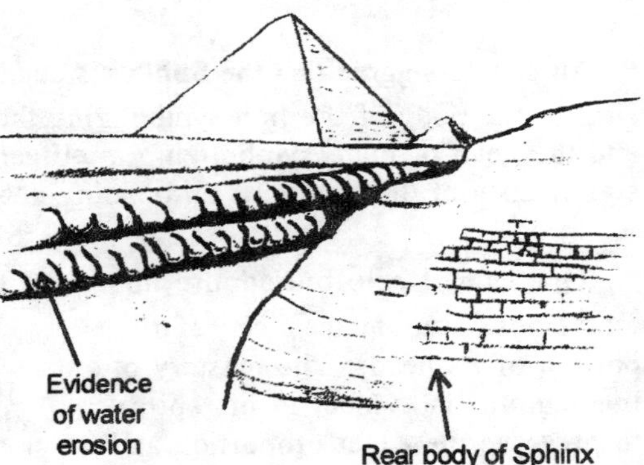

C- The base of the Sphinx, as well as the bottom of the original quarry site are made of a harder limestone which is resistant to the effects of the natural elements.

The Eroded Body

The question is: what caused the erosion of the body?
There are two possible causes:

A- Possible weathering by wind and sand.
Since the body of the Sphinx is located in a hollow, it takes less than twenty years to fill the hollow and cover the body totally.
The Sphinx has been covered by sand since the time it was created thousands of years ago. Therefore the Sphinx was not subject to weathering exposure to wind and sand, instead it was actually protected

from such natural elements.

B- Possible water erosion.
Geologists agree that Egypt was subject to severe flooding, at the end of the last Ice Age, c. 15,000-10,000 B.C.

So, if the erosion was caused by water, the Sphinx must have been carved before Egypt was under water i.e. more than 12,000 years ago. This, in turn, is too radical for scholars to swallow, as they prefer not to change their theory that Chephren built the Sphinx.

Never mind the egos, let us study the evidence regarding the water erosion.

The Repaired Paws

Researchers have found out that the extended front paws of the Sphinx were repaired three times in three distinct operations.
The research also concluded that each repair operation was intended to replace or reinforce prior repair operations. In short, the eroded condition of the paws has never worsened since the earliest repairs were made, i.e. it was a single event and not a continuous process which caused this erosion.

The study by Mark Lehner, Field Director for the American Research Center in Egypt, showed that no substantial damage occurred to the Sphinx since its original weathering event. Lehner wrote:

> *"It seems necessary to conclude ... that the core-body of the Sphinx was already in a severe state of erosion when the earliest level of masonry was added ....*
>
> *If we assume that a sand covering would act more to protect than to erode the statue, this leaves less than a millennium, or perhaps half a millennium, for the core to have eroded to the conditions shown by the profiles under the added masonry."*

Lehner estimated that the earliest of the three repairs occurred during the New Kingdom. He, however, never provided any historical or physical evidence to support his suggested time era. Some scholars are inclined to believe that the earliest repair was done by Chephren who was more of a restorer of the Sphinx than its builder.

Did the Ground Water Do It?

Most scholars have resigned themselves to the fact that the water caused the erosion to the body of the Sphinx. However, it was suggested that ground water may have risen, through capillary action, to react with the limestone of the Sphinx body causing this one-time erosion event. After 500 years the ground water dropped back down, and this phenomenon was never to occur again!

The evidence is overwhelming against the ground water theory. Here is why:

A- Over the course of thousands of years, the inundation of the Nile had gradually deposited additional silt, on the ground of the Valley. Whenever the ground rises, so does the ground water table. It is estimated that the ground water table was thirty feet lower in Chephren's time than its present level.

It is impossible for the ground water:

(i) to rise from a much deeper level than its present level.

(ii) to erode two feet deep channels into the body of the Sphinx, and the walls of the quarry pit, in the span of five hundred years.

(iii) to drop, after this 500 years, and not to occur again.

B- Additionally, why didn't this ground water theory have any effect at the following places:

(i) The bedrock of the quarry pit where the Sphinx rests? This area was never eroded and therefore was naturally never repaired.

(ii) Any other structure which was built during the Old Kingdom, and there are scores of them throughout the country?

C- The Mortuary Temple of Chephren stands 150 feet (46m) above the plateau and had a similar erosion pattern to the body of the Sphinx.

There was definitely no ground water in the case of this temple. So how do we explain the similar erosion pattern?

There is no other rational answer except that the water erosion occurred at the end of the last Ice Age c. 15,000-10,000 B.C.

The Figure of the Head

• We were told again and again that there is a resemblance between the face of the Sphinx and the statue of Chephren at the Cairo Museum. Nobody questioned the assumed resemblance for centuries.

A graphic outline to the same scale of both Chephren and the Sphinx' head was made and both were superimposed on each other, on a U.S. Television network and **there was no resemblance whatsoever.**

• Herodotus, who wrote about the pyramids in detail, did not mention the Sphinx. Since it takes less than twenty years to fill the Sphinx' hollow, Herodotus could only see a colossal head above the sand while the whole body was totally below the ground surface. With many things to see in Egypt, a single head would not have excited Herodotus.

Other writers of antiquity mentioned the Sphinx without attributing it to any particular Pharaoh.

• Twthomosis IV (1413-1405 B.C.) established a stela and placed it between the paws of the Sphinx. The stela described his dreams as a prince and how he cleaned the sands around the Sphinx' body, ...etc. It is a long text, but the name of Chephren appears on it, in hieroglyphs. The text surrounding the name was illegible. As such, no one knows why the name Chephren was mentioned on Twthomosis IV's stela. This is the only place the name Chephren is mentioned, at the site of the Sphinx.

2- The Temple of the "Sphinx"

This ruined temple, is located in front of the Sphinx, and is closed to the public.

It is worth noting that a recent drill hole in front of this temple, revealed the presence of red granite at a depth of 54 feet (16.5m). Granite is not native to northern Egypt and could have only come from Aswan. The presence of granite, at such a depth, is an additional proof of construction activities much earlier than 3,000 B.C.

3- The Valley Temple of "Chephren"

There is a causeway between the Mortuary Temple of Chephren and the Valley Temple, approximately 1650 feet long. Even though there are no inscriptions on the Sphinx or in this Temple, the presence of the causeway indicates some kind of a connection with that pharaoh. Later excavations found a number of Chephren statues in this temple.

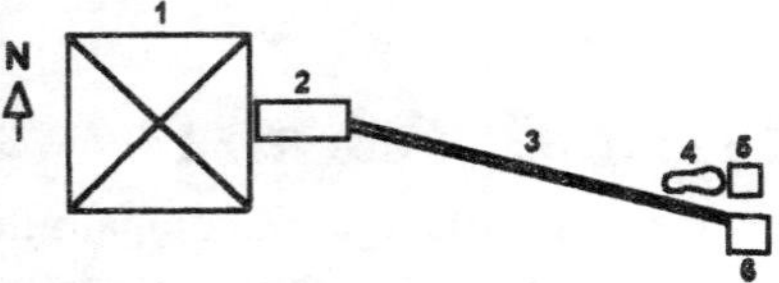

Profile of causeway.
1 Pyramid of Chephren (Khafre). **2** Mortuary Temple of Chephren. **3** Causeway to Valley Temple. **4** Great Sphinx. **5** Temple of the Sphinx. **6** Valley Temple of Chephren.

Chephren, Builder or Restorer

- The mentioned causeway, the Chephren statues and a claimed resemblance between the Sphinx and the statue of Chephren: all these factors caused many scholars to attribute the Sphinx and its temple complex to Chephren.

- Not only did these scholars rely on very weak reasons, in their Chephren attributions, but they also chose to dismiss an important piece of evidence, namely the "Inventory Stela" which was found in Giza, in the nineteenth century.

This stela describes events during the reign of Cheops, Chephren's predecessor and indicates that Cheops ordered the building of a temple alongside the Sphinx. This means that the Sphinx was already there before Cheops and therefore could not have been built by his son, Chephren. The stela was dismissed by some, because its stylistic features appeared to be from the New Kingdom. This is not a sufficient cause to dismiss it, since <u>there are many stelas and texts from the Old Kingdom that were later copied in the New Kingdom and no one dismissed them on such a basis.</u>

- The overwhelming physical evidence, as detailed above, leads us to the rational conclusion that Chephren did not and could not have built the Sphinx.

The found statues of Chephren, the mention of his name on Twthomosis IV's stela, and the causeway may lead us to the conclusion that Chephren was probably one of the restorers of the Sphinx, which was damaged at the end of the last Ice Age c. 15,000-10,000 B.C.

The Corroborative Evidence

Other physical and historical evidence throughout Egypt supports the physical evidence in Giza, in proving a much greater antiquity of the Egyptian civilization.

1- The Oseirion Structure at Abydos

- The Oseirion Structure, or Tomb of Osiris, is located in Abydos. Much of what is known of the pre-dynastic centuries comes from the funerary remains of Abydos.

- The Legend of Osiris is much older than dynastic Egypt.

- Abydos was the chief seat of worship of Osiris, Lord of the Underworld.

- King Seti I (1333-1304 BC) built the Temple of Osiris, which was completed by his son Ramses II, next to the Oseirion Structure.

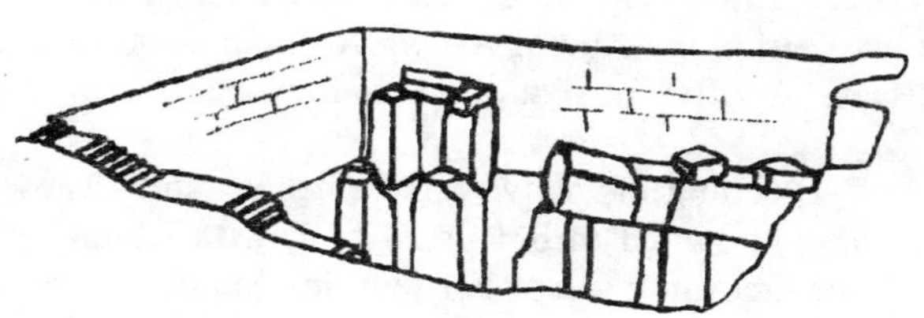

- The Oseirion Structure is located much below the elevation of Seti's Temple of Osiris and is partially submerged underneath the ground water table. The Oseirion's foundations are cut many feet below the present level of the water table, which has risen some twenty feet since New Kingdom times.

- Some scholars attributed the building of the Oseirion to Seti I. However, the style of Oseirion, being massive, bare, and simple, is very different from the elegant Seti temple with its acres of exquisite carvings. The difference in style between the two structures is too extreme to be built by one Pharaoh.

- The tremendous difference in elevation between the Oseirion and Seti's Temple as well as the dramatic difference in style between the two, suggest to many scholars that the Oseirion is a much older building.

• The evidence at the Oseirion is consistent with the evidence at Giza and elsewhere regarding the greater antiquity of the Egyptian civilization.

2- The Hathor Temple at Dendara

The signs of the zodiac are represented in two locations of this temple.

The first location is the ceiling of the temple where the sign of Cancer, the Crab, is shown first in the order of the twelve signs. Cancer is located opposite the leg of Nut, the sky, as she stretches over the universe.

The second location is the ceiling of the upper level of the temple, where the signs are arranged in a spiral with the Crab prominently shown at its center.

The placement of the Cancer sign, at the beginning of the order of the zodiac signs, is additional proof that the Egyptian civilization started recording history under the sign of Cancer, which astronomically occurred between 10,000 and 8,000 B.C. Incidentally, when this temple was built, it was during the Age of Aries. At the present time we are in the Age of Pisces. A different sign of the zodiac occurs every two thousand years.

> The ceiling of many of the Theban tombs show Nut, the sky, stretched in her usual arch with Kheper, the newly born morning sun at her feet, instead of Cancer, as shown at Dendara Temple, signifying that the Cancer sign at Dendara represented the new sun of the Egyptian civilization.

Kheper

3- The Early Historian Accounts

The Greek and Roman writers of antiquity, basing their accounts on information either first or second-hand from Egyptian sources, claimed a greater antiquity for Egyptian civilization than that currently established by Egyptologists. These Egyptian sources called for antiquity ranging from 24,000 to 36,000 years during which Egypt was civilized.

Read more about it in the chapter 'The First Pharaoh of Egypt'.

Part IV

Ancient Egypt and the Bible

Chapter 20

The History of the Bible

General

• The biblical accounts of the encounters between the Israelites and ancient Egypt have saturated the minds of the human race, for a long time. Ancient Egypt became the permanent casualty of the Chosen People. This book is an attempt to present both views of what happened.

• Ancient Egypt and the Israelites had generally a good relationship until Moses and his mother arrived on the scene. Their actions resulted in the Exodus, which was a bitter divorce between the Egyptians and the Israelites. Just like any bitter divorce, there are charges and counter charges. The two sides typically ignored each other, but it is the generations which followed (like the children in a divorce case) who have paid and will continue to pay the price.

If we review what happened rationally we will find that Egyptian historical evidence will place certain Old Testament stories in logical settings. As such, many biblical stories, which are considered by many to be fairy tales, will become credible.
However, we need to have an open mind and not allow egotism and stubbornness to stand in the way of being rational.

- The world was excited in 1947 and the following years, when the Dead Sea Scrolls were discovered. The results of the majority of these findings are being kept secret from the world. The contents of the few released scrolls contradict presently held biblical beliefs. The released scrolls will be discussed in the coming chapters.

- The purpose of this book is to identify historical figures of the Bible. It is NOT to argue theological interpretations of their lives and teachings that subsequently developed.

- The Bible, which is notorious in stating names of persons, sites, and water wells which in many cases have no impact on the story whatsoever, never named a pharaoh or his residence, when an event occurred.

  Among the many Pharaohs mentioned in the Bible, one married Abraham's wife. Another hired Joseph and made him his vizier (the highest officer in the country). The succeeding Pharaoh kept Joseph in his post. There were several Pharaohs in Moses' story. Solomon married a Pharaoh's daughter. The Bible would say, ***"The Pharaoh who knew not Joseph"***, or ***"Pharaoh of Oppression"***. Wouldn't it have been easier and more logical to use the name of these Pharaohs? Why did they leave <u>all</u> their names out? They must have been left out intentionally. But why?

  Egyptologists who tried to identify these Pharaohs were shocked to find the answers. Many of them tiptoed around the subject and left us to read between the lines. A conflict between historical facts and religious convictions is treading touchy, sensitive ground.

- Lack of historical evidence to support the stories we find in the Old Testament has resulted broadly in three schools of thought.

  1.) Some people expect every word of the Old Testament to be taken literally, despite the many contradictions. Often, these same people demand rational or scientific explanations for the events they encounter, in their everyday lives.

  2.) Some consider it to be basically a historical work which became distorted as a result of its initial long oral tradition as well as its eventual writing by several biblical editors.

  3.) Some consider it to be a collection of fairy tales/fables/myths that can be used as inspiration.

  The first view belongs to the religious idealists and is based on blind faith which does not require logic and/or reason in order to justify it. Blind faith is fine, so long as it is admitted.

  Rational observers will promptly find the contents of the Bible to fall somewhere between the second and the third views. <u>The Bible is a blend of history and fiction shaped by the political and religious disputes of ancient times.</u>

Sources of the Old Testament

• For two thousand years, there has been, and still is, an on-going debate over the sources of the Old Testament. Inquiring minds want to know:

- The number of biblical sources?
- When was each source written? and by whom?
- The number and extent of editing and alteration?
- Does the Bible describe actual historical events?

• The Biblical dates and ages are so badly off that no rational person can take them seriously. God created the world, according to the Bible chronology, in 4004 B.C. However, we know from other evidence that the earth was already inhabited in 4004 B.C. The ages of many biblical characters are unbelievable. The explanation that they may have attached a different meaning than we do to the word *'year'*, does not explain errors in biblical chronology. For example, we are told that Terah, Joseph's great-great-grandfather, was seventy when his son, Abram, was born. Terah, we are later told, died at the age of two hundred and five. Astonishingly, a few biblical verses later we learn that Abram was seventy-five when his father died, when according to biblical calculations, Abram should have been one hundred and twenty-five years old and not seventy-five.

• Because of its long oral tradition, biblical narration often confuses the names of places and people as well as the chronology of events. By careful examination, a rational conclusion could be drawn that many of these events took place chronologically in a different order to that described in the biblical account. Several examples of such confused chronology will be detailed in the following chapters.

• In reading the Old Testament and particularly the five books of the Pentateuch, one should consider the following facts:

- These stories were transferred by word of mouth over several centuries, before they were written down. It is inevitable to end up with distorted stories as a result of this long oral tradition.

- Upon writing the stories, the priests and the editors made their own contribution to the text that we have now.

- Translators have altered portions of the texts so as to comply with their *'standard of morality'*.

- Translation is difficult. <u>One Hebrew word may need a dozen English words to explain its exact meaning.</u>

• Ancient tradition ascribed the authorship of the Pentateuch to Moses: ***"Then the Lord said to Moses, 'Write this on a scroll as something to be remembered and make sure that Joshua hears it ...'"***

• The view that Moses composed the Pentateuch — the first five books of the Old Testament — from composite sources, which had been transmitted over several centuries, is no longer a valid opinion among the biblical scholars.

The Pentateuch includes the account of Moses' death. It is naturally impossible that Moses could have written about his own death. Therefore, it is logical to conclude that the writing of the Pentateuch took place long after Moses' death.

• The Pentateuch is essentially composed from the following five sources:

1- A Jehovistic source, dating from the ninth century B.C.
2- An Elohistic document, dating from the eighth century B.C.
3- The book of Deuteronomy, to be considered as a separate source, dating from the seventh century B.C.
4- A priestly source, dating from about the fifth century B.C.
5- The work of an editor who revised and edited the entire collection around the second century B.C.

The Hebrew Text of the Bible

Our standard translations of the Old Testament are based on the Massoretic Hebrew text, which came into existence in the ninth or tenth centuries A.D. This text was originated in the second century A.D. after a council had been assembled at Jamnia, a small town near Jaffa, in A.D. 70. At Jamnia the council agreed to the form and content of the Old Testament.

Hebrew, like hieroglyphics and other Semitic languages, does not have any written vowels. The true pronunciation and interpretation of the texts were accomplished by a body of Jewish scholars, who formulated a standard pronunciation of the Massorah (tradition of measure), between the seventh and tenth centuries A.D.

The Greek Text of the Bible

The Hebrew Massoretic text is not the only Canon we have for the Old Testament. The Greek text of Alexandria is even older.

In a letter written by an unknown author about 100 B.C., Ptolemy II, the King of Egypt (285-247 B.C.), ordered a Greek translation of the Bible. The High Priest of Jerusalem sent seventy-two elders to Alexandria, six scholars from each of the twelve tribes of Israel, together with an official copy of the Pentateuch. They worked for seventy-two days to produce the final copy of the Pentateuch in Greek. Later, the other books of the Old Testament were also translated into Greek by other scholars and the whole work became known as the *Septuagint*, which means *'The Seventy'*. The Greek text was adopted as the Bible of the early Church, but was abandoned later in favor of the Hebrew Massoretic text.

The Septuagint is, however, still used today by the Greek Orthodox Church as its authorized Bible.

The Biblical Ancient Egyptian/Israelites' Encounters

There is no doubt that there are serious problems with the chronology of many events in the Bible. This came as a result of the many narrators and editors working along the span of centuries, as well as the bad blood between the Jews and Egypt, after the Exodus. The encounters between the Israelites and ancient Egypt can be divided into three eras:

1- Pre Sojourn in Egypt

- Abram and Sarai entered Egypt for a period of time. Upon Abram and Sarai's return from Egypt to Canaan (present-day Israel/Lebanon), major changes began to occur to their small tribe. The Bible tells us that the Lord told Abram,

> *"Know for certain that your descendants will be aliens living in a land that is not theirs, and they will be enslaved and ill-treated for*

four hundred years...The fourth generation will return here..."

God also made a covenant with Abram, saying,

> *"To your descendants I give this land, from the river of Egypt to the great river, the Euphrates..."*

- Sarah gave birth to Isaac who was not allowed to go to Egypt.
- Isaac begat Jacob in Canaan.
- Jacob begat Joseph.

The evidence from the ancient Egyptian history, as detailed in later chapters will show that:

> **✧ Twthomosis III was the Pharaoh in the Abraham and Sarah story and that Twthomosis III and the biblical King David are one and the same.**

2- Israelites' Sojourn in Egypt

- Joseph's half brothers sold him as a slave, in Egypt. He later became the second in command to the Pharaoh. The Pharaoh allowed Joseph to bring his family to Egypt.

- Jacob (Joseph's father) who was also known as Israel, took his tribal family of seventy to settle in Goshen, east of the Nile delta.

- When did the Israelites enter Egypt and how long did they remain there before the Exodus?

It is generally accepted that they were in Egypt at the end of the Eighteenth Dynasty, and into the Nineteenth (c. 1308 BC). Scholars will disagree on when they arrived and when they departed.

The Old Testament does not provide any dates, or the name of the Pharaoh's capital city at the time, or the name of the Pharaoh, referring to him only as *'Pharaoh'*, *'King'* or *'Pharaoh, King of Egypt!'*

• The Old Testament provides two contradictory accounts about the length of time the Israelites spent in Egypt:

1- Duration of 430 years:
"Now the sojourning of the children of Israel, who dwelt in Egypt, was four hundred and thirty years." (Exodus 12:40)

2- Duration of four generations:
The warning to Abraham
"... Know of a surety that thy seed shall be a stranger in a land that is not theirs, and shall serve them; and they shall afflict them four hundred years ... But in the fourth generation they shall come hither again." (Genesis 15:13,16)
In Hebrew it reads *'wa dor rabi'i yashwbw hena'*.

The duration of four generations, and not 430 years, is the correct duration for the following reasons:

A- The exact translation of this Hebrew verse is: *"And the fourth (dor) return they here."* Grammatically *'the fourth dor'* is the subject of the verb. Therefore, *dor* can only mean *'generation'*. The word *dor* was never used to mean a hundred-year cycle in Hebrew or Assyrian, or Ugaritic texts.

B- What confirms the biblical word *'dor'* to mean *'a generation'* is the fact that the Pentateuch names only four generations between the time of the Descent into Egypt and the Exodus.

C- The Talmud does not agree with 430 years either as the length of the Israelites' sojourn in Egypt; *"And the children of Israel journeyed from Raamses to Succoth. Two hundred and ten years after their entrance into Egypt, the Israelites departed therefrom, six hundred thousand men, with wives and children."*

The evidence from the ancient Egyptian history, as detailed in the following chapters will show that:

- **Joseph entered Egypt and became the vizier (second in command) to Pharaoh Twthomosis IV (1413-1405 B.C.) and was the vizier for the succeeding Pharaoh, Amenhotep III (1405-1367 B.C.).**

✧ **Joseph's daughter, Tiye, was married to Amenhotep III. Tiye gave birth to Akhenaton and Semenkhkare.**

✧ **Akhenaton begat Twtankhamen.**

✧ **The four generations of the Sojourn are actually**
- **Joseph**
- **Tiye**
- **Akhenaton (to be identified later as the biblical Moses)**
- **Twtankhamen (to be identified later as the biblical Jesus)**

✧ **Amenhotep III and the biblical King Solomon are one and the same.**

3- The Exodus and Living in the Promised Land

• Moses (Akhenaton), who lived in exile in Sinai for several years, went back to Egypt to challenge the authority of the self-appointed Pharaoh. He was allowed to leave with the Israelites from Egypt in what is known as the Exodus. After wandering in the desert, Moses died and the Israelites settled in their promised land.

• They were ruled by King David whose empire extended from the Nile to the Euphrates.

• King David begat Solomon, who sat on his father's throne after his death.

• The new Israelite Kingdom vanished after Solomon's death as quickly as it was created by King David.

The historical evidence from ancient Egypt, in the following chapters, will show that:

✧ **Moses was killed by King Seti I (1333-1304 B.C.) and the Israelites wandered the desert for forty years before settling in Canaan. The occupation of Canaan was a gradual process, as also confirmed in the Book of Judges.**

✧ **King David's war accounts match precisely with those of King Twthomosis III (1490-1436 B.C.).**

✧ **King Solomon's life and lack of wars match precisely with those of King Amenhotep III (1436-1413 B.C.).**

CHRONOLOGY OF THE EIGHTEENTH DYNASTY

King	*Length of Reign*	*Dates*
Ahmosis	22	1575-1550 B.C.
Amenhotep I	21	1550-1528 B.C.
Twthmosis I	4 or 9	1528-1510 B.C.
Twthmosis II	18	1510-1490 B.C.
Hatshepsut	20 or 22	1490-1468 B.C.
Twthmosis III	54	1490-1436 B.C.
Amenhotep II	23	1436-1413 B.C.
Twthmosis IV	8	1413-1405 B.C.
Amenhotep III	38	1405-1367 B.C.
Amenhotep IV (Akhenaten)	6	1367-1361 B.C.
Semenkhkare	-	1361-1361 B.C.
Twtankhamun	9	1361-1352 B.C.
Aye	4	1352-1348 B.C.
Horemheb	13	1348-1335 B.C.

CHRONOLOGY OF THE NINETEENTH DYNASTY

King	Length of Reign	Dates
Ramses I	2	1335-1333 B.C.
Seti I	29	1333-1304 B.C.
Ramses II	67	1304-1237 B.C.
Merenptah	10	1237-1227 B.C.

These dates are given here to be helpful to the reader: the difference between them, and other lists will be resolved later when the co-regency periods between some kings are clarified.

The Names of God in the Old Testament

It is important that we review the Hebrew names, their meanings and how each is translated into English. The Hebrew word *'Lord'* may be construed to mean *God* in English, but in its original Hebrew may mean a *man* as a *Lord.*

The Israelites' God was identified in a variety of terms, such as:

El: (Genesis, 33:20);
El 'Elyon (The Most High): (Psalms, 73:11);
El 'Olam (The Everlasting God): (Genesis, 21:33);
El Shaddai (God Almighty): (Genesis, 17:1);
El Ro-i (The God Who Sees Me, or The God Of Vision): (Exodus, 6:3);

Other names and their meanings are:

Elohim: is the plural of Eloho, meaning *'a god'*, and is used in the Bible more than two thousand times. **Eloho** is usually translated to *'God'* in English.

Elohim is also used for *'pagan'* gods and goddesses (Exodus, 12:12 and I Kings, 11:5).

Jehovah: is the personal name of the God of Israel, and is written in Hebrew with four consonants, YHWH, which is understood to mean *'I am'*. This name occurs frequently in the Bible. Jehovah is usually translated to *'Lord'* in English.

Strangely, the Hebrew word 'YHWH' could be written, but is not supposed to be read aloud by the Jews and had to be pronounced as *'Adonai'*. This Jewish practice started just before Moses returned to Egypt to challenge the Pharaoh. (Read more about it under the chapter 'The Exodus, the Bitter Divorce'.) The Jewish standard explanation is that a ban on uttering God's personal name was intended as a sign of respect. Such an explanation is contradicted by the fact, that all the other names given to the Israelite God before the time of Moses, as well as *Adonai*, are spoken aloud by the Jews.

Adonai: It is used in the Bible to refer to human beings (***"The man, who is the Lord of the land ..."***, Genesis, 42:30') as well as God.
Adonai is translated to *'Lord'* in English (meaning *God* or a *man*).
Adonai Jehovah: as a combined form is found in Genesis, 15:2, Genesis

15:8, and Deuteronomy 3:24.
It is translated to *'My Lord Jehovah'* in English.

Barren Women and Miracles

Barren women who later have children are a recurrent theme in the Old Testament. At such times, and still in some parts of the Middle East, it was not uncommon for a girl to get married before she reached child-bearing age. Therefore, the wife would be considered barren until she reached an age when she could get pregnant. Historical records support these early marriages, such as the case of Tiye, who was only about eight years old when Amenhotep III made her his Great Royal Wife.

Meaning of Key Words

When ancient writings are translated and/or interpreted incorrectly, one will find oneself on the wrong track of relationships between individuals, their actual roles, and/or a wrong chronology of events. In order to be able to understand and/or to realize the cause for some of the discrepancies in ancient writings, the following are some keywords which have several meanings.

Lord — This word could mean God, or *a person in a high position.* Taking this lingual fact into account will lead us to read many parts of the Bible, in a different and interesting light.

Worship — This word could mean *reverence or devotion* for a deity or *"extreme devotion"* or intense love or admiration of any kind, i.e. it could be for God or for a human.

Father — This word can mean *ancestor*, leader, God, *a biological father*, grandfather, founder, or any man deserving respect or reverence because of age.

Holy — This word can mean *sacred* as belonging to or coming from God, or *spiritually pure,* or deserving of great respect and adoration.

Nurse — Two of the many meanings of this word are:

a. to suckle a child

b. to tend the sick

Mother In the Middle East, it is not (and has not been) infrequent forwomen to suckle children who are not theirs. In this part of the world, the act of suckling a child will make the woman a mother to that child, and henceforth her offsprings will be brothers and sisters to the nursed (suckled) child.

Sister Many ancient writings refer to wives as sisters and husbands as brothers. In ancient Egypt, a wife-sister judicial status existed whereby a woman, in addition to becoming a man's wife was adopted by him as a sister. In such a case, two separate documents were drawn up, one for marriage, and the other for sistership, and the woman concerned, merited higher social status and greater privileges than the ordinary wife.

Piecing the Puzzle

Throughout our daily life, we make decisions and form opinions about events we have not witnessed personally, based on available evidence, experience and common sense. Therefore, we should not accept the biblical stories, figures and dates as historical fact without other corroborative evidence.

Let us open our minds and review the available evidence. For the truth is a composite of different and complementary pieces of a puzzle. Let us put the pieces in the right location, time and order.

Chapter 21

Abraham and Sarah

General

• Thousands of years ago in Canaan (same area as modern Israel and Lebanon), famine was a regular occurrence. It was at a time of famine, according to the Bible, when Abram and Sarai traveled to Egypt, a journey that began the relationship between the Egyptian royalty and, what was to become later, the tribe of Israel.

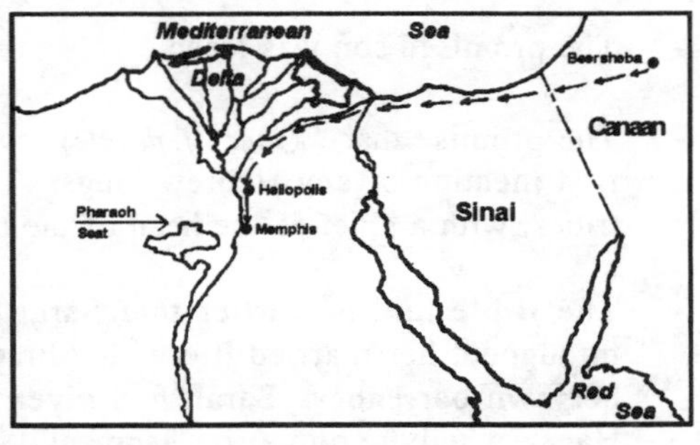

Compared to Canaan, Egypt was a rich and sophisticated country. Abram and Sarai did not stop in the eastern delta of the Nile, which one might have expected it they were simply seeking food, but traveled hundreds of miles to Heliopolis or Memphis where the pharaoh was residing. Apparently, Abram and Sarai may have been looking for more than just food. **They traveled unnecessarily deep into Egypt, of their own free will.** We are told however, in the Bible, that Abram was afraid of the pharaoh murdering him because of his beautiful wife. Abram told Sarai to tell others that she was Abram's sister ***"so that I shall be treated well for your sake and my life will be spared because of you"***. Subsequently the Pharaoh married Sarai (according to the Hebrew version of the Bible) and Abram was rewarded generously for the hand of his *'sister'*.

Even though the Pharaoh did not know that he married a married woman, the Bible tells us that the Lord ***"inflicted serious diseases"*** on the Pharaoh and his household. Once the Pharaoh found out the truth about Abram and Sarai, he told Abram to take his wife and leave.

The behavior of Abram and Sarai in Egypt, according to the Bible's version, can hardly be considered ethical or moral.

- Abram and Sarai returned to Canaan and major changes began to occur to their small tribe. The Bible tells us that the Lord made a covenant with Abram saying: *"To your descendants I give this land, from the river of Egypt to the great river, the Euphrates"*. Later, the Lord told Abram, *"...No longer will you be called Abram, your name will be Abraham, for I have made you a father of a host of nations...Kings will come from you"*. The Lord continues, *"As for Sarai your wife...her name will be Sarah. I shall bless her and give you a son by her...Kings of people shall come from her"*.

- Some observations of the above passages are worth noting:

- The promised son was Isaac.

- The promise that *"Kings of peoples"* will descend from Sarah is the first mention of any Hebrew kings. The Hebrews lived as nomadic tribes, with a chief as the head of the tribe and not a king.

- The Bible told us earlier that Sarai had been unable to conceive throughout her married life with Abram. In fact, to compensate for her own barrenness, Sarah had given Abraham her Egyptian maid Hagar, who bore him a son, Ishmael. So it must have been surprising to Abraham to learn that Sarah would bear a son, as stated in the Bible.

Isaac's Father

Who was Isaac's father? As Sarah was married to both Abraham and the Pharaoh, the child could have belonged to either of them. The following points should assist in answering this pivotal question.

- The Talmud, which is considered second in authority to the Old Testament, suggests that when Isaac was born, he did not look like Abraham. *"On the day that Abraham weaned his son Isaac, he made a great banquet, and all the peoples of the world derided him, saying: "Have you seen that old man and the woman who brought a foundling from the street, and now claim him as their son! And what is more they make a great banquet to establish their claim!"*

- We are told, by the Bible, that after the birth of Isaac, Abraham built an altar and was ready to slaughter him with a knife as a sacrifice to the Lord. At the last minute, a voice came from heaven, *"Do not raise your hand against the boy"*.

Firstly, it is difficult to believe that Abraham would kill his own son, if Isaac was really his son.

Secondly, it is a fact that human sacrifices were not the custom of the time, in this area of the world, and even if it was the custom why not sacrifice your eldest son, Ishmael?!

- The question of Isaac's father and the threatened sacrifice was raised between Jesus and the Jews, when they were seeking to kill him at Galilee, and he was trying to persuade them otherwise, as described in the Gospel of St. John (8:31-44):

  "...I know you are Abraham's descendants. Yet you are ready to kill me, because you have no room for my word. I am telling you what I have seen in the Father's presence, and you do what you have heard from your father."

  "Abraham is our father", they answered.

  "If you were Abraham's children," said Jesus, "then you would do the things that Abraham did. As it is, you are determined to kill me, a man who has told you the truth that he heard from God. Abraham did not do such things. You are doing the things your own father does."

  "<u>We are not illegitimate children</u>", they protested. "The only Father we have is God Himself."

  Jesus said to them: "If God were your Father, you would love me, for I came from God and now am here. I have not come on my own, but He sent me. Why is not my language clear to you? Because you are unable to hear what I say. You belong you father, the devil, and you want to carry out your father's desire. He was a murderer from the beginning, not holding to the truth, for there is no truth in him..."

The above passage indicates the following:

1- The Jews referred to Abraham as their father instead of making such a reference to Israel (Isaac's son).
2- Later on, the Jews accepted in their argument, that they <u>were not physically</u> the descendants of Abraham. Instead, they are the spiritual children of God.
3- Jesus is wondering why, when Abraham did not kill Isaac, the Jews want to kill him.

But who was the ruling Pharaoh when Abram and Sarai went to Egypt? All evidences lead to Twthomosis III, as the Pharaoh who married Sarai and who fathered Isaac. More details will follow in the next two chapters.

A Special Son

In Genesis 26:2, the Lord addressed Isaac, ***"Go not down into Egypt ...."***. It is logical to assume that there is no reason for this instruction except to forbid him to seek his real father's inheritance.

Away from Egypt, Isaac grew to manhood and married Rebekah. He had twins, both boys, from her. They were Esau and Jacob. The name of his second boy was Jacob (*Y'qwb* means *'the one who follows'*). The Bible tells us that Esau sold his birthright to Jacob.

Jacob had eleven children. The youngest was Joseph, who began the Israelite's sojourn into Egypt. As a point of interest, coincidentally just after the birth of Joseph, the Bible tells us, in Genesis 35:9-10, that God said unto Jacob ***"Thy name is Jacob: thy name shall not be called any more Jacob, but Israel shall be thy name: and he called his name Israel"***. The new name is significant as explained below.

We shall follow Jacob/Israel as he enters Egypt with his tribe, when Joseph, his son, becomes the second highest official in the land, after the Pharaoh.

Glossary of Interesting Names/Words

1- ***Abraham*** (in Egyptian) means *'heart of the majesty of Re'*.

2- ***Sarah*** (in Hebrew & Egyptian) is the feminine form of *'Sar'*.

3- ***Ysra/Sar*** (in Hebrew & Egyptian) means *'Prince/High Official'*.

4- ***El*** (in Hebrew) is the short form of ***Elohim*** [God].

5- ***Ysrael (Israel)*** means *'Elohim* [God] *rules'*, which is the same title given to the ruling Pharaoh of Egypt.

Chapter 22

Twthomosis III
The Warrior King

The Name

As discussed earlier, the ancient language didn't have short vowels. The first element of this king's name was always written as *Twt*, i.e. with three consonants. For some mischievous reasons the middle consonant letter was changed to the vowel *'u'*, by some Egyptologists. When *Twt* is written, in the equivalent Hebrew alphabetical characters, it becomes *Dwd*. When *Dwd* is pronounced phonetically it becomes *Dawood* which is the Hebrew name for *David*.

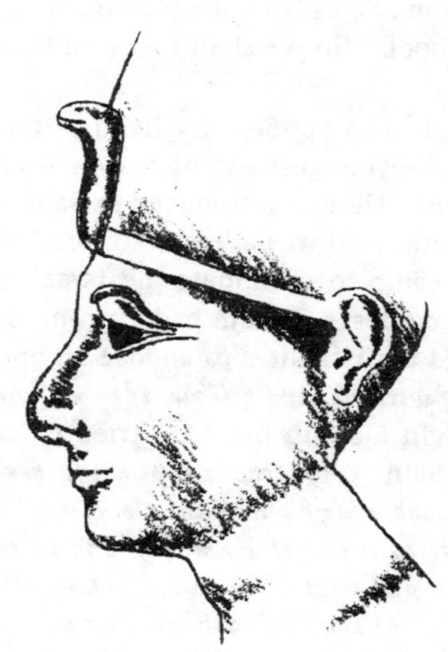

Is there any chance that the Egyptian warrior king was actually the biblical warrior King David? Let us study the accounts of the Egyptian David (Twthomosis III) and the biblical David.

The life of the biblical David can be divided into two parts:

I As a youth rising into prominence among his people.
(We shall prove that the biblical account of his youth was borrowed from an ancient Egyptian tale and that the biblical account is historically baseless.)

II As a warrior king of his people.

(We shall prove that basically the biblical war accounts of King David match precisely the war accounts of Twthomosis III.)

(I) His Youth

Biblical Account

Before we start we should mention that there are major differences between the early Hebrew text and the Greek text of the Bible. The English version comes from the Hebrew text. The differences are not the subject of this book. So we shall focus on the main sequence of events.

David, who supposedly lived in the first half of the tenth century B.C., was the youngest son of Jesse. As a young boy he was a shepherd and a harpist. He was introduced to Saul who appointed him as his armorbearer. Goliath, who was a huge, armored and strong giant, came from the Philistine camp to intimidate the Israelites, by challenging them to a man-to-man contest. Goliath had a strong iron spear, sword and a shield. Goliath asked the Israelites to choose an opponent and promised: *"If he be able to fight with me, and kill me, then we will be your servants"*. David volunteered to fight Goliath but Saul tried to persuade him otherwise. Then David told Saul: *'Thy servant kept his father sheep, and there came a lion, and a bear, and took a lamb out of the flock; And I went out after him, and smote him, and delivered it out of his mouth: and when he rose against me, I caught him by his beard, and smote him, and slew him. Thy servant slew both the lion and the bear . . . . The Lord has delivered me out of the paw of the lion, and out of the paw of the bear, he will deliver me out of the hand of the Philistine'*. I Samuel 17:34-7

David refused to wear armor or carry a sword and went to face Goliath; David then knocked Goliath down with a stone from his sling and took Goliath's sword and cut off his head. The Bible tells us then, *"David took the head of the Philistine (Goliath) and brought it to Jerusalem, but he put his armor in his tent"*. I Samuel, 17:54

Historical Analysis of the Biblical Account

1- The Bible tells us that Goliath was a Philistine. But when did these Philistines settle and establish themselves in Canaan?

The evidence indicates that the Philistines became an established community after the reign of Ramses III (c. 1182-1151 B.C.).

The Harris Papyrus, in the British Museum, states that Ramses III built a temple for Amen in Canaan. The mass invasion of Canaan by the 'Peoples of the Sea', of the coastal plain of Canaan, began around 1174 B.C., which coincided with the Greek war against Troy. The walls of Ramses III's funerary temple in western Thebes depicts the fact that the invading people were after permanent settlement, for they consisted of whole families. The wall inscriptions also indicate that the Peoples of the Sea were a combination of Peleset (which are Philistines - the word Palestine came from Peleset), Tjekker, Sheklesh, Danu and Weshesh. Ramses III defeated the invaders in a naval battle and many of the captives were allowed to settle in southwest Canaan.

After the reign of Ramses III, Egypt lost control over Palestine and the Philistines established themselves in the coastal plains of Canaan and started expanding towards the Dead Sea and the River Jordan. It was at the same time that the Israelites were trying to establish themselves in the area. Because of the vacuum left after the reign of Ramses III, both Philistines and Israelites began fighting and thus the stories of Saul, David and Goliath.

Historically speaking, if David did do battle with the Philistines, he could not have lived before the twelfth century B.C., because that was when the mass invasion of the coastal plain of Canaan by the Philistines took place. Therefore, historical facts contradict the biblical time period of the David and Goliath duel, to occur during the first half of the tenth century.

2- Many scholars have noted the similarities between the most famous ancient Egyptian tale The Autobiography of Sinhue and the biblical account of David and Goliath.

Readers are encouraged to read this beautiful ancient Egyptian tale, which was used in ancient Egyptian schools as an example of literary excellence.

William Kelly Simpson wrote, *"The account of the fight between the champion of Retenu (Sinhue) has frequently been compared to the David and Goliath duel, for which it may have served as a literary prototype".*

3- Some factual observations of Sinhue and David stories:

a- The Sinhue tale existed in many texts as far back as the twentieth century B.C. Therefore, it was developed a thousand years before the biblical account of David and Goliath was supposed to have occurred.
The Israelites, during their sojourn in Egypt, must have been influenced by the Egyptian Sinhue tale.

b- Sinhue's opponent in the famous tale, was a giant. Giant people were said to have lived in Canaan around the twentieth century B.C., when this tale was first developed.

The Bible, in the Second Book of Samuel speaks of Goliath as having been born to the giants. The Raphaim (giants) and the Philistines are totally different people who lived in two different eras.

c- As a result of Sinhue's win, he was appointed the commander of the army. Similarly, David was given an identical position, as per the First Book of Samuel 18:5, ***"Saul set him (David) over the men of war"***.

d- The biblical account of David and Goliath occurred, according to the Book of Samuel, when Jerusalem was not yet under Israelite control. Why and how did David take Goliath's head to a foreign city under enemy's control? ***"David took the head of the Philistine, and brought it to Jerusalem, but he put his armor in his tent."?!*** I Samuel, 17:54

Based on all the above, the story of David and Goliath is a fictional story which was inserted in the Bible in an attempt to enhance King David's trait as a hero and a warrior, and that the events of the duel between David and Goliath was actually borrowed from the Egyptian literary work The Autobiography of Sinhue.

Twthomosis III As A Youth

In order to understand the episode of Hatshepsut and Twthomosis III, we must start with his father, Twthomosis II.

Twthomosis II (c. 1510-1490 B.C.) was born of a minor wife, and not the Great Royal Wife. In order to inherit the throne, he married his half-sister, Hatshepsut, the heiress daughter of his father and Queen Ahmose (the Great Royal Wife).

Twthomosis II had a son, Twthomosis III, by a concubine named Isis. Twthomosis II also had a daughter, Neferure from Hatshepsut. Twthomosis II died shortly thereafter. Since the line of the throne inheritance went through the eldest daughter, the normal method for Twthomosis III to inherit the throne was for him to marry Neferure, who was the heiress. The marriage did not occur, possibly because of Hatshepsut's refusal to consent. Hatshepsut continued to insist that Neferure was the legal Heir, **'Lady of the Two Lands, Mistress of Upper and Lower Egypt'**. It was then necessary for Twthomosis III to receive the approval of the priesthood, so as to get himself "adopted" by Amen in order to ensure his right to the throne.

Twthomosis III was only five years old when his father died. However, he was not allowed to succeed his father on the throne, instead Queen Hatshepsut appointed herself as his guardian. Two years later, Hatshepsut began sharing kingship with Twthomosis III and dressed as a man. Twthomosis III was kept powerless until Year 16 of the co-regency, when the legal heiress died. After Neferure's death, Twthomosis III gained increasing importance. He joined the army as a young man and there is evidence to suggest that he fought in the area of Gaza (the same area of the Sinhue story and the David and Goliath account) towards the end of the co-regency. When Hatshepsut died, after 22 years of the co-regency, Twthomosis III became the sole ruler of Egypt.

> **Many people like to view the Hatshepsut/Twthomosis III story as a contest of man against woman. Hatshepsut and/or Neferure refused him as a husband for Neferure. Was he refused because of Hatshepsut's ambitions or was he paying the price for his father's personal deeds, or was it just a typical family feud. We have no knowledge of the answers to these questions. However, we know that Egyptian women achieved the highest regard in soci-**

ety, throughout history. (Read the chapter '*Women*'.)

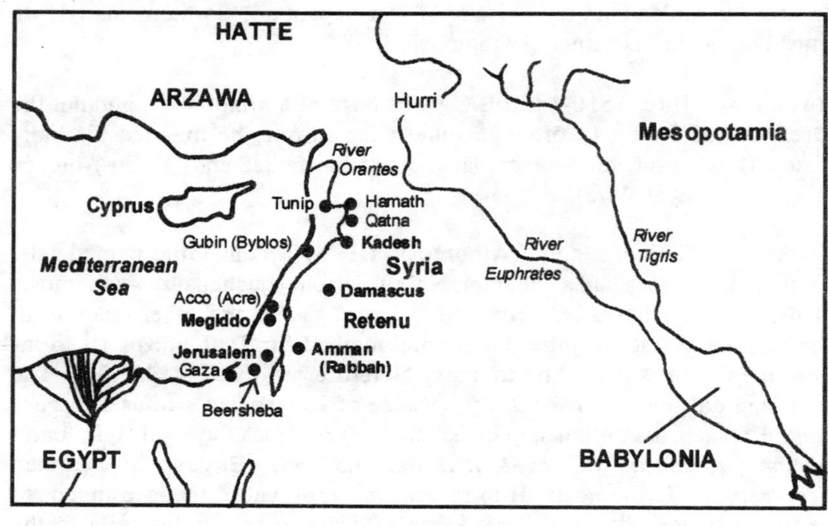

(II) The Warrior King

The Biblical Warrior King

After the David and Goliath event, David was suddenly transformed into a mighty warrior, at the head of Saul's army. The biblical accounts of the campaigns fought by David are described in the Second Book of Samuel. It shows an account of a series of wars in northern Palestine, Syria (up to the limits of the Mesopotamian river, the Euphrates) as well as Moab, to the east of the Dead Sea.

A few discrepancies in his biblical campaigns need to be discussed and clarified. As a result of long oral tradition, the biblical narration had confused one sequence of events, and the name of two places, in these campaigns.

A- *Confused Chronology*

1- The Bible tells us that David defeated the confederate Syrian Kingdom, which was led by Hadadezer. *'David slayed twenty thousand of them, put garrisons in Aram of Damascus, and the Syrians became his servants and paid tribute.'*

The second book of Samuel (8:3) specifically tells us that David *"smote also Hadadezer ... King of Zobath* (located near Hamath in northern Syria), *as he went to recover his border at the river Euphrates."*

2- Two biblical chapters later, however, in describing David's campaign against the Ammonites, we find the Syrians and Zobath (who were just totally wiped out) are fighting David!

We are now told that the Ammonites were asking the Syrians for military support (!) and that Zobath (the defeated city) was among the Syrian allies (!)

We are also told that after David defeated the Ammonites' allies, they fled and sought refuge in their city, Rabbah (present-day Amman, the capital city of Jordan), and that David's army returned to besiege Rabbah.

- **This situation is impossible, if Zobath had already been defeated and David had established garrisons in Syria.**

- **Geographically and logically, these two events must have taken place chronologically in the reverse order to that described in the biblical account.**

B- Confused City-Names

1- Rabbah- is present-day Amman, the capital city of Jordan. The Bible claims that David conquered Rabbah after a long siege in the first half of the tenth century B.C. However, no walls or other archaeological evidence were found to support that claim.

The biblical editor made a mistake in naming *Rabbah* as the city besieged and attacked by David. The correct name is *Megiddo*.

The Bible itself disputes the validity of the Rabbah story.

a- The military importance of Megiddo and its legend, as an international battleground, is reflected in John (Revelation, 16:16). **Armageddon (*Har Meggiddon*, the Mount of Megiddo)** is the site where, at the end of days, all the kings of the world will fight the ultimate battle against the forces of God.

b- In the second book of Samuel (10:2), we are told that David took the city of Rabbah whose king was Hanun.
Seven chapters later, we find Rabbah independent under its king, Shobi, who felt pity on David and his followers because they were ***"hungry and weary, and thirsty in the wilderness"*** II Samuel, 17:28-9.

Rabbah was a minor insignificant location at that time.

c- Solomon, David's successor, who inherited the empire without war, raised a levy so as ***"to build the wall of Megiddo"*** I Kings 9:15.

d- **Megiddo** is also mentioned as one of Solomon's possessions in I Kings, 4:12.

2- Zobath- No traces of a locality with this name have been found in either Syria or Canaan at the supposed time of David (tenth century B.C.) or Twthomosis III (fifteenth century B.C.).

Zobath is actually the city of Qadesh, the northern Syrian stronghold, on the River Orontes. This true identification will be verified later in this chapter.

The Egyptian Warrior King

When Twthomosis III became the sole ruler of Egypt, after the death of Hatshepsut, four decades had passed without a major Egyptian military campaign in western Asia. During this period, the Syrian King of Qadesh led a Syria-Canaanite confederacy in a general rebellion against the Egyptian presence, which was secured since the reign of Twthomosis I (c. 1528-1510 B.C.).

In response to the rebellion, Twthomosis III led a total of seventeen campaigns in western Asia over the next twenty years. The daily events of these wars fought by Twthomosis III, were recorded by the scribe who accompanied the army on its campaigns. These records are to be found in the Annals, a 223-line document that covers the inside of the walls enclosing the corridor surrounding the granite holy of holies, which Twthomosis III built at the Karnak temple.

> **The historical details of the wars fought by the Warrior King Twthomosis III, in the Karnak temple match precisely the biblical accounts of the wars fought by the Warrior King David, in the second book of Samuel, except for the discrepancies in chronology and the two city names, mentioned earlier.**

The common denominator of the events at the biblical Rabbah and the Egyptian Megiddo, as evident from both the war annals of Twthomosis III and the biblical account of David's campaigns, are:

* The king fought against a major fortified city in Canaan that was aided by a Syrian confederation led by a king of one Syrian city;

* The king's army defeated the coalition near the city gates and the enemy sought sanctuary within its fortified walls;

* The king's army surrounded the city for a long time before they attacked it and took it;

* After the defeat of the Syrian confederation at (Rabbah/Megiddo), the main Syrian city went on threatening the king. The king and his army therefore conquered that Syrian city and went further to regain the borders at the River Euphrates. He then erected a stela in celebration of his triumph.

Twthomosis III always looked back on the battle of Megiddo as the most important military campaign of his life. That is why in all his military inscriptions, on the walls of the Karnak temple and other locations, he gives more details about that military campaign than any others.

As mentioned earlier, Megiddo is the site, according to John (Revelations 16:16) where the kings of the world will have their final battle against the forces of God.

Historical and archaeological evidence confirms that these military campaigns occurred during the reign of Twthhomosis III. There is no evidence to support the biblical account that these events occurred five centuries later, at the supposed time of the biblical David in the first half of the tenth century B.C.

David and Abraham

Did Abraham and the biblical David live at the same time? A thorough examination of Abraham's story in the Bible, provides the evidence supporting such a case.

1- The story of Abraham is to be found in the Book of Genesis, 11:26 to 25:10. There are certain peoples mentioned in Genesis, such as Philistines, Moabites, Ammonites, Aramacans, Edomites, Amalekites and Canaanites.

These are the very same people who were incorporated in David's Empire, according to II Samuel 8.

2- We are told, in the second book of Samuel, that while David was staying at the fortress of Jerusalem, at the time of the siege of the fortified city, he sent for Bathsheba, the wife of Uriah the Hittite, who was serving with the king's forces at the siege, so as to take her to his home where *'he lay with her'* (II Samuel, 11:4). As a result of this affair, Bathsheba became pregnant. We are told later in II Samuel that the child of sin got ill and died.

a- The similarity between Abraham and Uriah is of interest, for both of them:

i- are foreigners, Abraham was a Canaanite in Egypt and Uriah a Hittite in Jerusalem.

ii- had their wives made pregnant by a King and gave birth to a son, who were destined to die, except that Isaac's life was spared at the last minute.

b- The husband of Bathsheba, in the biblical story of David, is identified as Uriah the Hittite. If the name is actually Uriah, it is composed of two elements

Ur- a Hurrian (northern Mesopotamian) word meaning *'city'* or *'light'*.
Yah (iah)- is the short form of Jehovah, the Israelites' God.

Therefore, the name, accordingly, means *'Jehovah's Light'*. However, he is described as being Hittite. How can we expect a Hittite, a traditional enemy of Egypt and the Israelites to be one of the heroes of David's army?
It is therefore reasonable to conclude that Uriah was a fictional character, as a Hittite.

c- Is it possible to tie the name Uriah to Abraham?

Let us take a look:

Ur- birth place of Abraham (according to the Bible).
Yah (iah)- short form of Jehovah (the Israelites God).

It is therefore more logical to conclude that the name Ur-iah may belong to Abraham, as it relates to both his birth place and to his God.

d- Is it possible to tie Sarai (or Sarah) to Bathsheba?

The name Bathsheba was originally read Beth-Sheba.

Beth- means *'a girl'* or *'a daughter'*.

Sheba- An area south of Canaan that takes its name from the local well, Beer-Sheba.

Therefore the name Bathsheba means *'a girl (or daughter) of Sheba'*.
The Bible tells us that Sarah was from Sheba and that she returned to it, with her husband Abraham, after they were deported

from Egypt.

Therefore Sarah and the *'girl (daughter) of Sheba'* are one and the same person.

It is reasonably logical to relate Uriah to Abraham and Bathsheba to Sarah, in their names and lives. The evidence mounts on the true character of Uriah (Abraham), Bathsheba (Sarah), and their relationship to the Warrior King. The big questions become: Is it possible that Abraham and Sarah never went to Egypt and that Sarah's liaison with the Pharaoh took place while the Pharaoh lived, at the hills of Jerusalem, while laying siege to Megiddo? Was it this area where Abraham was to sacrifice Isaac? Was it the Lord of those mounts, the Pharaoh, who persuaded Abraham to let Isaac live? Was it also this Lord (Pharaoh) who instructed the son,Isaac *"Go not down into Egypt..."* **as per Genesis 26:2?**

Chapter 23

Old Jerusalem
City of Peace

The Holy Place

Situated in the Judaean hills, thirty-five miles east of the Mediterranean Sea and at an elevation of 2,440 feet, an obscure fortress, at the southeastern hill, was the beginning of what was to be Jerusalem.

It was the Warrior King David/Twthomosis III who transformed this obscure place to a holy place, when he stayed there for seven months, while his army was surrounding the enemies at Megiddo (wrongly named Rabbah in the Bible).

Let us follow the events of this transformation, in the biblical and historical accounts.

The Biblical Evidence

1- The second book of Samuel, 5:6-7 describes how David took Jerusalem, *"and the King and his men went to Jerusalem unto the Jebusites, the inhabitants of the land ... David took the strong hold (fortress) of Zion, the same as the City of David."*

These verses don't necessarily mean that David took the place by force for the *"... the King and his men ..."* could mean the King and his close advisors and guards. Therefore it could be interpreted as a peaceful surrender of the fortress.

This interpretation is reinforced in II Samuel 24:22-3, when David went to buy a piece of land from the *King* of the territory. The

The Historical Evidence

1- The annals of Twthomosis III, at the Karnak temple, indicate that while his army was surrounding Megiddo, Twthomosis III stayed "**at a fortress east of this town**". The siege lasted seven months before Twthomosis III made his final offensive attack on Megiddo.

The annals don't indicate any hostility at the fortress.

recognition of the Bible that the King of the territory was still in power, indicates that David never conquered this place to start with. (More about it under item no. 3 of this chapter.)

2- Shortly after David's arrival, the Israelites *"brought in the ark of the Lord, and set it in his place, in the midst of the tabernacle that David had pitched for it ...."* (II Samuel, 6:17)

The idea of a holy Ark was introduced to the Israelites by Moses, from Egyptian practices of worship.

The consequences of bringing the Ark to Jerusalem is said to have made the location, the holy center for the Israelite tribes.

2- The annals of Twthomosis III, at Karnak: "**... awakening in [life] in the tent of life, prosperity and health, at the town of Araunah. Proceeding northward by my majesty, carrying my father Amen-Re, Lord of the Thrones of the Two Lands [that he might open the ways] before me.**"

Twthomosis III carried the Ark of the neter (god) Amen-Re with him to war, and it stayed with him near the fortress. The presence of the holy Ark, transformed this location into a holy ground.

3- The Bible tells us that David was directed to build an altar to the Lord on the threshing floor of Mount Moriah, the high ground north of the city. This area was then under the control of Araunah, the Jebusite king, when King David went to buy the threshing floor. Araunah made David an offer *"... Let my Lord the king take and offer up what seemeth good unto him: behold, here be oxen for burnt sacrifice, and threshing instruments and other instruments of the oxen for wood. All these things did Araunah, as a king, give unto the king ..."* (II Samuel, 24:22-3).

3- The annals indicate that Twthomosis III established a site for a shrine to God.

The relationship between the two kings, Twthomosis III and Araunah, is made quite clear from the Tell el-Amarna letters, dating from the fourteenth century B.C. In one of these letters from the ruler of Jerusalem to Akhenaten, the son and successor of Amenhotep III, it states: **"Behold, this land of Jerusalem, neither my father nor my mother gave it to me; the mighty arm [of the king] gave it to me"**. While in another letter the ruler of Jerusalem confirms his royal ancestry: **"... the mighty arm of the king set [me] in the house of my father"**. This echoes the relationship we find in the biblical account of David's purchase of the threshing-floor on Mount Moriah from the local king, Araunah, who said: *"All these things did Araunah, as a king, give unto the king . . ."* (II Samuel, 24:23). It is evident that, after King Araunah cooperated peacefully with the Egyptian military, Twthomosis III kept him and his descendants as rulers. So, when Twthomosis III went out to fight against the confederation of Canaanite and Syrian princes at Megiddo, Jerusalem was not part of the rebellion. The king was therefore able to go from Gaza to Megiddo, and to seek safe sanctuary in Jerusalem during the long months that Megiddo was under siege.

4- Psalms 2:6-8 celebrates the new altar by calling David, as being the 'Son of God' similar to Egyptian Kings, *"Yet have I set my king upon my holy hill of Zion. I will declare the decree: the Lord hath said unto me, Thou art my Son; this day have I begotten thee. Ask of me, and I shall give thee the heathen for thine inheritance, and the uttermost parts of the earth for thy possession"* (Psalms, 2:6-8).

4- The Egyptian king was the only king to be identified as the **'Son of God'**.

5- Verse 5:7 of the second book of Samuel introduces us to a new name *'Zion'*. Zion was originated in the Bible and has not been found in any other historical source. The name *'Zion'* has different and conflicting biblical meanings. Here are some of the meanings:

a- Zion: *"Originally a Canaanite fortress."*

Biblical Source: ***"David took the stronghold of Zion: the same as the City of David"*** (II Samuel 5:7).

Two verses later, a somewhat different meaning ***"So David dwelt in the fort, and called it the City of David ..."*** (II Samuel, 5:9).

b- Zion: *"The hill in Jerusalem on which a temple was built."*

Biblical Source: ***"So shall ye know that I am the Lord your God dwelling in Zion, my holy mountain: then shall Jerusalem be holy ..."*** (Joel, 3:17).

c- Zion: *"A holy place."*

Biblical Source: ***"The Lord hear thee in the day of trouble, the name of the God of Jacob defend thee; Send thee help from the sanctuary, and strengthen thee out of Zion"*** (Psalms, 20:1-2).

In this case Zion means a sanctuary.

d- Zion: *"Heaven or Heavenly City."*

Biblical Source: ***"For the Lord hath chosen Zion, he hath desired it for his habitation. This is my rest for ever: here will I dwell; for I have desired it"*** (Psalms, 132:13-14).

5- *Zion* is not an original Hebrew word. It consists of two elements, *Zi* and *On*.

'Zi' Is a Hebrew word, meaning a barren place.

'On' is the name of the ancient Egyptian holy city of Heliopolis (a suburb of Cairo). The Bible tells us that Joseph married ***"the daughter of Potipherah, priest of On"*** (Genesis, 41:45).

Therefore Zion is a combination of Hebrew-Egyptian word meaning the **On (holy place) of the desert.**

e- Other meanings for Zion are:
- *Jerusalem*
- *Land of Israel*
- *The Jewish people*
- *Theocracy of God*

The Names Of Jerusalem

The Tell el-Amarna Letters, were written in the Akkadian language, and were dated from 1400 B.C. They contained six communications from the ruler of Jerusalem to the Egyptian King. These letters are the first documented historical evidence naming the city as **'mat Urusalim'**, meaning **'the Land of Jerusalem'**. The letters state clearly that Jerusalem was under Egyptian control with an Egyptian military garrison stationed locally.

Urusalem is the Akkadian name for Jerusalem, and can be divided into two elements (Uru & Salem)

Uru- is derived from the verb yarah meaning *'to found'* or *'to establish'*.

Salem- means peace, as also identified by the Jewish rabbis in the Haddadah, the legendary part of the Talmud.

Thus the meaning of Urusalim is *'foundation of peace'* or *'establishing peace'*.

The name Jerusalem, however, does not appear on any list of conquered locations, during Twthomosis III or any of his successors, during the period when Canaan was part of Egypt's empire. The Egyptians recognized Jerusalem by another name - **Qadesh**. It is *Qadesh* that is mentioned in the lists of subdued Asiatic cities, of most Egyptian kings of this period.

The first verse of Chapter 11 of the Book of Nehemiah speaks of *'Jerusalem the holy city'* (in Hebrew, *Yurushalayim ha Qudesh*). The modern Arabic name for Jerusalem is el-Quds, which becomes ha-Qudesh in Hebrew. This word means, both in Arabic and Hebrew, the holy (ground).

Both the Bible and Koran use the name Qadesh as a synonym for Jerusalem.

Other Cities called Qadesh

There was more than one location bearing the name Qadesh at the time of Twthomosis III. It is not difficult to figure out which Qadesh is meant, from the sequence of events. One Qadesh was the northern Syrian stronghold on the River Orontes (modern-day Tell Nabi Mind) south of Lake Homs.

The other Qadesh is located in Upper Galilee, north of Hazor and has an insignificant strategic location. According to Yohanan Aharoni, the prominent Israeli archaeologist, the *"rough, hilly and relatively inhospitable terrain of Upper Galilee was almost uninhabited in the Late Bronze Period (1550-1200 B.C.)."* Both from archaeological and historical evidence it seems to have been a small unfortified settlement at the time.

Since the Twthomosis III annals identified Qadesh first, followed by Megiddo as the main objectives of his first campaign, this will logically exclude identification of the insignificant and uninhibited northern Palestine city, in Upper Galilee, as Qadesh.

Chapter 24

Joseph
and the Beginning of the Sojourn

Joseph in the Bible

Isaac's son, Jacob, we are told, loved Joseph, his youngest child, more than any of his other children. Joseph's half-brothers, naturally, hated Joseph because of this favoritism. The Bible tells us that his half-brothers got rid of Joseph by selling him as a slave, but told their father that a wild beast devoured him. Joseph was sold to Potiphar, one of the Pharaoh's officials, the captain of the guard. We are told that Potiphar's wife tried to seduce Joseph, and when he refused, she claimed that he attacked her. Joseph was promptly sent to jail, and there he established a reputation as an interpreter of dreams. The biblical story goes that after no one could interpret the Pharaoh's dreams, Joseph was called from jail to interpret them for him. The Pharaoh was so pleased with Joseph, that he made Joseph his second in command, gave him an Egyptian name and gave him an Egyptian wife. Joseph's family rejoined him eventually in Egypt. Both he and his father died and were embalmed in Egypt.

The Egyptian Historical Account

There are no historical records of the biblical Joseph and his family, in any place in the Middle East. There is, however, historical evidence, in Egypt, of Yuya and his family, which parallels the biblical story of Joseph.

The tomb of Yuya was found in the Valley of the Kings, on the west bank at Luxor, in 1905. One must wonder why a man like Yuya, who is not of royal blood, and moreover not even an Egyptian, but a Semite, was buried in the Valley of the Kings. Yuya, as a minister (vizier) to both Tuthomosis IV (c. 1413 - 1405 B.C.) and Amenhotep III (c. 1405 - 1367 B.C.) would have expected to be buried among his peers in the Valley of the Nobles.

Yuya must have been a very special person. Among the many impressive titles attributed to him in the tomb, is **'nṯr n nb tawi'**, which means **'the holy father of the Lord of the two lands'**. The Pharaoh's title in Egypt was the Lord of the Two Lands, and therefore Yuya's title indicates that he fathered a Pharaoh.

The hands of Yuya's mummy were not crossed in the usual Osiris form, over his chest. Instead, the palms of his hands were facing his neck under the chin. No Egyptian mummy was ever found with his hands in this position.

The Time of Joseph

It should be emphasized that the story of Joseph, in the Bible, was written, rewritten, and added to, three times between the ninth century B.C. and the second century B.C., at which time an editor came along and made one story out of the three prior accounts, and even added another section dealing with Joseph's death and his desire to be re-buried (?!) in Canaan.

There is absolutely no reference in the Bible to the time when Joseph was in Egypt. After the Exodus, which is in essence a case of a bitter divorce between Egypt and the Jews, both parties proceeded to erase their ties to each other. There is not a single reference to the name of any Pharaoh throughout the Bible.

Biblicists, however, choose to believe and popularize the account of the Jewish historian who suggested in his book, Contra Apionem, written towards the end of the first century A.D., that the Israelites' Descent into Egypt and their Exodus took place during the Hyksos rule (c.1663 - 1550 B.C.). Josephus, who was writing about events 1700 years old at the time, relied on some information provided by Manetho, an Egyptian priest of the third century B.C. (1300 years after the Hyksos era).

Manetho provided a complete history from the Egyptian records of the thirty-one royal dynasties that ruled Egypt from C. 3100 to 332 B.C. Manetho, according to Josephus, provided a separate account about Moses and the Exodus based soley on Egyptian folk tales.

Some theorized that the Hyksos and the Israelites are one and the same, but when such theory contradicted many parts of the Bible, biblicists adopted a modified theory of Josephus' account. The current modified and unfounded theory was that Joseph was sold into slavery, during the Hyksos era, and that all his family followed him later to Egypt.

On studying the Bible carefully and marrying it to Egyptian history, the generally accepted theory will be proven to be a mirage.

Joseph and Yuya

Let us compare the biblical account with the historical evidence.

A. The Pharaoh released Joseph from jail and said, ***"Since a god has made all this known to you, there is no one so shrewd and wise as you. You shall be in charge of my household, and all my people are to submit to your orders. Only in respect of the throne shall I be greater than you."*** Genesis 41:40.

The Hebrew narrator described Joseph's position as ***'mshna'.*** This word means *'to double'*.

One of Yuya's titles, as inscribed in his tomb is **"whom the king has made his double"**.

B. The Pharaoh gave him an Egyptian name. ***"And Pharaoh called Joseph's name Zaphnath-pa-a-neah..."*** Genesis 41:45

1- It should be noted that both Joseph's biblical name and the name of Yuya are composite names, i.e. *Yu-seph* - *'Y'* in Egyptian and Hebrew becomes *'J'* in English, and in both languages, *'O'* and *'U'* are written with the same sign.

2- Let us analyze <u>the Egyptian name given in the Bible</u>. Since both Hebrew and ancient Egyptian have no written short vowels, the consonants of the Hebrew name will be

[Z ph] nth ph 'nh

The Egyptian original of this Hebrew name is

[S ph] nṯr iw-f 'nh

↕ ↕ ↕ ↕

<u>Translation</u> - *success/creation god is-he live*

Notice that the first two elements *'s'* and *'ph'*, or *'seph'* form the second part of Joseph's name.

The word *'seph'* has no Hebrew origin, and therefore it is likely that the name Joseph was not his birth name, but a later name in his life. *'Seph'*, however, was a common Egyptian name at that time.

The whole name could mean *'creation/success/ medicine of god, may he live'*.

3- Let us analyze the biblical name, *Yu-seph* (Joseph in English) and the name of *Yu-ya.*

- Yuya's name was spelled in eleven different ways, on the items inside his tomb. But the spelling always begins with the letter *'Y'*, which has to be read as a consonant because an Egyptian syllable cannot start with a vowel.
The variety of spellings suggests that Yuya's name was a foreign one, which the scribes found difficult to translate into hieroglyphics.

- It was a common custom and therefore possible, in the case of Joseph, that a person's name would indicate the god under whom the person concerned was placed. If Joseph's God was Yhwa (Jehovah), then that would comprise the first part of Joseph's name.

- There is no way of knowing the name of Joseph when he first arrived in Egypt from Canaan and/or what name, if any, was given to him by his master or when he was in jail.

- It should also be noted that it was a common practice at the time for Egyptians to have several names, some of which were kept secret. It was also the custom to use pet names, as well as abbreviated forms, for longer and more complex names.

- Finally, to drive the point home, the biblical *'John'* in English speaking countries is equated in Arabic speaking countries to *'Yeh-ya'*. The sound similarity between *Joseph* (or *Yu-seph*) and *Yuya* is much closer than *John* and *Yeh-ya*.

C. The Pharaoh gave Joseph an Egyptian wife, Asenath, daughter of

1- Even though the name of Yuya's wife, Tuya, cannot be transcribed into Asenath, this could be a situation where an Egyptian had more than one name.

Potipherah, the priest of On (present day Heliopolis, a suburb of Cairo, and the center of worship in lower Egypt of the neter (god) Re.)

(A similar example of possible name discrepancies is that Queen Elizabeth I and Queen Bess were the same person. If most of the relevant documents have been destroyed, as in the case of Tuya and Asenath, it would be difficult to prove that Bess and Elizabeth I were one and the same person.)

2- The position of Joseph's father-in-law, as ***'priest of On'***, contradicts the theory of Joseph living during the Hyksos era.
Most scholars, if not all of them, affirm that the Hyksos honored only one Egyptian neter, Seth. Manetho has reported that the Hyksos razed the temples of the other gods (neterw) to the ground.

If the Hyksos were governing Egypt during the time of Joseph, can we expect a Hyksos ruler, who himself worshipped Seth, to marry his deputy to a daughter of a priest of the hated (by the Hyksos) neter Re?

It is almost beyond doubt that the story of this marriage occurred many years after the Hyksos' times.

D. The Bible states that Joseph became the father of two sons, Manasseh and Ephraim. There was no mention made of any daughter.

The absence of mentioning a daughter, in the Bible, is not proof that Joseph had no daughter. The Bible mentions very few women and no one can then conclude that the Hebrews fathered only male descendants. The Bible, however, gives us an indirect indication that Joseph had a daughter:

1. When Joseph revealed himself to his brothers, on their second trip to Egypt, ***"And [Joseph] wept aloud and the Egyptians and the house of Pharaoh heard."*** Genesis 45:2

In both ancient and a large portion of modern Egypt, it is improper to refer to a married woman by her name. She was and is always referred to as *"the house of xxx"*, *xxx* being the husband's name. Therefore, the *house of the Pharaoh* meant the *Pharaoh's wife*.

2. When Jacob died and Joseph wanted to bury him in Canaan, he sought a mediator to ask the Pharaoh's permission. Even though we know already that Joseph was close to the Pharaoh, his action indicates that the mediator was even closer to the Pharaoh. The queen would have more influence on the Pharaoh than the vizier would, so Joseph would naturally go to his daughter, Queen Tiye. ***"And when the days of his mourning were past, Joseph spoke unto the house of the Pharaoh saying, 'If now I have found grace in your eyes, speak, I pray you, in the ears of the Pharaoh'".*** Genesis 50:4

3. In Genesis 46:27, it is stated that the total number of the members of Jacob's family, including Joseph and his two sons, is seventy. If we add up the number of Jacob's descendants form Genesis 46:15, 18, 22, and 25, in addition to Jacob himself, the total is only sixty-nine.

Also in Genesis 46:26, the number of Jacob's descendants, who went down to Egypt, is given as sixty-six, which means that four were already in Egypt. However we are given the names of only three.

It is reasonable to conclude that the seventieth person was already in Egypt, and it was Joseph's daughter, Queen Tiye.

It appears that the omission of her name was the work of later Hebrew scribes, who wanted to disassociate the Hebrews from the royal Egyptian family. However, they forgot to change all related verses of Genesis.

• • •

Joseph was thirty when he entered the Pharaoh's service, and he served the Pharaoh and the people very well.

When famine came, which affected many countries, including Canaan (same area as modern Israel and Lebanon), Jacob sent his sons to Egypt to buy corn.

E. When Joseph met his brothers, he concealed his identity and accused them of spying. In Genesis 42:9, Joseph said ***"...Ye are spies, to see the nakedness of the land ye are come."***

Since the Hyksos included Canaanites, and **if** the Hyksos were in control of Egypt, why would they suspect spies from their own kind?!

This accusation can only be justified if the danger to Egypt is from the Canaan region. This was the case after the Hyksos left Egypt and not during the time they were still there.

It makes sense to deduce that Joseph was in Egypt after the Hyksos left Egypt. It was therefore natural to be wary of Canaanites.

F. When Joseph visited his brothers later on, he disguised himself by speaking to them through an interpreter. Therefore he was able to overhear a conversation between them. ***"And they knew not that Joseph understood them, for he spoke unto them by an interpreter."*** Genesis 42:43

Since Canaanite was the language of the Hyksos, an interpreter was not needed.

Yet more proof that Joseph was in Egypt after the Hyksos left it.

The biblical editor was not knowledgeable of all the facts when he wrote the story of Joseph, a few centuries later.

• • •

Per Joseph's instruction, they took the food provisions back to Canaan, but had to leave their brother Simeon, in Egypt as a ransom. They were instructed to bring their youngest brother Benjamin to Joseph, before he could release Simeon.

When Jacob's household ran out of food, he was forced to abide by Joseph's order and he sent his sons, together with his youngest Benjamin.

G. When Joseph saw Benjamin with the brothers, he invited them all to dinner. He said to his steward ***"Bring the men into the house, and slaughter an animal and make ready, for the men are to dine with me at noon."*** Genesis 43:16.

A few biblical verses later, Joseph changed his own plan by ordering the food to be served separately, Genesis 43:32 ***"They served him by himself, and them by them selves, and the Egyptians who might not eat bread with the Hebrews, for that is an abomination unto the Egyptians."***

It is hard to believe that a Hyksos, who himself is a shepherd, would hate to eat with other shepherds.

The Egyptians developed their hatred of shepherds only after the Hyksos rule. It is therefore logical to conclude that Joseph was in Egypt after the Hyksos left Egypt.

H. Finally, Joseph revealed himself to the brothers, Genesis 45:8. *"...So then it was not you who sent me hither, but God, and he hath made me a father to Pharaoh."*

The biblical Hebrew edition of the second portion of the statement reads *(wa-ya sim-ni la-ab la-Phar 'a)*, which literally means, *'And placed he me for a father to Pharaoh'*.

The most impressive title in Yuya's tomb is **nṯr n nb tawi (the holy father of the Lord of the Two Lands)**. The Lord of the Two Lands was the formal title of the Pharaoh. **Therefore, Yuya's title is 'the holy father of the Pharaoh'.** Which is exactly the same title mentioned in Genesis 45:8.

Yuya's daughter, namely Tiye, was married to Amenhotep III (c.1405-1367 B.C.), and bore him a son who was the next Pharaoh of Egypt, namely Amenhotep IV (Akhenaton). That is how Yuya fathered a Pharaoh.

I. With the Pharaoh's permission, Jacob (Israel) and his family were allowed to settle in the Land of Goshen (east of the Nile Delta). Genesis 46:34, *"...ye may dwell in the Land of Goshen, for every shepherd is an abomination unto the Egyptians."*

Once again, it is hard to believe that a Hyksos who is a shepherd himself, would hate other shepherds, especially that the majority of the Hyksos were Canaanites.

The logical conclusion is that Joseph lived in Egypt after the Hyksos' departure.

J. When Jacob felt that the time of his death was approaching, he sent for Joseph and said to him, *"Do not bury me in Egypt, but when I die, carry me out of Egypt and bury me where my forefathers are buried."*

1. Mummification was limited to the Royal family until the eighteenth dynasty, because of its prohibitive expense. Nobles and high officials were mummified from the eighteenth dynasty on, i.e. after the Hyksos left Egypt.

2. The mummification process took seventy days, about forty days of which were required for the dehydration of the body.

Upon Jacob/Israel's death, Genesis 50:2,3 tells us *"And Joseph commanded his servants, the physicians, to embalm his father and the physicians embalmed Israel. And forty days were fulfilled for him; for so are fulfilled the days of those who are embalmed: and the Egyptians mourned for him threescore and ten days."*

3. Mummification was associated with the belief in the resurrection of Osiris. Osiris remained the symbol of resurrection until the belief in Jesus Christ replaced the ancient Egyptian doctrine.

4. **None of the Hyksos rulers were ever mummified, simply because they did not believe in Osiris.** They only believed in Seth, the enemy of Osiris.

5. If Jacob died when the Hyksos were in control, one cannot expect mummification of Jacob or Joseph, because it runs contrary to Hyksos' beliefs.

J.

1. The Book of Genesis ends with Joseph's death, *'being an hundred and ten years old, and they embalmed him, and he was put in a coffin in Egypt.'* Genesis 50:26.

Ancient Egyptians considered old age to be a sign of wisdom, and accordingly, gave to those who lived to be wise, the age of 110 years, for symbolic purposes, notwithstanding their actual age. Some scholars were able to count, from Egyptian texts, at least twenty-seven characters who were said to have reached the age of 110 years.

The Pharaoh praised Joseph *'...there is none so discreet and wise as thou art'*. Genesis 41:39.

1- This is a complete about-face by Joseph towards the land which elevated him from a slave to the deputy of the Pharaoh!

2. Before he died, Joseph predicted the Exodus, *"...I die: and God will surely visit you and bring you out of this land unto the Land which he swore to Abraham, to Isaac, and to Jacob. And Joseph took an oath of the children of Israel, saying, God will surely visit you, and shall carry up my bones from hence."* Genesis 50:24,25.

2- When Joseph married an Egyptian woman, he knew that **his children would not be brought up as Hebrews**, because Israeli children follow their mother and not their father.

3- If Joseph foresaw trouble for the Israelites, one should expect him to tell them to leave early, before the trouble.

4- It is illogical to believe that Joseph wanted to be buried in Egypt and in the same time wanted the Israelites, while they were running for their lives, to find his '*secret tomb*', three generations after his death, so that they could fulfill his wish to ***"carry up my bones from hence"***. Genesis 50:25.

5- The use of the word, **'bones'**, shows that the scribe who edited the story had no idea of how an embalmed body would look. Finding bones means that there was no embalmment to begin with, because embalmment means the preservation of the body.

Once again, in the aftermath of the bitter divorce between the Israelites and Egypt, the biblical editors tried to disassociate themselves from their host country. However, no matter how much they tried, they only confused themselves and their followers, who continuously struggle to make sense out of nonsense.

Joseph and His Adopted Land

Joseph was rescued and honored in Egypt. He was allowed to practice his religious beliefs freely. He was allowed to bring his tribe to Egypt. Joseph was the nice beginning of the Israelites' sojourn in Egypt.

How and why did the Israelites' sojourn in Egypt, which started on such high notes, end in the Exodus? Why did the Jews, who were wandering in the desert with Moses, yearn to go back to Egypt, and even conspired to get rid of their leader Moses, as the Bible tells us?

It was Joseph's grandson, Akhenaton, who caused the upheaval. His story will be told in the coming chapters.

Chapter 25

Amenhotep III
Man of Peace

General

Thirty-two years after the death of the warrior King, Twthomosis III, his great-grandson, Amenhotep III, sat upon the throne of Egypt.

King	Length of Reign	Dates
Twthomosis III (David)	54	1490-1436 B.C.
Amenhotep II	23	1436-1413 B.C.
Twthomosis IV	8	1413-1405 B.C.
Amenhotep III (Solomon)	38	1405-1367 B.C.

Egypt was the universal leader of the known world with a vast empire between the Nile and Euphrates. Amenhotep III later became known as *'king of kings, ruler of rulers ...'*

The details of his life and achievements match that of the biblical Solomon. The name Solomon means *'safety'* or *'peace'*. Amenhotep III's reign was almost entirely peaceful except for a minor military operation in northern Sudan during Year 5 of his reign. He developed alliances and diplomatic ties between himself and other leaders of the then-known world, to create a peaceful international climate.

Biblical Solomon

Solomon, according to the Old Testament, followed David to the throne at Jerusalem. Biblical scholars have assigned c. 965-925 B.C. as the dates of Solomon's forty-year reign. His supposed accession to the throne occurred during the Egyptian rule of King Siamun (c. 976-956 B.C.).

There is no historical record of a ruler named Solomon at any time. Furthermore, both the Old Testament and the Talmud agree that Solomon was not the king's original name. According to II Samuel 12:25, at the time of his birth, the prophet Nathan gave Solomon the name of Jedidiah, meaning *'because of the Lord'* or *'by the word of the Lord'*.

The evidence points to Amenhotep III, as being the historical figure, identified in the Old Testament as Solomon. This evidence is described below.

Coronation of the King

- The idea of kingship, originally foreign to the Hebrews, was introduced into the Israelite theology from the time of David onward. In their case, as in Egyptian tradition, the king is regarded as the son of the deity. Jehovah tells King David in Psalms 2:7, *"Thou art my son; this day have I begotten thee."* He also says of Solomon, *"I will be his father, and he shall be my son"* (II Samuel, 7:14) The Israelite Lord now also refers to his kingly son as *"his anointed"*. Psalms, 2:2, 18:50, 20:6.

  Regarding the king as the son of the deity is a purely Egyptian concept which found its way into the Bible from the time of David.

- According to the Bible, David ordered Solomon to be anointed *'king over Israel'* (I Kings, 1:34). Anointing the king was an Egyptian, not a Hebrew custom.

  The Hebrew word **'MeSHeH'**, meaning *'the anointed one'*, is borrowed from the Egyptian word **'Meseh'**.

- After Solomon was anointed, then David said that Solomon should come and *'sit upon my throne'* (I Kings, 1:35). The German biblical scholar Otto Eissfeldt has made the point, *"It is comparatively easy to visualize the throne of gold and ivory with its six steps which stood in the audience chamber as it is described in I Kings, (11:11-20) ... The lavish use of gold can be compared without hesitation with the wonderfully-preserved chair of Twtankhamen."* Twtankhamen was Amenhotep III's grandson.

  The mirror image similarity between the biblical description of Solomon's throne and the actual throne of Twtankhamen, cannot be coincidental.

- Other aspects of the account of Solomon's coronation in I Kings — trumpet blowing, the acclamation *'God save king Solomon'*, and the royal procession — are descriptive of the ancient Egyptian traditions.

The King's Egyptian Wife

Amenhotep III

He married his baby sister Sitamun (an Egyptian), in order to inherit the throne, since the line of royal descent was through the eldest daughter.

Solomon

According to the Bible, Solomon *"made affinity with Pharaoh king of Egypt, and took Pharaoh's daughter, and brought her into the city of David"* (I Kings, 3:1).

Points of interest in the biblical account:

1- The reference to Pharaoh's daughter as being Solomon's first and principal wife indicates that, as in the case of Amenhotep III, that she was the wife of his own nationality. If Solomon was the king of Israel, he should have had an Israelite wife to bear his successor, since, according to Israelite tradition, the line of descent is from the mother.

Solomon married only foreign wives, beginning with the Pharaoh's daughter. Even his crown prince, Rehoboam, is said to have been the son of an Ammonite (I Kings, 14:21).

2- The Pharaoh whose daughter was married to Solomon was never named. The Pharaoh in question however is said to have *"gone up, and taken Gezer, and burnt it with fire, and slain the Canaanites that dwelt in the city, and given it for a present unto his daughter, Solomon's wife"* (I Kings, 9:16).

This biblical verse has no historical validity.

None of the Egyptian kings, who lived during the supposed reign of Solomon, were involved in military campaigns in western Asia. The kings of this period belonged to the very weak Twenty-First Dynasty.

The King and Foreign Wives

- Solomon is said to have had seven hundred wives and three hundred concubines (I Kings, 11:3). They were all foreigners: *"But King Solomon loved many strange women, together with the daughter of Pharaoh, women of the Moabites, Ammonites, Edomites, Zidonians and Hittites"* (I Kings, 11:1).

- This love of foreign women is mirrored in the life of Amenhotep III who, after marrying Sitamun to inherit the throne, married Tiye, the daughter of Yuya (Joseph), an Israelite. Amenhotep III issued a scarab in celebration of his marriage to Tiye. Copies were sent to foreign princes, reading in part **"... the Great King's Wife, Tiye, who liveth. The name of her father is Yuya, the name of her mother is Tuya ..."** This scarab clarified the identity of Tiye. Earlier she had been thought to be a Mesopotamian princess from Mitanni, sent to Egypt to marry the king.

He also married two women from Mitanni, two from Babylonia as well as a princess from Arzawa in south-western Asia Minor.

Troubles in the Empire

- According to the Bible, the empire inherited by **Solomon** was weakened, to a certain extent, during the course of his reign. Solomon left the empire somewhat smaller than he inherited it.

- Similar weaknesses and rebellions are echoed in the Amarna diplomatic archives relating to the reign of **Amenhotep III**. Letters sent by Palestinian kings, especially Abdi-Kheba of Jerusalem, speak of continuous trouble in the area.

Frederick J. Giles, the Canadian Egyptologist who studied the Amarna letters, wrote that *"At the time of the death of Twthomosis III [the Empire] was, to be sure, of somewhat greater extent than that at the death of Amenhotep III. Yet the apparent decrease may have been due to policy rather than military defeat."*

Therefore the biblical account of the weakening of King David's empire during the time of Solomon agrees with historical records during the reign of Amenhotep III.

The Government

Pre-Solomon Rule

- During the period between the entry into Canaan in the thirteenth century B.C., and the era of Saul at the end of the eleventh century B.C., Israel existed as a confederation of twelve tribes. Each tribe was living separately in its own land, and governed by its elders. All twelve tribes were, however, sharing a common spiritual center.

- When the Philistines started competing for occupation of the same territory as the twelve tribes, the Israelites felt the need for a common leader to unify them against their enemies: *"Then all the elders of Israel gathered themselves together, and came to Samuel unto Ramah, And said unto him, Behold, thou art old, and thy sons walk not in thy ways: now make us a king to judge us like all the nations"* (I Samuel, 8: 4-5). So, Samuel chose Saul and declared him king. He was accepted by all the tribes, but this did not change the political system overnight, each tribe continued to govern its own affairs as before.

- There is no evidence, during the time of the biblical David, of a political system for administering such a vast empire; no taxation system; and no organized army to guard its boundaries.

Solomon Rule

According to the Bible, Solomon did away with the tribal divisions and united Israel, together with other parts of the empire

The bible would have us believe that the tribal society of the Hebrews, was integrated overnight into a sophisticated political system, under the control of the King and his central government. Furthermore, we are told that this political system, vanished at the end of his forty-year reign, as abruptly and as mysteriously, as it began!

Amenhotep III Rule

The administrative system attributed to Solomon does not belong to the

Palestinian Israel, but to the period of the Egyptian Empire. Such a government structure is a purely Egyptian system which existed more than 5,000 years ago.

During the empire period, and in particular during the time of Twthomosis III, the political system was reorganized to suit the needs of the age, and was later developed further by Amenhotep III. The empire was arranged in twelve administrative sections, an arrangement that the biblical narrator borrowed for his account of the Solomon story.

Bureaucracy

The governmental positions during David and Solomon, as stated in II Samuel, 8:16-18, 20:23-6, and I Kings, 4:2-6, are similar to appointments made by Twthomosis III and Amenhotep III.

Taxation

• From its earliest history, Egypt had a tax system.
As mentioned earlier, the Empire during Twthomosis III's reign, including Egypt, was divided into twelve areas. Each area was expected to contribute sufficient tax to cover the country's needs for one month of the year. Each district had its own supervising official.

• The supposed Empire of Solomon also had twelve districts, requiring each to furnish victuals and materials for one month of the year. Both the Egyptian tax and the levy on the Israelites were for the purpose of provisioning: *"And Solomon had twelve officers over all Israel, which provided victuals for the king and his household: each man his month in a year made provision"* (I Kings, 4:7)... *"And those officers provided victual for king Solomon, and for all that came unto king Solomon's table, every man in his month"* (I Kings, 4:27)

Almost all scholars agree that the taxation system, which the Bible says was introduced by Solomon, matches precisely the system that was used in Egypt at the time of Amenhotep III.

The Great Builder

Solomon is reputed as being a master builder. He built ***"the house of the Lord, and his own house, and Millo, and the wall of Jerusalem, and Hazer, and Megiddo, and Gezer"*** (I Kings, 9:15) and numerous other building activities throughout the Empire.

Let us review the construction activities at the sites mentioned above in I Kings, 9:15, in their same order.

1- The Temples

• The Bible tells us that Solomon built a temple on Mount Moriah, north of Jerusalem. The site is now occupied by the Dome of the Rock mosque and therefore no excavation can be carried out to search for this temple.

There are, however, some remarkable similarities between this biblically described temple and the mortuary temple of Amenhotep III in western Thebes.

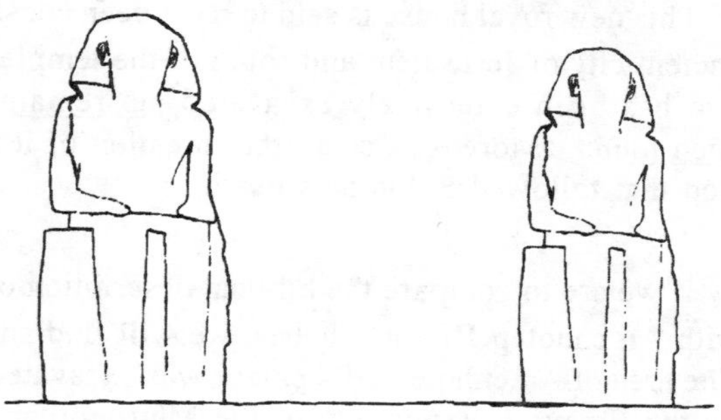

A- Even though no remains of the mortuary temple have been found, two colossal statues of the seated king, just under seventy feet tall, stood at the front of the temple, and still exist in western Thebes. They are comparable to the two pillars of the biblical Solomon's temple. The two Egyptian statues have names, like the mentioned biblical pillars.

B- On a stela which came from this temple, we find the original inscription of Amenhotep III, in which he describes the temple as ***"an everlasting fortress of sandstone, embellished with gold throughout, its floor shining with silver and all its doorways with electrum. It is extended with royal statues of granite, of quartzite and precious stones, fashioned to last for ever."***

Similarly, much precious material were also used in the biblically described Solomon temple.

• Amenhotep III is known to have built many other temples, both in Egypt and in Canaanite cities. Archaeological evidence supports the belief that several of the biblically described Solomonic temples were built in Canaan during the reign of Amenhotep III. There are purely Egyptian aspects of this Solomonic temple, such as:

A- The two pillars, or representations, at the entrance of the temple. They signify the split of the spiritual One into two and that one has to pass through it in order to reach the inner element.

B- The practice of carrying the deity in an ark, and its placement in the Holy of Holies.

2- The Royal Palace

• This new royal house is said to have been constructed to the north of the ancient city of Jerusalem and south of the temple area. Although Jerusalem has been extensively excavated, no remains of such a palace have been found. Moreover, no further mention of it was made during the period that followed Solomon's death.

• If we are to compare the biblical description of Solomon's royal palace with Amenhotep III's at Thebes, we will find an identical picture.
The area of Amenhotep III's palace was excavated between 1910 and 1920 by the Egyptian Expedition of the Metropolitan Museum of Art of New York. The result of these excavations found the layout of Amenhotep III's palace to match precisely the biblical account in I Kings, 7:2-12 where Solomon's palace consisted of five elements: 1) The King's palace, 2) The house of Pharaoh's daughter, ***"whom he had taken to wife"***, 3) The throne room, 4) A hall of columns, and 5) The house of the forest of Lebanon.

3- The Millo

The British archaeologist Kathleen Kenyon was able, in 1961, to uncover the remains of the Millo (filling), which was utilized in the widening of the ground level below the ancient fortress of Jerusalem. She was able to date the first construction of the Millo to the fourteenth century B.C., the time of Amenhotep III.

No evidence was found, to relate the Millo to the tenth century B.C., during Solomon's supposed reign.

4- Sites of Fortifications

There is archaeological evidence of fortifications at Hazor, Megiddo and Gezer. The remains of these fortifications indicate that there were two cycles of destruction, and each was followed by a rebuilding operation.

Here are the sequences of these cycles:

Destruction - in the middle of the fifteenth century B.C. This was the time of the Twthomosis III campaigns. All three cities are contained in the list of western Asiatic cities which were conquered by Twthomosis III.

Rebuilding - Occurred approximately fifty years later during the reign of Amenhotep III. Egyptian objects, including a cartouche of Amenhotep III, were found in the strata belonging to this period.

There is also other evidence of wealth and trading activities, in this area, during this prosperous period.

Destruction - in the twelfth century B.C. This was the result of the invading 'Peoples of the Sea' who included the Philistines.

Rebuilding - in the middle of the tenth century B.C. by the Philistines. Their special pottery and iron objects were found in the strata belonging to this period.

After checking the archaeological findings of the rebuilding operation, some archaeologists attributed found pottery and iron objects (at Hazor) to Solomon. Their conclusions were based on the biblical historical sequence and not on credible physical evidence. None of the items found bore any inscription that identified a king named Solomon, or anything else related to his supposed kingdom. Furthermore, the Old Testament did not give us any description matching the archaeological findings.

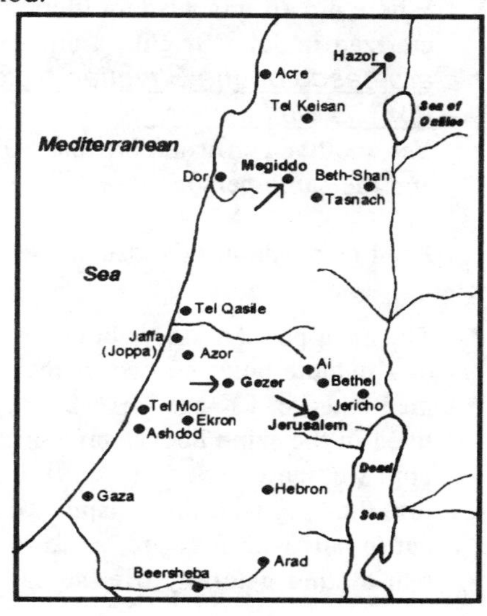

The construction work attributed to Solomon was the work of the Philistines, who were rebuilding Hazor, after their initial destruction of the city in the twelfth century B.C.

> **To summarize, there is historical and archaeological evidence of building during the reign of Amenhotep III that matches those ascribed to Solomon. However, none of them are dated to the tenth century B.C., the supposed time when Solomon ruled.**

The Wisdom of The King

Solomon is described in the Bible as being very wise. ***"King Solomon exceeded all the kings of the earth for riches and for wisdom"*** (I Kings, 10:23).

The reasons given for his wisdom brings forth more similarities between Solomon and Amenhotep III. Two areas will be discussed here:

1- The authoring of the Books of Hebrew wisdom and poetry were attributed to Solomon. It is hard to believe that the king was the composer of all these books of Proverbs, of Ecclesiates and Wisdom, and of Psalms!

Where did all this wisdom literature come from? The answer is summarized in John Bright's finding: *"That parts of the Proverbs ... are based on the Egyptian Maxims of Amenemope (Amenhotep III) ... is well known".*
Yet another confirmation that Solomon and Amenhotep III are one and the same person.

Read more about this issue under the chapter 'Literature'.

2- The most popular story about the wisdom of Solomon is his resolution of a dispute between two mothers, over the parenthood of a child, as mentioned in I Kings, 3:16-28. The story goes that two women, who lived in the same house, gave birth to baby boys. One baby died and both women claimed the surviving child as her own. They went before the king with their dispute. Solomon then ordered the child to be cut in half with a sword, so as to give one half to each woman. The real mother naturally tried to save the boy's life by letting the other woman have the boy. That is how Solomon identified the real mother.

It is hard to believe that the king, who had professional judges and officials, would involve himself personally in such a dispute between two women who are described in the Bible as *"harlots"*. The king would not have personally sat in judgment of such a case, unless he had a personal interest. The women involved were his wife, Queen Tiye, the mother of Moses (Akhenaton), and Tiy, Moses' nursing mother, who was already nursing Nefertiti, his sister. Both women were living in the royal palace, at that time. Read more about it in the following chapter.

The King and Foreign Gods

• The Bible tells us that Solomon was diverted to other gods: *"King Solomon loved many strange women, together with the daughter of Pharaoh, women of the Moabites, Ammonites, Edomites, Zidonians, and Hittites; Of the nations concerning which the Lord said unto the children of Israel, Ye shall not go in to them, neither shall they come in unto you; for surely they will turn away your heart after their gods: Solomon clave unto these in love"* (I Kings, 11:1-2).

"For it came to pass, when Solomon was old, that his wives turned away his heart after other gods: and his heart was not perfect with the Lord his God, as was the heart of David his father. For Solomon went after Ashtoreth the goddess of the Zidonians, and after Milcom the abomination of the Ammonites" (I Kings, 11:4-5).

• Amenhotep III was also diverted and converted to the worship of the Aten, the God of the Amarna kings. He also continued his belief in the Egyptian gods (neterw).

Different Eras

Despite the hard work of biblical scholars, historians and archaeologists, no single piece of evidence has been found to support the period of the supposed United Monarchy of David and Solomon. Scholars have been confused by the biblical chronology, which present David and Solomon as having belonged to the period following both the Exodus and the settlement in the "Promised Land".

Many of these biblical events occurred four to five centuries earlier than what the Old Testament would have us believe. Both Twthomosis III, the historical King David, and his great-grandson Amenhotep III, the Biblical Solomon, belonged to the Egyptian's Eighteenth Dynasty.

Chapter 26

Akhenaton and Moses

General

• The drama of Akhenaton is the second most controversial subject in Egyptian history, next to the Great Pyramid.

• Akhenaton has been called by many *'the first monotheist'*. He glorified one of the neterw, namely *'Aten'*, over and above all the other neterw (gods) but mostly he wanted to challenge Amon and his establishment at Thebes. His vendetta with Amon was motivated as much by politics as by religion.

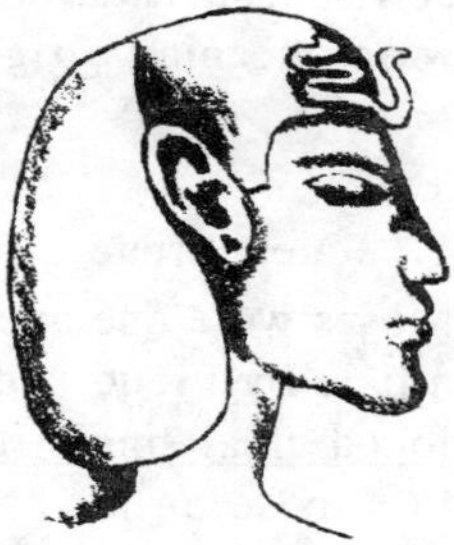

• Throughout Egypt, he ordered the name of Amon, the supreme deity of Thebes, to be erased from the inscriptions of the temples. Akhenaton's reign extended eighteen years, much of it as co-regent. After he abdicated the throne, the worship of Amon was reinstated. The works of Akhenaton were destroyed. His name was deleted throughout the rest of Egyptian history. He was referred to as *'the criminal'*, *'the rebel'* and *'mos'* which means *'rightful person/heir'*.

• In order to judge his behavior, one must ask the people of any country what their reaction would be if their leader decided that his church, of all the churches, was the only right one. Would they call him an enlightened monotheist? Furthermore, what if this leader decided to actually close all other churches, because, in his view, they were no good? Would he be called an enlightened monotheist?

The people of any country would surely react as ancient Egyptians reacted, because their leader would not be an enlightened monotheist, but a tyrannical dictator.

Sigmund Freud Research

• Sigmund Freud, the Jewish father of psychoanalysis, was interested in reading about Akhenaton and Moses. He later wrote a book called Moses and Monotheism. Sigmund Freud argued that Moses was an Egyptian, a follower of Akhenaton, who later led the Jews out of Egypt.

• Freud also came to the conclusion that *'Moses'* was itself an Egyptian name.
Even though the Bible in Exodus, 2:10 tells us that Moses' royal mother, who adopted him, called him **Moshe** because, she said, ***"I drew him out of the water"***, Freud demonstrated that *Moshe* had a different meaning. In fact, the Hebrew word *m sh a*, as a verb, can mean either *'to draw'* or *'one who draws out'*. The name **Moshui**, is the one which means *'one who has been drawn out'*. It was then Freud's conclusion that the name of the Jewish leader was not of Hebrew origin, but comes from the Egyptian word, **mos**, meaning a rightful person.

• Later, Freud came very close to demonstrating that Akhenaton and Moses were one and the same person. In 1937 Imago published another article by Freud under the title **'If Moses was an Egyptian'**. Freud found great similarity between the new religion that Akhenaton had tried to impose on his country and the religious teaching ascribed to Moses. Sigmund Freud wrote: *"The Jewish creed says: 'Schema Yisrael Adonai Elohenu Adonai Echod'."* ('Hear, 0 Israel, the Lord thy God is one God'.) The Hebrew letter *'d'* is equivalent to the Egyptian letter *'t'* and the Hebrew *'e'* becomes the Egyptian *'o'*. Therefore this sentence from the Jewish creed could be translated: *"Hear, 0 Israel, our God Aten is the only God."* Akhenaton, as stated earlier, declared that Aten is the only God.

• The similarity between the religions of Moses and Akhenaton as raised in Sigmund Freud's book, Moses and Monotheism, has caused endless argument about this subject.

Childhood

• Akhenaton's father, Amenhotep III, met and fell in love with Yuya's daughter, Tiye. In order to inherit the throne, Amenhotep III married his half-sister Sitamun. He shortly thereafter married Tiye, the half-Egyptian. To add insult to injury, he made Tiye rather than Sitamun, his Great Royal Wife (queen).

Amenhotep III's marital actions were irresponsible and must have created a poisonous atmosphere.

Later, Tiye had a son, Twthomosis, who was educated and trained at Memphis and who held the title of the High Priest of Ptah, as did most heirs-apparent during the Eighteenth Dynasty, but then he disappeared suddenly from the scene.

There may have been an imminent danger awaiting Tiye's sons. She was of mixed Egyptian-Israelite blood, and if her son succeeded to the throne, this would be regarded as forming a new dynasty of non-Egyptian, part-Israelite rulers over Egypt.

Her second son was born, probably in 1394 B.C., at the fortified frontier city of Zarw. He was named Amenhotep IV (later to be known as Akhenaton).

• Upon Akhenaton's birth, Tiye sent him by water to the safety of her Israelite relations at nearby Goshen. This event is echoed in the biblical story of Moses being found by a princess in the bulrushes by the bank of the Nile.

The imminent danger to Tiye's sons is echoed in the Talmud which provides a different reason for the attempt to kill Moses at birth. It was Moses specifically (not all other Hebrew children) who was to be murdered because he posed a threat to the throne of Egypt.

• The Bible gave the impression that Moses was the first-born in his family. We find out later that he already had an elder sister, Miriam, who was quietly watching him floating on the water. She approached the Pharaoh's daughter and offered: ***"Shall I fetch one of the Hebrew women to nurse the baby for you?"*** When the offer was accepted, the sister got her mother. The mother agreed to nurse her own baby in return for payment.

Later, when the child grew older, she took him back to the Pharaoh's daughter, who adopted him as her son. Then she, we are told, gave him the name Moses.

Some comments about these biblical events:

1- As we can see from the case of the Patriarch Joseph, when the Pharaoh appointed him as his vizier he gave him an Egyptian name to go with his new Egyptian identity. Does it make sense for the royal mother of Moses to give her adopted Egyptian son a Hebrew name?!

2- Can we expect the Egyptian royal mother to have sufficient, or any, knowledge of the Hebrew language to be able to choose a special Hebrew name for the child?

3- The biblical claim that the Pharaoh's daughter adopted the child is inherently improbable. The customs of the time would not have allowed an unmarried princess to adopt a child.

4- Finally, the biblical story of two mothers fighting over the parenthood of a child who went to Solomon to resolve their dispute (I Kings 3:16-28) is strikingly similar to the account of Moses growing up in the Pharaoh's palace, where he had "two mothers". Solomon, the King of Kings, would not have gotten involved in a dispute between two women, unless the dispute was in his household.

Tiye

• In either case of Akhenaton or Moses, we know very little of their early years beyond the fact that both had an extremely close relationship with their mother.

• Akhenaton, spent most of his youth in the Eastern Delta and at Heliopolis. In the Eastern Delta area he was influenced by Aten, a God without an image. At Heliopolis, he was educated by the priests of Re, the ancient Egyptian solar deity.

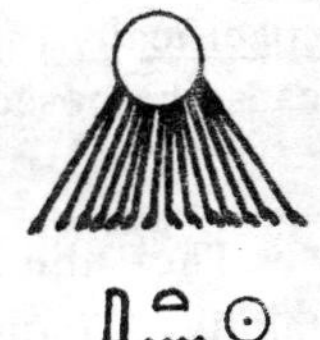

Early historians stated that the biblical Moses spent his early youth at Heliopolis.

• There is no evidence that Akhenaton/Moses spent his early days at Memphis, where his father had his main residence at the time and where the heirs apparent were normally trained and educated with the sons of the nobles.

• When he was in his very early teens, Amenhotep IV was finally allowed to take up residence at Thebes. The Amonite priests and nobles of Egypt, the protectors of old traditions, regarded Akhenaton with contempt for his mixed race. It was not he who first rejected them, it was they, the Amonists, who refused to accept him as the legitimate heir to the throne.

When Amenhotep III's health began to deteriorate, Tiye's power increased correspondingly. In order to ensure her son's inheritance of the throne, she arranged for him to marry his half-sister, Nefertiti. She was the daughter of Amenhotep III by his sister, Sitamun, the legitimate heiress. Thus Nefertiti is recognized in the Bible as Miriam, Moses' sister.

Tiye prompted her husband, Amenhotep III, to appoint Amenhotep IV (Akhenaton) as his co-regent.

• Queen Tiye was definitely the power behind the throne, at the time. Her name, unlike that of earlier queens, was placed regularly in a cartouche, a distinction previously limited to the ruling monarch. Furthermore, she was represented as being of equivalent stature to the king, Amenhotep III.

The Name "Moses"

• As explained earlier, the biblical explanation of the name is incorrect.

• In Ancient Egyptian, this word, meaning a rightful person/heir, consists of two consonants, *'m'* and *'s'*. If we take away the two vowels *'o'* and *'e'* from Moshe (the Jewish name for Moses) we are left with only two consonants, *'m'* and *'sh'*. As the Hebrew letter *'sh'* is the equivalent of the Egyptian *'s'*, one is able to conclude that the Hebrew word came from the Egyptian word. In both Hebrew and Egyptian, short vowels, although always pronounced, were never written. Using long consonants for long vowels was a later development in both languages.

As for the name Moses, the *'s'* at the end of the name is drawn from the Greek translation of the biblical name.

• *Mos* was part of many compound Egyptian names such as *Ptah-mos* and *Twth-mos*. We also find some examples of the word *mos* being used on its own as a personal pronoun and which means rightful person. Such practice began during the Eighteenth Dynasty.

• Once Akhenaton was no longer on the throne, use of his royal names was forbidden, and he was referred to officially in later times as **'The Fallen One of Akhetaten (Amarna)'** and **'The Rebel of Akhetaten'**. The Israelites may have called him ***mos*** to indicate that he was the legitimate son of Amenhotep III and the rightful heir to his father's throne.

• Many generations later and in a different country, the biblical editor, who may not have had any knowledge of Moses' original name, attempted to provide a Hebrew explanation. It is also possible that the biblical editor was trying to remove any possible link between Moses and his position as the Pharaoh of Egypt.

Brother Aaron

• The Bible tells us that Moses has a brother called Aaron, <u>a long time</u> after Moses' birth.

Was Aaron a biological brother or a feeding brother? In the biblical era and even today, Bedouin mothers regularly nurse each others' babies when they get hungry. The children of both mothers know each other as brothers and sisters.

Thus, the woman who nursed Moses would have been called his mother. Her real son, Aaron, was simply what the Bedouins, call *'a feeding brother'* to Moses.

• Aaron played an important role, when Moses went back to Egypt to challenge the ruling Pharaoh.

Aten Worship

• There were very many neterw in Egypt. Some deities had only local distinction. Others, like Amon, Re and Osiris, were recognized throughout Egypt. Aten was among this multitude of deities, and it was not a new idea which was introduced by Akhenaton. Aten does appear in a few texts from the time of the Twelfth Dynasty. It appeared frequently since the time of Twthomosis IV (1401-1391 B.C.). Akhenaton exalted Aten over

and above the others. Aten is the disk of the sun as physical manifestation of Re. Aten had no image, unlike the other neterw.

- Adonai in Hebrew means *'my Lord'*. The last two letters *'ai'* of the word is a Hebrew pronoun meaning *'my'* or *'mine'* and signifying possession. *'Adon'* meaning Lord was correctly noted by Sigmund Freud, as the Hebrew word for the Egyptian *'Aten'*. As the Egyptian *'t'* becomes *'d'* in Hebrew and the vowel *'e'* becomes an *'o'*, *Adon* is the Hebrew equivalent of the Egyptian *Aten*.

Thus Adon and Aten are one and the same.

- The hymn to Aten which is attributed to Akhenaton is a mirror image of Psalm 104. Below, are both versions for you to compare:

Hymn to the Aten

The cattle are content in their pasture, the trees and plants are green, the birds fly from their nests. Their wings are raised in praise of your soul. The goats leap on their feet. All flying and fluttering things live when you shine for them. Likewise the boats race up and down the river, and every way is open, because you have appeared. The fish in the river leap before your face. Your rays go to the depth of the sea.

Psalm 104

He causeth the grass to grow for the cattle, and the herb for the service of man: that he may bring forth food out of the earth: and wine that maketh glad the heart of man and oil to make his face shine, and bread which strengtheneth man's heart. The trees of the Lord are full of sap: the cedars of Lebanon which he hath planted: where the birds make their nests: as for the stork, the fir trees are her house. The high hills are a refuge for the wild goats; and the rocks for the conies.... So is this great and wide sea, wherein are things creeping innumerable, both great and small beasts. There go the ships.

The similarity of sequence and of images in both compositions is so strikingly alike. As such, many believe that the earlier Egyptian hymn must have been known to the Hebrew writer.

• Akhenaton chose the Heliopolitan solar form of the Egyptian temple, to be used as the place for worship of the Aten.

Likewise, Moses was the first person to introduce a temple into Israelite worship, when he created the tabernacle in Sinai.

• Akhenaten adopted the Egyptian practice of a holy boat, which was usually kept in the temple. The ark was used to carry the deity during processions.

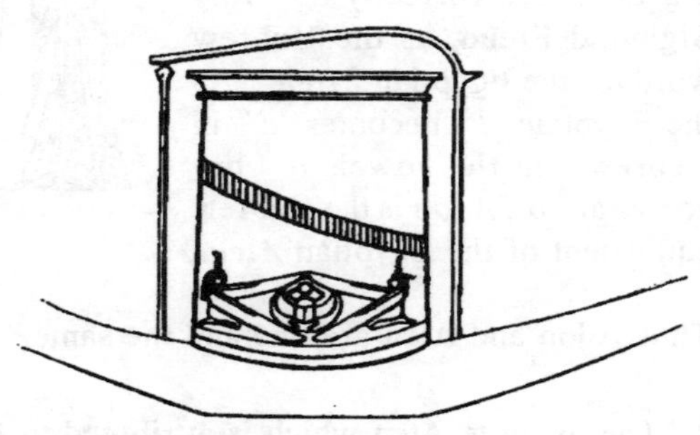

Moses also introduced the ark, where the Pentateuch scrolls were kept (Exodus, 25:10). The ark is respected as the second holiest part of the Jewish temple, after the Pentateuch itself.

• There was no Israelite priesthood before the time of Moses. Moses arranged the priesthood in two main levels, the high priest and the ordinary priests. Instructions were issued to them about their specific garment, purification, annointment and how to go about fulfilling the duties of their offices.

Rituals and worship of the newly-established Israelite priesthood were similar to those introduced by Akhenaton.

• Across the Nile from Tell-el Amarna, there is the city of Mal-lawi (Mallevi), which means literally *'The City of the Levites'*. The Levites, who held priestly positions with Moses, held the same positions with Akhenaton at Amarna. Such as:

1- **Meryre II** was the High Priest of the Aten, at the Amarna temple. The Hebrew equivalent of this name is ***Merari***, who is described in Genesis, 46:11 as one of the sons of Levi.

2- **Panehesy** was the Chief Servitor of the Aten at Akhenaton's temple. The Hebrew equivalent of this name is *Phinehas*, who was the son of Eleazar and grandson of Aaron according to Exodus, 6:25.

It is therefore evident that we are dealing with the same high officials who served Akhenaton at Amarna and then accompanied him to Sinai afterwards. Yet another confirmation that Moses and Akhenaton are one and the same.

The Ruler

Akhenaton's eighteen-year reign was mostly a co-regency. He reigned the first twelve years in conjunction with his father, Amenhotep III. It was very probable that the last few years of his reign was a co-regency with his brother Semenkhkare.

1- Early co-Regency Rule

Akhenaton became a co-regent in or about Year 28 of Amenhotep III. About Year 33, he transferred his residence to his new capital city, Tell el-Amarna, 200 miles north of Thebes. His reign had two groups of dated inscriptions. One related to the Thebes residence, which started at year 28 of Amenhotep III. The other one was related to the Amarna residence. A correspondence in date, year by year, between the two groups of inscriptions can be easily established. For example, Year 28 of Amenhotep III equals to Year 1 of Amenhotep IV. Year 33 of Amenhotep III is equal to Year 6 of Amenhotep IV, ...etc. Amenhotep III died in his Year 38, which was Akhenaton's Year 12.

From the start of the co-regency, Amenhotep IV offended the Amonite priesthood by building temples to his God, the Aten, within the boundaries of the established Amon-Re temples at Karnak. He also did not invite the traditional priests to any of the festivities. In his fifth year he changed his name to Akhenaton in honor of the Aten.

Because of the hostile climate which he created, Tiye, his powerful mother convinced both her son, Akhenaton, and her husband, Amenhotep III, to leave Thebes and go to their new capital city at Tell el-Amarna (two hundred miles north of Thebes). Amenhotep named his new city Akhetaten meaning *'the city of the horizon of the Aten'*. The co-regency ended when his father died in Akhenaten's Year 12.

• The issue of the co-regency between Amenhotep III and his son, Akhenaton, was further reinforced by the discovery of his vizier's tomb in late 1989. The main points to be drawn from these findings are:

1- Akhenaton could only have had a vizier, if he was ruling.

2- Since Amenhotep III was mentioned, in the vizier's tomb, by his praenomen, Neb-Maat-Re, and in accordance with Egyptian traditions, it must be concluded that Amenhotep III was still alive when Akhenaton was in charge.

2- Sole Ruler

• When Akhenaton became sole ruler after Amenhotep III died, Year 12 of Akhenaton, he shut down the other temples, stopped all financial support for them and sent the priests home. These actions made a bad situation worse.

• Throughout his reign, Akhenaton relied completely on the army's support for protection. The new capital city was an armed camp with parades and processions of soldiers, infantry and chariotry in their heavy gear. This military climate is depicted in the tombs of the nobles, at Tell-el Amarna.

• The loyalty of the army, which was controlled by Aye (son of Yuya/ Joseph), had kept Akhenaton in power, in the uneasy years that followed his coming to the throne, as sole ruler in his Year 12.

3- Late Co-Regency Ruler

• As a last resort or as a ploy, Akhenaton, in his Year 15, was forced to install his brother, Semenkhkare, as his co-regent at Thebes. This action only delayed the final outcome.

• As a sign of trouble between Akhenaton and Nefertiti, her official name Neferneferuaten, meaning *'beloved of Akhenaton'*, was given to Semenkhkare, upon his accession to the throne.

• Semenkhkare left Amarna for Thebes, where he reversed Akhenaton's hostile actions and began building a temple to Amon.

• In his Year 17, Akhenaton suddenly disappeared. At and about the same time, Semenkhkare died suddenly. The co-regency of Akhenaton and Semenkhkare was succeeded by the young prince, Twtankhamun.

• In his Year 17, Akhenaton may have been warned by his uncle, Aye, of a threat on his life. He abdicated and fled to Sinai, with a small group of followers, taking with him his symbol of Pharaonic authority, a staff topped by a brass serpent.

Although Sinai was part of Egypt from the early days of Egyptian history, there was no established governing authority there. It was more or less a buffer zone between Egypt and its neighbors.

• The sudden disappearance of Akhenaton is echoed in the biblical story of Moses when he escaped to Sinai, after he slew an Egyptian. The account of how Moses slew an Egyptian may have been mentioned in the Amarna Tablets. Among them is a letter, sent from Abd-Khiba, King of Jerusalem, to Akhenaton, in which Abd-Khiba accuses Akhenaton of not punishing some Hebrews who killed two Egyptian officials: "**... the Khabiru (Hebrews) are seizing the towns of the king ... Turbazu has been slain in the very gate of Zilu (Zarw), yet the king holds back ... Yaptih-Hadad has been slain in the very gate of Zilu, yet the king holds back.**"

Was letting the Israelites get away with two murders, the final blow to Akhenaton's reign?

4- King Without Power

Even though Akhenaton abdicated and fled from the scene, he was still regarded as the legitimate ruler. As long as he was alive, the Pharaoh was regarded as being the lawful ruler of his lands, even if he was weak and had no authority.

When the ten-year old Twtankhamen became the official Pharaoh, he was assigned and controlled by a guardian. This would be similar to any monarchy nowadays when the legal heir is a minor. As such, the rule of Akhenaton, his father, continued for four years and during this time the boy King was still called Twtankh**aten**.

Four years later, Year 21 of Akhenaton, the Boy King abandoned the Aten (at least officially) and returned to be the son of Amon. Simultaneously, he changed his name from Twtankh**aten** to Twtankh**amen**. The Amon priesthood accepted this return in a crowning celebration. Only then did he become the legitimate monarch.

At this point in time, the Aten lost its power in Egypt, and Akhenaton, who was still alive, was king no more.

Akhenaton's Vizier

- Late in 1989, the tomb of Aper-el, Akhenaton's vizier, was discovered almost intact in Saqqara.

- The name Aper-el consists of two parts. The first part *'Aper'* corresponds to the Egyptian word for *'Hebrew'*. The second part of the name *'el'* is the short form of *'Elohim'*, which means *'the Lord'* in Hebrew. Similar names are known to have existed in Egypt at this time, but never in the case of high officials.

- The fact that Akhenaton's vizier was a worshipper of El confirms the strong bond between the king and the Israelites living in Egypt at the time. Such a bond is also evident in the many pieces of funerary items, which were found, in Aper-el's tomb. They included a box given to Aper-el by Amenhotep III and Queen Tiye, as well as Amenhotep III's cartouche.

Nefertiti The Beloved

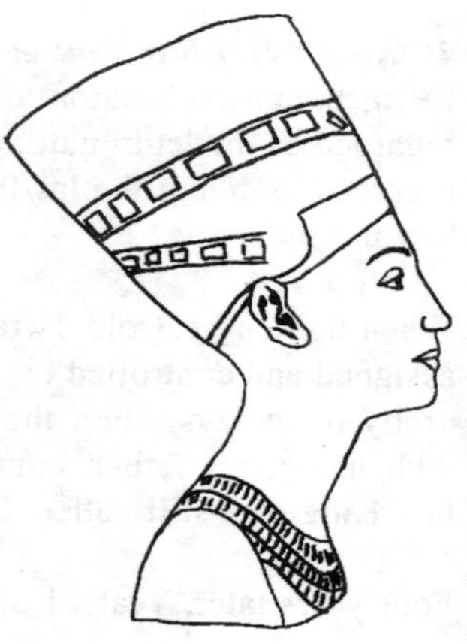

- Queen Nefertiti is described in the tomb of one of the officials of Akhenaton as the one who **"unites her beauties and propitiates the Aten with her pleasant voice and with her beautiful hands holding the sistra"**. Nefertiti means **'the beautiful one has come'**.

- When Semenkhkare became co-regent, Nefertiti disappeared mysteriously and some scholars suggested, without any evidence, that she must have died around that time. There is evidence that she moved to the north City of Amarna where Twtankhamen was also resident. Objects inscribed with the queen's name have been found at the residence in the city of Amarna. One can deduce that she may have disagreed with her husband, and that her views proved to be right after all. There is no evidence that she was buried in her royal tomb.

• There is conclusive evidence that Akhenaton had at least six daughters with Queen Nefertiti, in addition to Twtankhamen. Akhenaton's parenthood to Twtankhamen will be proven in the next chapter.

• When Akhenaton abolished the worship of Isis among other deities, Nefertiti's image was used in place of that of the mother netert (goddess) on Amarna funerary objects. Nefertiti's image is to be found, in place of the image of Isis in the sarcophagus of Akhenaton.

Akhenaton's Capital City Akhetaten (Amarna)

• Contrary to the general view, the name Amarna was not derived from a Moslim Arab tribe which settled in the area. No evidence exists to substantiate that. The name is, however, derived from the name in the second cartouche of Akhenaton's god, namely *Im-r-n*.

Amram, or Imran, was the name given in the Bible to Moses' father, and it is precisely the same name Akhenaten gave to his *'father'*, the Aten. Yet another confirmation that Moses and Akhenaton are one and the same.

• The city was well-planned, with temples to Aten, residences for all classes, and tombs for the royal family and their high officials.

• The house of the high priest **Panehesy** was located prominently in the city. He was never buried in his assigned tomb. He is equated to the biblical ***Phinehas***, the priest, who according to the Talmud, killed Jesus.

• The main themes, in all the tombs, repeat themselves. At the entrance there is always a hymn to the aten disk.

• No evidence of burial, or even of sarcophagi, have been found in any of the nobles' tombs.

The principal theme in the tombs is not the typical Egyptian daily activity, as in other noble tombs, but the relationship between the deceased and Akhenaton and other members of the royal family. Sometimes the king is shown as being accessible to his subjects. Other times Akhenaton has replaced the neterw.

In Egypt, the king always represented the divine in man. Akhenaton thought that it was he, Akhenaton the man, who was divine.

Amarna Letters

The Amarna letters were discovered in 1887. They consist of a collection of several hundred clay tablets written in Babylonian cuneiform. The letters were sent to Akhenaton and Amenhotep III from other kings and rulers of the adjoining lands. Egypt's replies to these letters were destroyed, so we have only one side of the correspondence. By inference however, it is quite possible to guess many subject matters of concern.

The Aftermath

- Semenkhkare died suddenly and mysteriously at Thebes. It was impossible to give him a proper burial especially with so much turmoil in the country. Semenkhkare was therefore buried secretly, and in a hurry, using some objects meant to be used by Akhenaton, who had already fled from Amarna to Sinai.

- Incidentally some of Semenkhkare's funerary equipment at Amarna, were later used for Twtankhamen who also died suddenly. Semenkhkare was succeeded in his turn by the young king Twtankhaten, the son of Akhenaton (Moses).

Twtankhamen ruled for at least nine, and perhaps ten years (c. 1361-1352 B.C.) before meeting an early death. He was succeeded by Aye (Ephraim), his great-uncle and the last of the four Amarna kings.

- Aye ruled for only four years before he disappeared. Nothing much is known about his death. His mummy — if he was ever mummified — was never found. His tomb, in the Valley of the Kings, was usurped by his successor, Horemheb.

The Exile

• According to the Talmud, when Moses was 18, he fled Egypt, after killing an Egyptian. He then became a soldier and fought on the side of the King of Ethiopia, against a rebellion led by an Egyptian native, Bi'lam. After the King won, Moses became very popular. As a result, when the king died, Moses was appointed as their new king and ***"they gave him the widow of their king for a wife."***

Moses reigned ***'in justice and righteousness'***. But the Queen of Ethiopia, Adonith wanted her own son by the dead king to rule. She said to the people: ***"Why should this stranger continue to rule over you?"*** The Talmud account goes, that even though the people loved and wanted him, Moses resigned voluntarily, and departed from their land. The people of Ethiopia bestowed great honors upon him.

There are so many similarities between The Talmud story of Moses and the Akhenaton story at Amarna:

1- Moses was elevated to the post of king for some time before going to Sinai. Akhenaton likewise.

2- Moses officiated as the high priest. Akhenaton likewise.

3- The Talmud reference to Ethiopia, which is described as being a city, was mistaken for the Amarna location.

4- The name of the Egyptian queen who became the wife of Moses is given as Adonith (Aten-it). Her name is clearly derived from the Aten, who was Akhenaton's god.

5- The queen's desire to place her son on the throne instead of Moses is similar to Twtankhamen replacing his father, Akhenaton.

The Tomb of Akhenaton

No evidence has ever been found regarding the date of Akhenaton's death. The evidence, however, is consistent with the Talmud account of the reign of Moses, as a king of Nubia (Ethiopia), that he resigned his post, but did not die.

Here is some of the supporting evidence:

1- Akhenaton's city, including the royal tomb, were substantially destroyed. However, archaeologists were able to reconstruct, from many small fragments, Akhenaton's sarcophagus which is the outermost of a series of coffins that would protect the royal mummy. (Three series of coffins enclosed each of the mummies of Yuya and Twtankhamen). The presence of the inner coffins would indicate burial. This absence indicates otherwise. No fragments of the inner coffers were ever found.

2- There was no trace of other funerary items such as chariots, chairs, and magic bricks which were normally buried in royal tombs, only after the king's death. The found funerary items, which belonged to Akhenaton, are the sarcophagus lid, the ushabti and the canopic chest. Such objects were normally placed in the tomb prior to the time of actual death.

3- Enough original fragments were found of the canopic chest. The fragments have been used to reconstruct the chest, which is now in the Cairo Museum.

It was customary to anoint the canopic chest and other funerary objects with bitumin or resin, at the time of burial. These anointing rituals did not contradict Akhenaton's religious beliefs, and therefore the chest should have been stained, if Akhenaton was ever buried there. Almost all experts have confirmed the complete absence of such stains.

4- The actual canopic jars which would have contained the viscera of the deceased have not been found.
The absence of these jars, or their fragments, from Akhenaton's tomb, is more strong evidence that he was never buried there.

Chapter 27

Twt Ankh Amen
The Redeemer

General

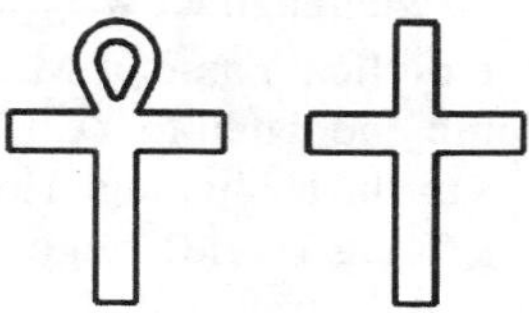

• This chapter will establish the identity of the historical figure of Jesus. Many went down this road before, but most of them pulled back because they reached areas of conflict between history and religion which is usually a touchy area. Please have an open mind and judge the evidence.

Twtankhamen is the historical figure of Jesus.

One will ask how can that be since the two characters Jesus and Twtankhamen lived "apparently" in different places and different times. Let us go through the evidence:

✞ There is not a shred of contemporary evidence to support the New Testament story of the birth, life or death of Jesus. However, there is an expanse of evidence proving that Jesus had lived many centuries earlier.

✞ One wonders, if Jesus lived, suffered and died during the period of Roman rule in Palestine, why did **not** his name appear in the writings of three distinguished contemporary authors of that time — Philo Judaeus, Justus of Tiberias and Flavius Josephus?!

No reference to Jesus was made in the thirty-eight works left behind by Philo Judaeus, who was born c. 15 B.C. and died about twenty years after the supposed date of the Crucifixion. Philo's brother was the head of the Jewish community living in Alexandria. His son was married to a granddaughter of King Herod.

How can we expect a man like Philo Judaeus with all his family connections not to mention Jesus in all his voluminous writings, if Jesus ever existed?!

✞ The Talmudic rabbis do not relate Jesus to the time of Herod or Pontius Pilate. Instead they say that a priest named Pinhas killed him. Pinhas was a contemporary of Moses. Read more about Pinhas in the previous chapter and later in this chapter.

His Birth

Twtankhamen

• Twtankhamen was born in the city of Amarna, which was named after the biblical name of Moses' father. A linen shirt found in Twtankhamen's tomb and dated to Year 7 of Akhenaton, indicates that this was the year of his birth. He belonged to the Twthmosside royal family of which Twthmosis III (King David) reigned four generations earlier. A text on a lion of red granite in the British Museum refers to Twtankhamen **"He restored the monuments of his [ancestor] Amenhotep III."**

• The holy virgin birth of the Egyptian king is a recurring theme in temples and writings throughout ancient Egypt (see the chapter, 'The Pharaoh, Our Holy Father', for details).

Jesus

✞ Luke describes the forthcoming birth of Jesus in the following terms:

> ***"He shall be great, and shall be called the Son of the Highest: and the Lord God shall give unto him the throne of his father David: And he shall reign over the house of Jacob for ever; and of his kingdom there shall be no end".*** 1:32-3.

Twtankhamen, like Jesus, can also be described as:

- Son of the Highest
- seated upon the throne of his father (father here means ancestor)

The Virgin Birth & The Church

✞ The birth of Jesus is not mentioned in New Testament writings of the first century A.D., only the later Gospel-writers refer to it. His death and resurrection were the main focus of interest rather than his birth.

- ✞ By the year 200 A.D., the Church issued a Creed for its members. The Creed stated that Jesus Christ was *"conceived by the Holy Ghost"* and *"born of the Virgin Mary"*.

- ✞ The virgin concept evolved further, when the Council of Trullo in 692 A.D. declared that Mary, the mother of Jesus was 'ever-virgin'. [This declaration contradicts Matthew 1:25 and 12:46, Mark 3:31 and 6:3, Luke 8:19, and John 2:12.]

- ✞ The virgin idea reached its peak, in the writings of St. Thomas Aquinas, in the thirteenth century. The church endorsed his writing:

> *"Because she conceived Christ without the defilement of sin, and without the stain of sexual mingling, therefore did she bring him forth without pain, without violation of her virginal integrity, without detriment to the purity of her maidenhood."*

- ✞ The released Dead Sea Scrolls did not mention a virgin mother.

The Three Wise Men

The story found in Matthew, about the three wise men who came from foreign countries to offer tribute and presents to the newborn king, is of Egyptian origin. During the time of the Empire such visits and gifts were common practice.

A box was found, in the Valley of the Kings, which contained several pieces of gold leaf, bearing the names of Twtankhamun and Aye. One of these pieces of gold leaf has the two royal cartouches of Aye on one side, faced on the other side by three foreigners whose arms are raised in a position of reverence towards the king's names (shown above).

- The first man looks like a typical Syrian from the Mediterranean coast.
- The second man is undoubtedly from the Sudan.
- The third man represents the white-skinned races of the North, such as Libyans and inhabitants of the Mediterranean islands.

Here, then, is a representation of the three biblical races, Shem, Ham and Japhet. This, therefore, is the original idea of the three wise men, who represented the different people of the ancient known world.

His Father

Twtankhamen

The main questions are:

1- Was Twtankhamen the son or brother of Akhenaton?

- As mentioned in the previous chapter, 'Akhenaton and Moses', both Akhenaton and his father Amenhotep III had a co-regency, for twelve years, then Akhenaton ruled alone for three years. According to a shirt found in Twtankhamen's tomb, he was born during Akhenaton's Year 7 at Amarna. The shirt evidence provides two conclusions:

A- Since the date on the shirt refers to Akhenaton, therefore and in accordance with the ancient Egyptian practices, Akhenaton was his father.

B- Akhenaton's Year 7 would make Twtankhamen ten years of age when he came to the throne and nineteen when he died. These dates are confirmed by anatomical examination of his body, as well as by dated objects found in his tomb.

2- Was Akhenaton's mother, Queen Tiye, the mother or grandmother of Twtankhamen?

- As stated earlier, Twtankhamen was born in Year 7 of his father Akhenaton. During the co-regency of Amenhotep III and Akhenaton, Year 7 of Akhenaton corresponds to Year 33 of Amenhotep III. At such a time, Queen Tiye was about forty-one years old. Two years earlier she had given birth to a daughter, Baketaten.

So, hypothetically she could have been able to give birth to a son, at age forty-one. However, the evidence found in her steward Huya's tomb, indicate that Tiye's first visit to Amarna was during or after Akhenaton's Year 10, i.e. three years after Twtankhamen's birth.

The above mentioned shirt indicates a birth in Akhenaton's Year 7 and at Amarna, i.e. when and where Tiye was not present.

Therefore the logical answer is that Akhenaton was the father of Twtankhamen, and Queen Tiye was the grandmother.

Jesus

☦ Jesus is of a royal descendant, as per Matthew 1:1, *"Jesus Christ, the son of (King) David."*

☦ The order of the Messianic Banquet (Passover meal) said that God would *"beget"* the Davidic Messiah. The second book of Samuel 7:13-14 affirms the same point:

"I will establish the throne of his kingdom for ever. I will be his father, and he shall be my son".

The New Testament (Hebrews, 1:5) affirms the same idea of the Messiah as the Son of God, *"begotten"* of the Father.

☦ Other points related to Jesus' father were discussed under his birth.

His Mother

Twtankhamen

• Since Akhenaton fathered Twtankhamen (as proven earlier), his mother must have been Akhenaton's wife, namely Nefertiti.

Without any evidence to support their argument, some scholars have suggested a different mother from Queen Nefertiti for the young king. Some scholars have also been confused about the relationship between Twtankhamen and the royal family. This is simply explained as follows:

- Akhenaton and Nefertiti's eldest daughter married Semenkhkare (Akhenaton's brother and succeeding Pharaoh), who died shortly before the coronation of Twtankhamen.

- Their second daughter had died at sometime.

- The third daughter Ankhsenpa-aten, in the order of events, becomes the heiress. Twtankhamen married her and in so doing he ascended to the throne.

• Before the birth of Twtankhamen, Nefertiti had three daughters, and another three afterwards. No evidence of other sons has been found. Hiding the identity of sons was the prudent thing to do, so as to protect these mixed blood heirs from the Egyptian purists. From the archaeological remains of Amarna's northern palace, it can be concluded that Nefertiti remained there with her son, Twtankhamen, before and after he came to the throne. This ratifies the maternal relationship.

• Nefertiti's image was used in place of that of the mother goddess on Amarna funerary objects. For instance, after her death, Nefertiti's image can be found in place of the image of Isis in the sarcophagus of Akhenaten. Furthermore, there are statues in Rome, originally made to represent Isis and her son Horus, which were used by the Church to represent Mary and her son.

• The name, Nefertiti, means **'*the beautiful one has come*'**.

Jesus

- The Bible tells us in several locations that Mary, the mother of Jesus, had other children besides Jesus, (see Matthew 12:46, Mark 3:31 and 6:3, Luke 8:19, John 2:12), as well as the proclamation that Joseph ***"knew her not till she had brought forth her firstborn son ..."*** (Matthew 1:25).

- The biblical name of Jesus' mother is Mary. The name Mary is given to many women in the New Testament. The two closest women to Jesus were called Mary, his mother and Mary Magdalene. The origin of this name lies in ancient Egypt, where the word *'mery'* means *'the beloved'*.
The name Mary/Mery is one of the most repeated words in ancient Egyptian texts. It was used as an adjective before names of people, neterw, ...etc.

- Mary has been described as ***"the descendant of princes and rulers"*** (b.

Sanh. 106a). This description can only fit Nefertiti, the biblical Madonna.

☥ It was the 6th century B.C. statue of Isis and her son, now in the Turin Museum, which inspired the 15th century painter Masaccio, in his presentation of The Virgin and Child.

His Names

Here are some of his names, which he is known by:

1- The Living Image of the Lord

The young king-to-be was given the name Twt-ankh-aten when he was born. As shown elsewhere, the Egyptian word, Aten, is the equivalent of Adon — the Lord — in Hebrew. His birth name therefore means *'the living image of the Lord'*. Thus he was recognized from the time of his birth as the Son of God, **'the eldest Son of Aten (the Lord) in heaven'**.

2- Messiah/Christ

The English word *'Christ'* comes from the Greek *'Kristos'*, which is the equivalent of the Hebrew and Aramaic *Mesheh*. This word is derived from the Egyptian *MeSHeH*, which as a verb means *'to anoint'*. Thus *'the Christ'* means *'the anointed one', who is 'the king'*.

3- Essa

Essa is the Arabic name of Jesus and the only one used in the Koran. Essa was also the word used for Jesus in the Coptic Egyptian language in the first century A.D.

The name of the Jewish sect, the Essenes, indicates that they were followers of Jesus. Philo Judaeus, who wrote the earliest account of this sect around 30 A.D., called them Essaeans from the Greek *Essaios* but stated that the word was of non-Greek origin. The Essaeans were included among the Jewish divisions of Josephus' time, but he called them the Essenes, the same term that is used in English. However, it was recognized that the word *'Essene'* must have had a Semitic origin, which is *Essa*. *'Essaioi'* would therefore mean *'a follower of Essa'*.

The meanings of Essa and the Essenes were intentionally ignored because the

Essenes, as the followers of Essa (Jesus) existed before the time allotted to Jesus during the Romans' time.

4- Joshua

The names *Joshua* (*Ye-ho-shua* in Hebrew) and *Jesus* (*Ye-shua* in its short form), have the same meaning which is: 'Yahweh (the Lord) is salvation.' The Greek text of the Bible reports both names as *Jesus*. The King James Bible and many of the early Church Fathers of the second and third centuries A.D. refer to *Joshua* and *Jesus* as one and the same person.

The sudden revival of Joshua in the Bible, as the Jews entered the Promised Land, is part of the cover-up, which will be discussed at the end of this chapter.

5- Ben Pandira

The Talmud generally refers to Jesus as 'a certain person' and not by a name. In some Talmudic passages he is named 'Ben Pandira' (the son of Pandira). Since the Jews do not agree that Jesus was the Son of God, they suggested that Pandira was a lover, not the husband, of Mary.

The word Pandira is a Hebrew form of an ancient Egyptian royal term. The word in Hebrew is **Pa-ndi-ra**, and in its original form is **Pa-ntr-ra** (pronounced **Pa-neter-ra**). All Egyptian kings, since ca. 3000 B.C. had the title **Pa-neter-ra** which means **Son of Ra**. Thus *'Ben Pandira'* identifies Jesus as an Egyptian king.

The title **"son of Ra"** is engraved on the Twtankhamen's stele which was found in the Karnak Temple in 1905.

His Wife

Ankhsenpa-aten

There are so many similarities between Ankhsenpa-aten, Twtankhamen's queen, and Mary Magdalene. Mary meant *'beloved'* in ancient Egypt.

Alabaster ointment jars were found in the Twtankhamen tomb. His wife is shown anointing him with perfume, on the back of his throne, exactly as the evangelists described Mary Magdalene anointing Jesus.

The couple are shown together in several scenes, always in a relaxed, romantic mode. One can sense her love for Twtankhamen, similar to Mary Magdalene's love for Jesus.

As his wife and queen, she was the only person who could attend his funerary rites, witness the priests proclaim his resurrection, and inform the disciples of the news.

Mary Magdalene

The term *'Magdalene'* has been explained as belonging to or from the city of Magdala, an unidentified location on the western shore of the Sea of Galilee. The Hebrew word *migdol* means *a tower*. A city named Migdol was located on Horus Road, leading from Egypt to Gaza. Ezekiel 29:10 mentions it: "*... the tower (migdol) of Syene (in the Eastern Delta) even unto the border of Ethiopia*".

This Mary is described in the Bible, as a person who is emotionally related to Jesus. The Bible tells us of her first encounter with Jesus, "*there came a woman having an alabaster box of ointment of spikenard very precious; and she brake the box, and poured it on his head*" (Mark, 14:3). Luke described the very romantic scene of the two: "*And [she] stood at his feet behind him weeping, and began to wash his feet with tears, and did wipe them with the hairs of her head, and kissed his feet, and anointed them with the ointment*" (7:38).

As a result of this close relationship, Mary Magdalene became one of those who followed Jesus until after his death. She was very close to Jesus. She waited at his temporary burial place, after his death. She was the one who Jesus talked to after his resurrection: "*Jesus saith unto her, Mary. She turned herself, and saith unto him, Rabboni; which is to say, Master. Jesus saith unto her, Touch me not; for I am not yet ascended to my Father: but go to my brethren, and say unto them, I ascend unto my Father, and your Father; and to my God, and your God*" (John, 20:16-17).

The King

Kings of the Later Eighteenth
and Early Nineteenth Dynasties

King	*Length of reign*	*Dates*	
Twthmosis III (DAVID)	54	1490-1436 B.C.	
Amenhotep II	23	1436-1413 B.C.	
Twthmosis IV	8	1413-1405 B.C.	
Amenhotep III (SOLOMON)	38	1405-1367 B.C.	
Akhenaton (MOSES) (alone)	6	1367-1361 B.C.	Amarna Kings
Semenkhkare	-	1361-1361 B.C.	Amarna Kings
Twtankhamen (JESUS)	9	1361-1352 B.C.	Amarna Kings
Aye (EPHRAIM)	4	1352-1348 B.C.	Amarna Kings
Horemheb	13	1348-1335 B.C.	

Nineteenth Dynasty

Ramses I	2	1335-1333 B.C.
Seti I	29	1333-1304 B.C.
Ramses II	67	1304-1237 B.C.

Twtankhamen

The Coronation ceremony of the King included, among other things, anointing with the fat of the crocodile. This is the original source of the word *'Messiah'*. *MeSSeH* was the word for crocodile in ancient Egypt. The image of two crocodiles formed the title of the king which were given to him, at the time of his coronation. The letter *'s'* in Egyptian is equivalent to *'sh'* in Hebrew and Aramaic. It is therefore evident that the biblical word *Messiah* originated from *mesheeh*, the ancient Egyptian word signifying the ritual of anointing the King.

The young king was ten years of age when he started his rule in 1361 B.C. At this young age, a custodian or guardian must have been in charge of the state affairs. This would be the case nowadays too, if the legal heir is a minor. The following are the highlights of his nine year reign:

> For four years he continued to live at Amarna, the capital city built by his father. Nefertiti continued to live with her children in the northern palace at Amarna. She was still referred to as the **'Great King's Wife'**, indicating that Akhenaton was still alive and still influential.

There were building activities during this stage at Thebes which included additions to the existing Aten temples.

- During his Year 4, the young king moved his residence from Amarna to Memphis, southwest of modern Cairo. The temples of the ancient neterw of Egypt were reopened and they were allowed to be worshipped alongside the Aten.

He still adhered completely to the Aten worship, as evident from his recovered throne. At the top center of his throne, one can see the symbol of the Aten, with its extending rays, giving the ankh, the Egyptian key of life, to Twtankhamen and his wife. The Aten is represented here as the sole God. Two cartouches of Twtankhamen are shown on the throne. One of these cartouches proves that he used this throne after he had changed his name.

- He changed his name from Twtankh**aten** to Twtankh**amen**, and his queen's name changed to Ankhsenpa**amen**. The change was in recognition of Amon. The priesthood and temple income were restored. Restoration of buildings and grounds of the temples were carried out. A stela of Twtankhamen at Karnak includes the official work order: **"Now His Majesty appeared as king at a time when the temples of the neterw from Elephantine as far as the Delta marshes had fallen into ruin, and their shrines become neglected. They had turned into mounds overgrown [with] weeds, and it seemed that their sanctuaries had never existed."** This sounds very much like the complaint that Jesus is said to have made about the conditions of the temple at Jerusalem.

- In his Year 9 Twtankhamen, accompanied by Aye, went to Sinai to try to urge Akhenaton and his followers to return to Egypt. His message to them was to live in harmony, with people of a different belief. This mission is echoed in the Gospel account in Matthew, chapter 5, of the Sermon on the Mount given by Jesus:

  "Blessed are the peacemakers: for they shall be called the children of God ... Think not that I am come to destroy the law, or the prophets:

> *I am not come to destroy, but to fulfill ... Agree with thine adversary quickly ... Ye have heard that it hath been said, An eye for an eye, and a tooth for a tooth: But I say unto you, that ye resist not evil: but whosoever shall smite thee on thy right cheek, turn to him the other also ... Ye have heard that it hath been said, Thou shalt love thy neighbor, and hate thine enemy. But I say unto you, Love your enemies, bless them that curse you, do good to them that hate you ... That ye may be the children of your Father which is in Heaven."*

However, instead of his pleas being accepted, he was accused of betraying his faith — and was killed.

Jesus

✞ Both the Bible and the Talmud agree that:

- Jesus was in Egypt.
  - *"Out of Egypt have I called my son"* (Matthew 2:15).
  - *"Jesus the Nazarene who practiced magic in Egypt"* (b. Sanh., 107b).

- Jesus was a king.
  - Jesus, who is known as *"the King of Israel"*, was the descendant of the biblical King David, as per Luke 1:32-3 *"... and the Lord God shall give unto him the throne of his father [meaning his ancestor] David. And he shall reign over the house of Jacob forever, and his kingdom there shall be of no end."*
  - Jesus' mother, Mary, has been described as *"the descendant of princes and rulers"* (b. Sanh., 106a).
  - *"... It seems that the King is crucified"* (T. Sanh., 9.7).

His Death

Twtankhamen

- The violent nature of Twtankhamen's death is evident from the condition of his mummy. An extensive examination of Twt's mummy, including the use of x-rays, was carried out in 1968. The mummy was found to have many broken bones and joints. The tissues of the face were contracted. The teeth were tightly clenched together. There was no evidence of disease as the cause of death. It was also observed that Twt had some Semitic features.

- The funerary mask of Twtankhamen, the best likeness of a Pharaoh ever found, shows the suffering eyes of the young King, at his death.

- Howard Carter reported that he found many items in Twtankhamen's tomb that linked them *"to later Christian beliefs and practices"*, such as:

a- His scepter which was used in conjunction with offerings. It contains this text: **'The Beautiful *God*, beloved, dazzling of face like the Aten when it shines ... Twtankhamen.'**

  ✞ The text is very similar to the biblical accounts of the Transfiguration of Jesus and his ***"shining face"*** on the Mount shortly before he died.

b- Fruits and seeds of Christ-thorn, a tree like a hawthorn, native to ancient Egypt, used for food or medicine, and also said to have had some religious significance.

  ✞ These thorny shrubs said to have been used for Christ's crown of thorns: *'And the soldiers plaited a crown of thorns, and put it on his head . . .'* (John, 19:2).

c- Two ritual robes.

✞ Carter identified them as the "same priestly dalmatic worn by Christian deacons and bishops."

• The botanical evidence found in the tomb shows that Twtankhamen must have died in the spring and was buried seventy days later, the time required for the mummification process. Spring blossoms and fruits were found in wreaths, on top of the second and third coffins. These must have been dried out before use. The wreath on the third coffin included the mandrake fruits, sliced in half which were dried out before they were sewn on to the wreath. Additionally, the blue water-lily used in these wreaths does not bloom until the summer.

Twtankhamen most probably died in April, the same time as Christ's death.

• A frequently expressed comment refers to the obnoxious wealth in Twtankhamen's tomb. Egypt was extremely wealthy at that time. In a letter from Tushratta, the ruler in northern Mesopotamia, to Akhenaton (Twtankhamen's father), he wrote that gold in Egypt was *"as plentiful as dust"*.

Jesus

There are a conflicting accounts not only of how Jesus died, but also who condemned him.

How Did He Die?

✞ The Cross is identified as the symbol of Christ. The four Gospels are consistent in saying that Jesus was crucified:

"And they crucified him ..." (Matthew, 27:35)
"And when they had crucified him ..." (Mark, 15:24)
"And when they were come to the place, which is called Calvary, there they crucified him ..." (Luke, 23:33)
"Then the soldiers, when they had crucified Jesus ..." (John, 19:23).

Paul describes too: *"... Jesus, whom ye have crucified ..."* (Acts, 2:36).

However, crucifixion was a Roman, not an Israelite, form of execution. This form of execution would be expected had Jesus been tried and condemned by a Roman court. The Israelites hanged the condemned person from a tree: *"And if a man have committed a sin worthy of death ... thou hang him on a tree"* (Deuteronomy, 21:22).

♰ The Talmud refers to Jesus as having been both crucified :

"It seems that the king [Jesus] is crucified" (T. Sanh., 9.7).

and hanged:

"Jesus was hanged" (b. Sanh., 106b)
"They hanged him on the eve of the Passover" (b. Sanh., 43a).

There are also references in the New Testament to Jesus being hanged. Peter's account, for instance, reads:

"... whom they slew and hanged on a tree" (Acts, 10:39).
Paul also stated: *"... they took him down from the tree, and laid him in a sepulcher"* (Acts, 13:29).

♰ As a result, it could be that *'crucifixion'* and *'hanging'* are synonymous in this case.

Who Condemned Him?

♰ The New Testament clearly and totally blames the Israelite priests:

"... the Son of man shall be betrayed unto the chief priests and unto the scribes, and they shall condemn him to death" (Matthew, 20:18)
Peter pointed at the Jerusalem priests: *"... Jesus, whom ye slew and hanged on a tree"* (Acts, 5:30)
Paul said *"the Jews, who killed the Lord Jesus"* (I Thessalonians, 2:14-15).

♰ The Talmud clearly identifies Jesus' killer as Pinhas, the Israelite priest who lived in the fourteenth century B.C. and was a companion of Moses.

Phinehas looked upon Jesus' teachings of religious co-existence as blasphemy. On the eve of the Passover, Phinehas killed Jesus in the Tabernacle at the foot of mount Sinai.

Aye (Ephraim), the second son of Joseph the Patriarch, and Twtankhamen's successor, killed thousands of Israelites including Phinehas as a punishment for Jesus' death.

Nazarenes

It is an error to think that *'Jesus the Nazarene'* means Jesus from a location called Nazerah. *Nazarenes* signifies a religious sect and not a geographical location. The Nazarenes were one of many Gnostic sects. Hebrew Jews, to this day, use the term *Nazarene* for Christians. The Qumran community call themselves "Keepers of the Covenant", which translates to Hebrew as *'Nazrie ha-Brit'*. The word *'Nazrim'* was derived from the Hebrew name *'Nazrie ha-Brit'*. Nazrim, therefore is the earliest Hebrew name of the sect subsequently known as Christian.

Essenes

- The Essenes are the owners of the library of the Dead Sea Scrolls which date to 200 B.C., but contain some accounts of the Gospel accounts of birth, life and death of Jesus. In short, the Essenes and their scrolls are the best proof yet that Jesus lived seven centuries earlier than the common belief.

- The Essenes is a secret Jewish sect which separated from the Jewish community at large. They regard the beliefs and teachings of the Jerusalem priesthood to be untrue.

- The very name of the Essenes indicate that they were followers of Jesus. As explained earlier, Essenes means 'Follower of Essa'. Essa is the Arabic name for Jesus. Essa is the only name of Jesus to be mentioned in the Koran and was the name used in the Coptic Egyptian language, in the first century A.D.

- The Dead Sea Scrolls, which pre-date the Gospels, provide the following:

- An account of the Annunciation which reads almost exactly as Luke (1:28-35).

- A clear statement that the Essenes believed that the Messiah (their Teacher of Righteousness) had already lived and was later killed by the Wicked Priest.

- They, in 200 B.C., were awaiting the Messiah's Second Coming, not the first.

✞ The Book of Isaiah, dating from the eighth to sixth centuries B.C., introduced in the character of the suffering Servant, the Savior of the world, and the Redeemer.

The idea of Christ as the Redeemer proves that he had already lived his life and died.

The Gospels adopted the very same idea for the character of Jesus, almost seven hundred years later.

Cover-Up

✞ The killing of Joshua (Jesus) was always remembered by those who believed in him and later became his followers. The Jewish priesthood, however, deliberately concealed both his killing and its date. Here is how they did it.

Originally, both the Day of Atonement (Yom Kippur) and Passover were observed as one feast in Abib (Babylonian Nisan), in the spring time. Two major changes occurred:

1- The Day of Atonement is now observed in autumn and not in spring.

2- The significance of the Day of Atonement changed from a day of repentance, for the killing of the Messiah, to become a day for general repentance for sin.

Let us backtrack through this cover-up scheme.

1- After Moses left Egypt, he and his followers observed the feast of the

Passover: *"Thou shalt keep the feast of unleavened bread: (thou shalt eat unleavened bread seven days ... in the time appointed of the month Abib (Nisan); for in it thou camest out from Egypt ...)"* (Exodus, 23:15). The Passover is originally an Egyptian spring festival, which was observed for seven days, from the fifteenth to the twenty-first day of Abib (Babylonian Nisan). This was also the first month of the Israelite year.

After Jesus died, on the eve of the Passover, the fourteenth day of Abib, the Israelites offered a sacrificial lamb in atonement for the killing of Jesus: *"Thou shalt therefore sacrifice the Passover unto the Lord thy God, of the flock and the herd ... thou shalt sacrifice the Passover at even [evening], at the going down of the sun, at the season that thou camest forth out of Egypt"* (Deuteronomy, 16:2,6).

2- The Jewish sect, the Essenes, took the view that they had nothing to feel guilty about and regarded Christ as their sacrificial lamb. On the same day, the fourteenth day of Abib, the Essenes held a Messianic Banquet awaiting the return of their dead, Teacher of Righteousness, at the end of the world, when he would celebrate the meal with them. This Messianic Banquet is very similar to the Last Supper.

3- Later Christians stopped the practice of animal sacrifice because they regarded Jesus himself as the sacrifice: *"For even the Son of a man came not to be ministered unto, but to minister, and to give his life a ransom for many"* (Mark, 10:45) and *"... Behold the Lamb of God, which taketh away the sins of the world"* (John, 1:29).

4- During the Babylonian exile, in the sixth century B.C., the priests wrote the books of the Pentateuch, which had originated at the time of Moses. They referred to the date of the Passover as either 'the first month' or as Nisan.

The priests replaced, in exile, the solar calendar used previously with the Babylonian lunar calendar. As a result, Tishri (September - October), which was the seventh month of the Israelites' year, became the first month of a new calendar.

To manage the confusion caused by the calendar change, Ezekiel divided the year into two parts with the religious observances of the first month repeated in the seventh.

After their return from Babylon, the priests stopped the practice of two annual observations of the same event. This was the most opportune time to separate Atonement Day (in autumn) from Passover (in spring).

5- Splitting one event (Passover and Day of Atonement) into two separate events was followed by changing the significance of the Day of Atonement from a day of repentance, for killing the Messiah, to become a day for general repentance for sin.

It became increasingly interesting when they replaced the Messiah as the victim with an enemy of the Israelites, none other than an Egyptian Pharaoh. To top it all they made the Lord as the killer instead of him being the victim: *"The Lord smote ... the firstborn of Pharaoh that sat on his throne..."* (Exodus, 12:29).

In their attempts to cover up, they may have left important evidence. If it was simply the firstborn of a ruling Pharaoh who was smitten, there is no reason to add the words *"that sat on his throne"*. Therefore the biblical verse suggests that there was another Pharaoh who was not sitting on his throne.

Unintentionally, they left the evidence that the victim was none other than Twtankhamen (Jesus) who sat on his father's, Akhenaton/Moses, throne. Akhenaton was still alive, hiding in Sinai.

6- This would have been the perfect cover-up except that the Essenes worked secretly to keep the memory of their Teacher of Righteousness alive, until his return foiled the cover-up.

✞ The Bible itself confirms that Jesus and Moses were of the same era. That Jesus lived fourteen centuries earlier than had been thought would explain an event described in the Gospels of Matthew, Mark and Luke of the meeting of Jesus and Moses at the time of what is known as his Transfiguration:

> *"And after six days Jesus taketh with him Peter, and James, and John, and leadeth them up into a high mountain apart by themselves: and he was transfigured before them. And his raiment became shining, exceeding white as snow; so as no fuller on earth can white them. And they appeared unto them Elias (Elijah) with Moses: and they were talking with Jesus. And Peter answered and said to Jesus, Master, it is good for us to be here: and let us make three tabernacles; one for thee, and one for Moses, and one for Elias ..."* Mark, 9:2-5.

The biblical text is a straight forward factual description of an event. It is irrational to view the factual nature of this text as simply some kind of a "spiritual experience" and that it never actually happened!!

☥ When John the Baptist died many centuries later, the Essene leaders who had been waiting for the Second Coming of Christ, thought that John was the Messiah.

The evangelists (the writers of the Gospels) chose to ignore the Essenes' belief in John, as the Second Coming of Christ, and elected to use the time period of John the Baptist, to tell the story of Jesus Christ, as his First Coming. This led to the evangelists adopting the time of Herod the Great and Pontious Pilate for the birth and life of Jesus.

☥ After Jesus (Joshua) died at the foot of Mount Sinai, and the subsequent death of Phinehas, they both disappeared from the scene. However, later in the book of Joshua, we have both Joshua and Phinehas alive and as if they were never killed?! This is an unbelievable contradiction in the Bible.

Furthermore we are told that the Promised Land was conquered in a swift military campaign which is a total invention that cannot be supported by modern archaeological excavation. The occupation of Canaan was a gradual process, as also confirmed in the Book of Judges.

☥ The secrecy surrounding the hidden contents of the Dead Sea Scrolls is another clear indication that the cover-up is still continuing.

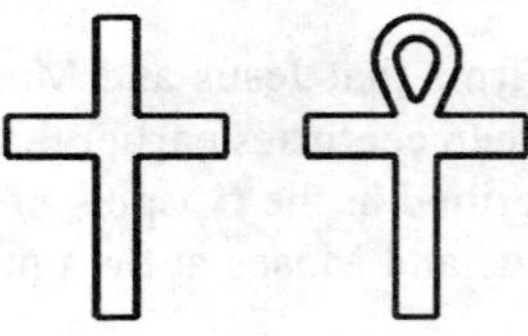

Chapter 28

Easter and Ancient Egypt

• In the Christian world, Easter is always celebrated in the first week after the full moon, following the vernal equinox (when day and night are of equal length in the spring). This religious occasion reflects the Christian conviction that Christ died, was buried, and subsequently disappeared on Friday, and was resurrected the third day after his death, i.e. on Sunday. It is the happiest day in the Christian calendar. The date of Easter Sunday was established by the Church Council of Nicaea in A.D. 325.

• The Webster's dictionary describes Easter as *"name of pagan vernal festival almost coincident in date with paschal festival of the church"*. The so-called *'pagan'* festival is the Egyptian Easter. But, how and why was this national holiday started in Egypt so long ago? How does it coincide with the Christian's Easter celebration?

• More than five thousand years ago, ancient Egyptians adopted a national holiday, which came at the end of a four day ceremony. According to Egyptian legend, Osiris died, was buried and then disappeared on Friday. They called that day the "Loss of Osiris". Osiris was resurrected, on the third day, i.e. on Sunday. The fourth day was and is the day of festivities.

Osiris was associated with both the lunar and solar cycles. The four day ceremony of the death and resurrection of Osiris was therefore held in the week following the full moon (lunar cycle), following the vernal equinox (solar cycle), which is exactly the same date set for the Christian Easter.

• It is interesting to know that Easter Monday is and has been a national holiday in Egypt for at least five thousand years! It is now called the "Breath of Life" day. It is the happiest day in the Egyptian calendar. People shed their winter clothes and wear their brightest outfits. Uniformed officers store their black wool uniforms, and don their white outfits. Springtime is here.

- One of the best-known Easter symbols is the egg, which has symbolized renewed life since ancient times, because all living creatures begin life in the egg. Egyptians continue to color eggs and eat them during their celebration.

- As you can see, the Christian Easter is a mirror image of the Egyptians' Breath of Life celebration except for one major difference: the Gospels tale of Jesus' death and resurrection is considered historical and the ancient Egyptian tale of Osiris is a legend.. You decide if you believe in the contents of the story, as a fact or as a fiction.

Chapter 29

The Exodus

The Bitter Divorce

General

After the death of Twtankhamen, his uncle Aye reigned for four years before he disappeared from the scene. Horemheb ascended to the throne at that time.

Horemheb was an army general and obtained his right to the throne by marrying Queen Nefertiti's sister, Mutnedjemet.

Kings of the Later Eighteenth
and Early Nineteenth Dynasties

King	*Length of reign*	*Dates*	
Twthmosis III (DAVID)	54	1490-1436 B.C.	
Amenhotep II	23	1436-1413 B.C.	
Twthmosis IV	8	1413-1405 B.C.	
Amenhotep III (SOLOMON)	38	1405-1367 B.C.	
Akhenaton (MOSES) (alone)	6	1367-1361 B.C.	Amarna Kings
Semenkhkare	-	1361-1361 B.C.	Amarna Kings
Twtankhamen (JESUS)	9	1361-1352 B.C.	Amarna Kings
Aye (EPHRAIM)	4	1352-1348 B.C.	Amarna Kings
Horemheb	13	1348-1335 B.C.	

Nineteenth Dynasty

Ramses I	2	1335-1333 B.C.
Seti I	29	1333-1304 B.C.
Ramses II	67	1304-1237 B.C.

Pharaoh of Oppression

The Bible never named this Pharaoh and referred to him only as the *"Pharaoh of Oppression"*. Based on historical circumstantial evidence he is identified, in Egyptian records, as Horemheb.

Horemheb appointed Pa-Ramses, the head of his army, as mayor of Zarw. It may have been Pa-Ramses who, on Horemheb's orders, treated the Israelites harshly and made them work to rebuild Zarw, as well as a new residence for himself, known later as Pi-Ramses. Pi-Ramses became the main residence in the Eastern Delta for Pharaohs of the Nineteenth and Twentieth Egyptian Dynasties, and it was also the starting point of the Exodus, according to the Bible.

Thirteen years passed before Horemheb, the biblical Pharaoh of Oppression, died:

> *"And it came to pass in process of time, that the king of Egypt died: and the children of Israel sighed under the bondage ..."* Exodus 2:23

At the death of Horemheb, Egypt was left without a legitimate heir to the throne. Pa-Ramses, by now an old man, found an opportunity to claim the throne for himself, as the first ruler of a new dynasty, the Nineteenth.

Pharaoh Who Knew Not Joseph

The Bible never named this Pharaoh and referred to him as *"Pharaoh Who Knew Not Joseph"*. Would it not been easier to call him by his name? Based on historical circumstantial evidence, he is identified in Egyptian records as Pa-Ramses (Ramses I).

The Bible tells us that when the Pharaoh of Oppression died, God sent Moses on a mission to lead the Israelites out of Egypt. God told Moses,

> *"Come now therefore, and I will send thee unto Pharaoh, that thou mayest bring forth my people the children of Israel out of Egypt."* Exodus 3:10

God also reassured Moses that his life would not be in any danger if he returned to Egypt because *"all those who wished to kill you are dead".*

The particulars of the events indicate that Moses/Akhenaton had different objectives. Moses/Akhenaton, who had been in hiding in the wilderness for about a quarter of a century, found an opportunity to restore himself to the throne, as the legal heir. He decided to try to reclaim his throne from Ramses I (same as Pa-Ramses).

Preparation for the Face-Off

After spending about twenty-five years hiding in the wilderness and fearful for his life, the biblical Moses began the preparation for a come-back. Strangely enough, his fear for his life was totally gone, and he was not worried about confronting Ramses I.
His only problems, according to the Bible, were how to succeed, in obtaining the support of the Israelites!

Logically, it was the Egyptian Akhenaton (not the biblical Moses) who needed the support of the Israelites. After being rejected by the majority of Egyptians, Akhenaton decided to choose the Israelites as his own people. When the time came to challenge the new Pharaoh, his main concern was not a confrontation with Ramses I, but to acquire the backing of the Israelites.

He had two problems:

His first problem was that he did not speak the Israelites' language sufficiently well. Moses/Akhenaton complained about the difficulty in communicating with the Israelites:

"And Moses said unto the Lord, 0 my Lord, I am not eloquent ... I am slow of speech and of a slow tongue." Exodus, 4:10

Aaron, the Israelite feeding brother of his early childhood, was called upon to be his spokesman:

"And the anger of the Lord was kindled against Moses, and he said, Is not Aaron the Levite thy brother? I know that he can speak well ..." Exodus, 4:14

His second problem was to reach a compromise between his religious beliefs and those of the Israelites. The following passages from the Old Testament, do not make any sense because one doesn't expect a Jewish leader to have such a religious problem with his own people.

Let us follow the strange passage from the Old Testament:

1- ***"And Moses said unto God, Behold when I come unto the children of Israel, and shall say unto them, The God of your fathers hath sent me unto you; and they shall say to me, What is his name? what shall I say unto them?"***

"And God said unto Moses, I AM THAT I AM: and he said, Thus shalt thou say unto the children of Israel, I AM (i.e. Jehovah) hath sent me unto you." Exodus, 3:13-14

2- Three chapters later, in the same Book of Exodus, we face a stranger passage:

"And I appeared unto Abraham, and unto Isaac, and unto Jacob, by the name of God Almighty, but by my name JE-HO-VAH was I not known to them." Exodus, 6:3

The contents of the last passage, in which God informs Moses that he never appeared to the patriarchs by the name *Jehovah*, is really strange, because the name *Jehovah* was used in several chapters, of the preceding Book of Genesis, in the Bible.

It seems that Akhenaton would not reject the name of his God, the Aten, for the purpose of gaining the support of the Israelites. Therefore an outlandish compromise was reached in Sinai, by which the Israelites continued to write their old personal name of God, Jehovah. However Jehovah could never be read aloud again and should, in every case, be pronounced *'Adonai'*. As mentioned earlier, *'Adonai'* is the same name of the God of Akhenaton.

The Site of the Face-Off

- It appears that both at the time of the birth of Moses and when he came back to confront Pa-Ramses, the ruling Pharaoh was in residence in the vicinity of Goshen, where the Israelites had been allowed to settle.

- We know from Joseph's (Yuya) story, that Jacob and his Israelite family were allowed to settle in Goshen, at the eastern side of the Nile Delta. This location allowed them to stay away from the Egyptian populous and also permitted them to have an easy access to travel back and forth, to their relatives in Canaan.

- Zarw was the major city in Goshen. Zarw occupied the old site of the previous Hyksos' capital city of Avaris.

- Akhenaton built his very first shrine of Aten, in the city of Zarw. This is yet another indication that Moses and Akhenaton are one and the same.

- At the end of the Eighteenth Dynasty, the town of Pa-Ramses was built at the same site of Avaris and Zarw.

- The archaeological investigation in this area, found three different walls at three levels, confirming what we know from literary sources of Pi-Ramses/Avaris/Zarw.

Therefore archaeologically Avaris, Pi-Ramses and Zarw occupied one and the same location. This area is the present-day Kantarah, and its neighborhood.

- Pi-Ramses became the Eastern Delta residence and capital of kings of the Nineteenth, Twentieth and early Twenty-first Dynasties. During the Twenty-first Dynasty, a new capital was established at Tanis, south of Lake Menzalah in the northern part of the Delta.

The Face-Off

Moses' mission was not just a case of getting the Israelites out of Egypt. There was some type of contest, as acknowledged in the biblical description of the events.

The following is the more logical sequence of events:

Moses went to Zarw (Goshen region) to present his case that after the death of Horemheb, he was the *'legitimate heir'* (which means *Mos* in ancient Egypt) and that Pa-Ramses had no just right to the throne. Since Moses was in hiding for twenty-five years, in Sinai, he had to prove his qualifications to the throne. The Egyptian priests and elders were there to judge and not to perform magic. Moses made his case as follows:

A- He showed that he was a King by presenting his staff topped by a brass serpent, the symbol of pharaonic authority which also identified him as the son of Amenhotep III.

There was no magic rod, as is also evident in the following documents.

1- The Hebrew word used in the Bible to indicate the rod of Moses is *'nahash'*, which has the meanings of both *'serpent'* and *'brass'*. The Haggadah, the legendary part of the Talmud, confirms the royal character of Moses's rod: ***"The rod which Moses used ... was shaped and engraved in the image of a scepter."***

2- More affirmation of the point is made in the second Book of Kings, 18:3-4:

> ***"And he did that which was right in the sight of the Lord, according to all that David his father did."***
>
> ***"He removed the high places and brake the images, and cut down the groves; and brake in pieces the brazen serpent that Moses had made; for unto those days the children of Israel did burn incense to it."***

It is clearly stated that Moses' magic rod was in reality a bronze serpent.

B- He also performed the sed festival rituals, which were not displayed before ordinary citizens.

During the sed festivals, which were attended by Egyptian kings, including Akhenaten, to rejuvenate their power, it was the custom to take part in rituals that included both the *'serpent rod'* and *'hand'* rituals performed by Moses.

Here, Moses does not sound like a magician, but more like someone who presents evidence of his royal background and legitimacy.

Pa-Ramses was not educated and trained to become a king, like Moses/ Akhenaton was, and therefore could not match the presentation made by Moses.

The wise men bowed the knee in front of him, confirming his superior rights to the throne. But Pa-Ramses used his army to crush the rebels. Moses was allowed to leave again for Sinai accompanied by the Israelites. In Sinai the followers of Akhenaten were joined subsequently by some Bedouin tribes (the Shasu), who are to be identified as the Midianites of the Bible.

• Incidentally, all the plagues of which we read about in the Bible, were natural seasonal events in Egypt, in the course of every year.

During the season of inundation, the Nile waters become reddish. If these events took place in the late days of summer, this change of color would have begun to affect the lower reaches of the river, in the eastern Delta.

Exodus

• Moses and his followers may have made their way to Sinai via the marshy area, to the south of Zarw and north of Lake Temsah and present-day Ismailia. This is the possible location for the biblical account of the "miraculous" crossing of the Red Sea by Moses and his people, and the subsequent drowning of the Pharaoh and his army, for the Egyptian chariots would get stuck in the mud. The Israelites, traveling on foot, would be able to cross safely.

Egyptian records show no evidence of this event, but the short reign of Ramses I (c. 1335-1333 B.C.) came to an end upon his death at this very time.

• The combination of the name, the life, the nature of reign and the sudden death of Ramses I, is one of the important pieces of the puzzle in the identification of the Pharaohs in the Bible.

The combination between matching available records, the process of elimination of other possible characters, and the records of such characters, identify Ramses I as the biblical *"Pharaoh Who Knew Not Joseph"*.

• Although Sinai was a part of Egypt, it did not have a resident governor. There was no army garrison stationed there. During the Eighteenth and Nineteenth Dynasties the area was placed under the control of two officials, the Royal Messenger in All Foreign Lands and the Royal Chancellor. It was more or less a buffer zone.

• After entering Sinai, the Israelites traveled for three days without finding water. When they found some water later on, it was so bitter that they could not drink it. They protested to Moses, asking: ***"What are we to drink?"*** **This protest, and at times threats to choose a new leader who would take them back to Egypt, is a recurrent event in the rest of the Pentateuch.** They really did not want to leave Egypt, in the first place, and wanted to go back.. It was Moses who forced them to follow him.

• Ramses I's son and successor, Seti I (C. 1333-1304 B.C.), received a message about the chaos in Sinai: '***The Shasu enemies are plotting rebellion. Their tribal leaders are gathered in one place, standing on the foothills of Khor*** (a general term for Palestine and Syria), ***and they are engaged in turmoil and uproar. Each of them is killing his fellow. They do not consider the laws of the palace.***'

Seti I did not wait for the burial of his father (Ramses I) or even his coronation, when he led his army promptly to Sinai.

The Shasu and the Israelites

• The descendants of Jacob (numbering seventy just seventy-five years before Seti I's reign) were of no significant number and/or stature to warrant a special name for them, in Egyptian records. When Moses/Akhenaton fled to Sinai and stayed there, for about twenty-five years, he had to establish alliances with the different and small Bedouin tribes in Sinai. The composition of this alliance is recorded in the Egyptian history, as the '***Shasu enemies***'.

• Seti I's war scenes, on the exterior north wall of the great Hypostyle Hall at Karnak, show that his first campaign against the Shasu occurred when they attempted to reach Canaan via the Road of Horus, the ancient highway connecting Egypt with western Asia. This took place immediately after the Exodus from Egypt, possibly when they trespassed to obtain water from military settlements along that road. Seti I chased them as far as the city of Canaan, Gaza, and, as a result, killed their leader, Moses, and many of his followers. Subsequently, they fled into Sinai for what the Old Testament calls ***'the forty years of wandering'***.

• To further prove that the Shasu and the Israelites are the same group of people, scholars studied:

1- The Shasu appearance in Sinai, in Year 1 of Seti I's reign, and their subsequent movements over the next 100 years. This information was provided from ancient Egyptian records.

2- The biblical accounts of the Exodus and their subsequent movements over 100 years.

Scholars concluded that both of them followed the same route at exactly the same time sequence, i.e. the Shasu and the Israelites are one and the same group of people.

• It was about a hundred years after the Seti I wars against the Shasu, and the settling of the Israelites in Canaan, over the span of many years, that the Egyptian records recognized the name Israel, on the so-called Israel Stela. (Read more about it under the chapter 'Israel Stela'.)

The Death of Moses

• The account in the Old Testament of the failure of Moses to reach the Promised Land, his death and his burial in an unmarked grave is another curious episode.

We are told initially that, when his followers complained of thirst, Moses used his rod to smite a rock and bring forth water. It was called ***'the water of Meribah'*** — a location in the north-center of Sinai, south of Canaan. It was this action that would later haunt him.

<u>Some time later</u>, when the Israelites were camped on the banks of the Jordan, near Jericho and opposite Canaan, Moses learned, according to

the Book of Deuteronomy, that he was to be denied the opportunity to cross the river, no matter how hard he pleaded:

> ***"I pray thee, let me go over, and see the good land that is beyond Jordan, that goodly mountain, and Lebanon."***
> ***"... the Lord said ... speak no more unto me of this matter ..."***
> ***"... thou shalt not go over this Jordan."*** Deuteronomy. 3:25-7

• Later in the Book of Deuteronomy we have an account of the actual death of Moses. The Lord said to him: ***"Get thee up into this mountain Abarim, unto Mount Nebo, which is in the land of Moab' (the borders between Sinai and eastern Jordan) 'that is over against Jericho; and behold the land of Canaan, which I give unto the children of Israel for a possession: And die in the mount ... Because ye trespassed against me among the children of Israel at the waters of Meribah-Kadesh, in the wilderness of Zin ... thou shalt not go thither unto the land which I give the children of Israel."*** 32:49-52

> It is irrational to believe that God would punish Moses for providing water for his thirsty people. It is more logical to believe that trespassing onto Egyptian water wells, may cause the authorities to punish him for such a violation.

• The Talmud provides a different account than the Old Testament of how Moses died. There is a Talmudic reference to a confrontation and a struggle between Moses and the ***'Angel of Death'*** on the Mount before he died. This had persuaded some biblical scholars to believe that Moses was killed.

> **It seems more likely that Moses, using his royal scepter (symbol of authority), entered one or more of the Egyptian fortresses along Horus Road to obtain water from their wells. Such actions were reported to Seti I, who reacted by chasing the Shasu, here identified as the Israelites, into northern Sinai. If these Talmudic references to the death of Moses are correct, it must have been there that Moses died, at the hand of Seti I, out of sight of his followers.**

Chapter 30

Ancient Egypt and Biblical Similarities

Similarities between the biblical accounts and ancient Egypt beliefs and life are shown throughout this book. Previous chapters identified some biblical characters as historical Egyptian characters. The following are a few similarities, as they relate to theological practices, between the Bible and ancient Egypt.

1- Egyptologist Sir E. A. Wallis Budge wrote, *"The new religion (Christianity) which was preached there by St. Mark and his immediate followers, in all essentials so closely resembled that which was the outcome of the worship of Osiris, Isis, and Horus that popular opposition was entirely disarmed."*

The similarities, noted by Budge and everyone who has compared the Egyptian Osiris/Isis/Horus myth to the Gospel story, are powerful. Both accounts are practically the same, e.g. the supernatural conception, the divine birth, the struggles against the enemy in the wilderness, and the resurrection from the dead to eternal life. The main difference between them is that the Gospel tale is considered historical and the Isis/Osiris/Horus cycle is a myth. The spiritual message of the Osiris/Isis/Horus myth and the Christian revelation are the same.

2- Gerald Massey, after studying the similarities between the Osiris/Isis/Horus myth and the Gospel story, concluded in his book Ancient Egypt, 1970, that the Christian revelation is Egyptian, in source. He believed that early Christians in their 'ignorance' (his word) took the Egyptian spiritual teaching and turned it into a spiritual and historical event.

3- According to ancient Egyptian legend, Osiris was said to have been killed on a Friday by his brother Set, who dismembered the body of Osiris in order to deny him a second life. However, Isis was able to collect the various parts of his body and, with her magic, restore him to life three days later in the underworld, where he became the judge of the dead.

The account of the Resurrection of Jesus in many ways is similar to that of Osiris. Like Osiris, he is said to have risen on the third day. The Osiris worshippers of ancient Egypt believed, as did the early Christians (Hebrews, 4:14), that ***"man cannot be saved"*** by a distant Almighty, but by one who has shared the experience of human suffering and death. Both Osiris and Jesus suffered and died. Both became the savior to whom men and women turned for assurance of immortality.

The fact that the Old Testament has no reference to resurrection until the writing of the Second Book of Isaiah, in the sixth century B.C., indicates that the account of the risen Christ came from another non-biblical source.

4- An ancient Egyptian festival celebrating the birth of Horus, was held towards the end of the Egyptian year, and it resembles the Christian festival of Christmas.

The celebration was called **"the Day of the Child in his Cradle"** and was held at the court and the chapel of the Dendara Temple.

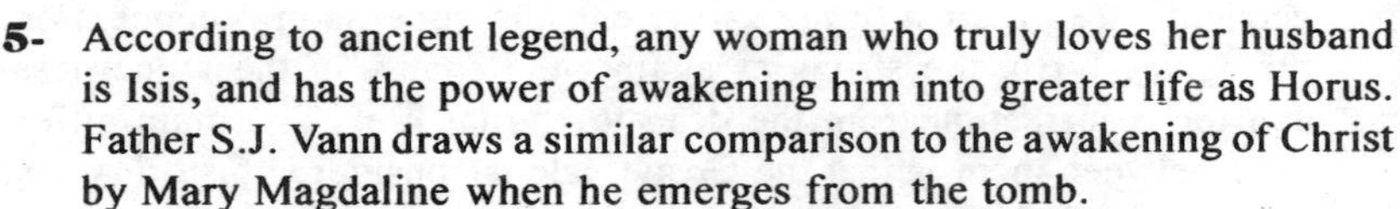

5- According to ancient legend, any woman who truly loves her husband is Isis, and has the power of awakening him into greater life as Horus. Father S.J. Vann draws a similar comparison to the awakening of Christ by Mary Magdaline when he emerges from the tomb.
(Read more about it under the chapters, 'Osiris', 'Isis' and 'Twtankhamen'.)

6- Opening the Mouth was a ceremony performed on statues, mummies, and temples. It corresponds to the modern Christian ordination.
(Read more about this Egyptian practice under the chapter, 'Art'.)

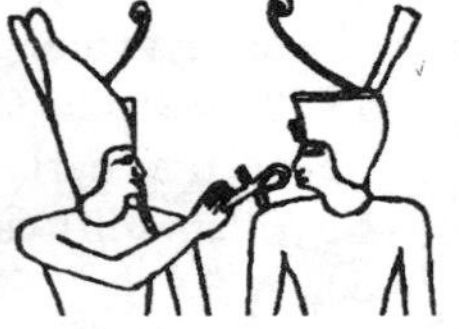

7- Dancing at the temples was common for both Egyptians and biblical characters.

- In the Hall of Offerings, at Dendara Temple, a song celebrating the taming of the lioness, goes:

> ***The King of Egypt, Pharaoh comes to dance***
> ***He comes to sing.***
> ***You, his Lady, see how he dances,***
> ***Wife of Horus***
> ***See how he springs.***

Similarly, Christ is celebrated as ***"Lord of the Dance"*** in a Christmas carol from the Middle Ages.

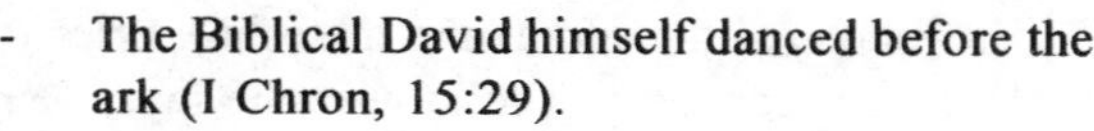

- The Biblical David himself danced before the ark (I Chron, 15:29).

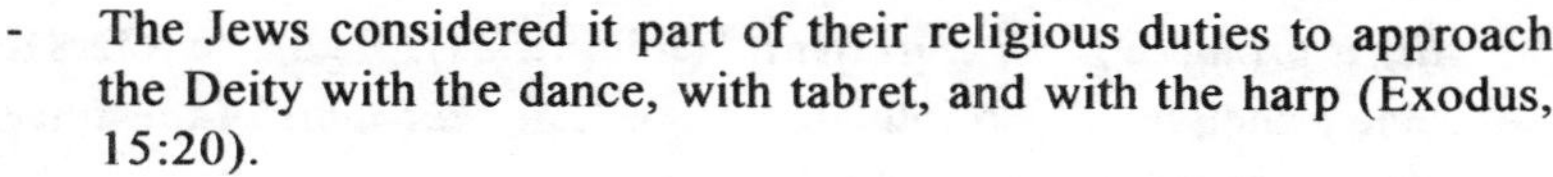

- The Jews considered it part of their religious duties to approach the Deity with the dance, with tabret, and with the harp (Exodus, 15:20).

- Their mode of worshipping the golden calf also consisted of songs and dancing; which was immediately derived from the ceremonies of the Egyptians.

8- There are many Egyptian texts which have notable parallels in the Bible, and outstanding among them is the hymn composed in honor of the Aten by Akhenaton, and Psalm 104. They are both amazingly similar in many particulars, sequence and images. (Read both under the chapter, 'Akhenaton and Moses'.)

9- Daily life activities are portrayed, on the walls of the tombs, in the presence of the neterw or with the assistance of the neterw. The typical sowing and reaping scene is symbolically similar to the Bible's ***"Whatsoever a man soweth, that shall he also reap."***

10- The walls of the tombs show vintners pressing new wine. The process of wine making is a metaphor for spiritual processes. Such is the case also in the biblical wine symbolism.

11- Various fishing nets and traps are portrayed on the walls of the tombs. In other texts, Horus becomes a fisherman and his four sons also fish for him. This is another parallel between Christian and Egyptian symbolism. Christ used the symbolism several times and he made his disciples fishers of men.

12- A recurrent theme, on the walls of some tombs, is the relief of a queen shown sniffing at the lotus. The lotus played a complex and significant role in the symbolism of Egypt. The perfume of the lotus is its spiritualized essence, similar to the ***"odor of sanctity"*** in Christian doctrine. Lotus symbolism is shown all over monuments in Egypt.

13- The theme in the Egyptian Book of the Caverns talks about the necessity for death and dissolution (of the carnal and material), prior to the birth of the spiritual. This is echoed by Christ when he says, ***"Except a corn of wheat fall into the ground and die, it abideth alone: but if it die, it bringeth forth much fruit"*** (John 12:24). Paul also refers to the same principle in I Corinthians 15:36, ***". . . that which thou sowest is not quickened, except it die."***

14- One of the texts, in the Egyptian Book of the Caverns, describes the unilluminated: "**They are like this, those who do not see the Great God, who do not perceive the rays of his disk, whose souls do not leave the earth, who do not hear the words of this Great God when he passes near to their cavern.**" The description is very similar to the Gospel references to those with ***"eyes to see and ears to hear."***

15- A text from the Egyptian Book of Night reads:

> **To come out of the Netherworld, to rest in the Morning Barge, to navigate the Abyss until the hour of Re, She who sees the beauty of her Lord, to make transformations in Khepri, to rise to the horizon, to enter the mouth, to come out of the vulva, to burst forth out of the Gate of the Horizon of the Hour, She who lifts up the beauty of Re in order to make live men, all cattle, all worms he has created.**

The description is very similar to Genesis 1:24, where God says, ***"Let the earth bring forth the living creature after his kind, cattle, and creeping thing ..."***

Chapter 31

The Israel Stela

• A stela is a carved or inscribed stone slab or pillar used for commemorative purposes.

• The so-called "Israel Stela" is a misinterpretation of the purpose and theme of this particular stela.

A granite stela was found in 1896 in the funerary temple of Merenptah. The stela had originally belonged to Amenhotep III (1405-1367 B.C.) who recorded some notations on it. The other side of the same stela was later used by Merenptah (1237-1227 B.C.) to record some of his achievements at Year 5 of his reign.

• Merenptah was about sixty years old when he came to the throne. In his ten year reign he had to fight a major war against the invading Libyans.

The main purpose and theme of the Merenptah's text, on the stela, was to record his triumph over the Libyan invaders. It was recorded in Year 5 of his reign. The details of his triumph were followed by a separate concluding section of twelve lines stating the peaceful and secured status of the Egyptian borders.

The following is a translation of the twelve lines:

The princes are prostrate, saying 'Mercy!' (The word used here is *shalom*, meaning *'peace'*).
Not one raises head among the Nine Bows.
Desolation is for Tehenu; Hatti is pacified;
Plundered is the Canaan with every evil;
Carried off is Ashkelon; seized upon is Gezer;
Yanoam is made as that which does not exist;
 **Israel is laid waste, his seed is not;**
Hurru is become a widow for Egypt!
All lands together, they are pacified;

> **Everyone who was restless, he has been bound by the King of upper and lower Egypt: Ba-en-Re Meriamon; the son of Re: Merenptah Hotep-hir-Maat, given life like Re every day.**

The twelve line epilogue makes reference to the lands of Hittites, Canaan (present day Israel and Lebanon) and some of its cities (Ashkelon, Gezer and Yanoam) as well as Libya (Tehenu).

• The mention of the name *'Israel'* in this epilogue caused some people to conclude that the Exodus took place during Merenptah's reign and subsequently they named the whole stela as the *'Israel Stela'* !!!

The line **Israel is laid waste, his seed is not** indicates that the people of Israel are quiet and not causing any trouble. It is a desperate act of grasping at straws to interpret the line, as a reference to the events of the Exodus.

• The twelve line epilogue on the Stela refers to the status quo which Merenptah inherited at the above listed locations. It stated the situations created by his grandfather Seti I and his father Ramses II.

• Nonwithstanding the clear intent of the twelve line epilogue, one cannot expect Merenptah, an old man of sixty years old, in his first five years of his reign to fight major wars in northern Syria, Syria and Palestine without leaving records of them, as he did in the case of the Libyan invaders.

There are no records of any campaign during Merenptah's rule except for his wars with the invading Libyans.

• The "Israel Stela" is a misleading name for a document which speaks of Israel as people, already in Palestine, at year 5 of Merenpath (son of Ramses II) reign. This stela has the first and only known mention of Israel in Egyptian text.

(Read more about the Exodus in the chapter entitled 'Exodus - The Bitter Divorce'.)

Part V

The Daily Life

Chapter 32

Justice System
The Search for the Truth

Nation of Laws

• Ancient Egypt was a nation of laws, from its earliest times. The superiority of their legislature has always been acknowledged, by the ancient Greek and other writers, as the reason for the long duration of their civilization.

• The Egyptian laws were attributed and/or inspired by **Thoth**. The neter Thoth personifies the divine intellect and it was he who uttered the words commanded by Re. His words were the first spoken and his words caused the creation of the world.

He was equated to the Greek Hermes and to the Roman Mercury.

• The main source of their laws came from a code of laws and jurisprudence, known as the "**Eight Books of Thoth**", which all judges had to be thoroughly skilled in. The Greeks, who equated Thoth to their Hermes, called these books the "Eight Books of Hermes" even though Hermes had nothing to do with them.

The number eight is associated with **Thoth** and he was called "**Master of the City of Eight**".

• Other laws and codes were subsequently and regularly added to the famous "Eight Books of Thoth". The names of the earliest monarchs and sages, who had contributed the additional codes, at successive periods, were acknowledged in historical records, with gratitude.

• The Greek Historian Diodorus informed us that the Egyptian laws were neither designed to arouse men's feelings about the prospect of distant rewards or punishments, nor to threaten the possibility of divine vengeance. They were, on the contrary, immediate in their effect.

- The laws and regulations were intended for the whole population, including the Pharaoh, who willingly complied, as Diodorus observed, with the rules of public and private life. Records show that close advisors of Pharaohs were prosecuted and punished, for non-political crimes.

The Judges

- The administration of justice was well organized and played an important part in the state affairs.

- The judges had a special patron saint, **Ma-at**, the netert of truth (similar to modern-day Lady of Justice). All judges of high rank served her as priests, and the chief justice wore a little figure of **Ma-at** around his neck as a badge of office.

- But who is this patron saint, **Ma-at**?

Ma-at personifies the principle of cosmic-order. She signifies all order, law, harmony, equillibrium and justice. The Egyptian texts recognize her cosmic power, as the source without which the other neterw are functionless.

The forty-two judges, at the final Day of Judgement, are under Ma-at's charge. (Read more about it under the chapter 'The Egyptian Religion').

Ma-at is often shown in a double form representing the two opposing sides of a litigation, because the scale of justice cannot balance without the equality of the opposing forces.

She is usually portrayed as a woman, with her symbol, the ostrich feather.

Entrusting this important heavenly attribute to a netert signifies the ancient Egyptian appreciation for women.

Ma-at was sometimes represented *'having her eyes closed'* to ensure equal justice for all. The modern-day blind-folded Lady of Justice is an imitation of Ma-at.

The high integrity of the Egyptian concept of justice is also represented by those statues at Thebes, of judges without hands, with the chief justice having his eyes turned downwards, signifying, as Plutarch says, *"that Justice ought: neither to be accessible to bribes, nor guided by favor and affection."*

- The Egyptian High Court consisted of thirty judges, who served as priests of **Ma-at**. Ten judges were chosen from each of the three cities—Thebes, Memphis, and Heliopolis. Diodorus said that this High Court was by no means inferior either to the Areopagites of Athens, or to the senate of Lacedoemon.

These thirty individuals constituted the bench of judges. At their first meeting they elected the president of the Court, with the title of Arch-judge. The city to which he belonged enjoyed the privilege of returning another judge, to complete the number of the thirty from whom he had been chosen.

- In addition to the High Court with the president and the thirty judges, each city, or capital of a nome, had its own "County Court," for the trial of minor and local offenses. The offices occupied by these local and regional courts were held by the most upright and learned individuals, to uphold the principles of **Ma-at**.

Court Proceedings

- Besides impartiality and the principle whereby each case should be treated according to its merits, another important feature of justice in ancient Egypt was the fact that it was administered free of charge.

- Depositions were taken before the trials. The complainant stated his case in writing. The writ included all related particulars, such as offenses, extent of injury, witnesses, points of law and requested judgements.

- The defendant then, taking up the deposition of the opposing party, wrote his response to each of the plaintiffs statements, either denying the charge, or arguing that the offense was not of a serious nature; and suggesting that the damages were incompatible with the nature of the crime.

- The complainant replied in writing; and the accused having brought forward all he had to say in his defense, the papers were given to the judges.

- When the trial convened, the president, or arch-judge, put on the emblem of Truth. The eight volumes which contained the laws of the land were placed close to him, in order to guide his decision, or to enable him to solve a difficult question, by reference to a code, or to former precedents, or to the opinion of some learned predecessor.

- After reviewing the written depositions and questioning the witnesses, if any, the judges made their decision. Their opinion only required to be ratified by the president, who then proceeded, in virtue of his office, to pronounce judgment on the case.

- They considered that this mode of proceeding was more likely to forward the ends of justice, than when the judges listened to the statements of pleaders. Eloquence often has the effect of fascinating, confusing and misleading the mind. Therefore, the persuasive arguments of oratory, which move the passions and excite the sympathy of the judges, were avoided.

Punishments

Here are a few of the known penalties for crimes. Such information was obtained from the very few cases which survived the ages as well as the writing of the Greek historian Diodorus.

- The deliberate killing of a free person or even a slave was punishable by death, regardless of the social status of the culprit.

- The prerogative of the royal pardon could be exercised on behalf of the guilty party; penalties were thus sometimes commuted by royal decree.

Chapter 33

Women

General

• No society, past or present, did or does value their women like the ancient Egyptians did. Whenever a society values women so highly, equality between men and women is the natural outcome.

- The most important aspects/attributes/principals of God were personified by women. The netert, Ma-at, personifies the cosmic-ordering principle. She keeps the universe in balance, order and harmony. Her cosmic power is the source without which the other neterw (gods and goddesses) are functionless and nil.

  And there are Isis, Mut, Sekhmet, Nephthys, Hathor, Seshat, and many other female neterw, who personify the greatest aspects of the One Universal God.

- The Egyptian women were entrusted with the civilization. The woman (princess), and not the male, was the legal heir to the throne, and the man she chose to marry, would become the ruling Pharaoh.

  Once again, the first statement in this chapter is not an exaggeration.

• Even though "beauty is in the eye of the beholder", not many will disagree that of all nations, there are no women as beautiful and as graceful as the ancient Egyptian women depicted on the walls of the ancient temples.

The beauties of Greece and Rome arouse our admiration, but they seem as cold as the marble from which they are formed.

The slim ladies of the fifteenth century are fashionable, but their faces are cold and distant.

The women of the seventeenth century, with their exposed masses of flesh, are lusty and earthy.

But if Nefertiti (her name means "**the beautiful one has come**"), were to enter an elegant establishment, all heads would turn, for truly she lives up to her name, and her beauty is timeless.

- The ancient Egyptian woman was described best by a widower, writing of his late wife:

> **She is profitable of speech, agreeable in her conversation, of good counsel in her writings; all that passes her lips is like the work of Ma-at, the netert of Truth, a perfect woman, greatly praised in her city, giving the hand to hall, saying that which is good, repeating what one loves, giving pleasure to all, nothing evil has ever passed her lips, most beloved by all....**

Power Behind the Throne

The royal authority and supreme direction of affairs were entrusted, without reserve, to women. Throughout Egyptian history, it was the princess who transmitted the solar blood. She was responsible for the purity of the line and for dynastic continuity. Egyptian kings claimed the right to the throne through marriage with the heiress. Egyptians knew that unless women were treated with respect, and made to exercise an influence over society, the manners and morals of men would suffer.

In High Positions

- As mentioned earlier, women personified major aspects/attributes of the One God. How much higher can a woman get than that?

- Since women were the legal heirs to the throne, they played an important part in the affairs of State, performing as a kind of power broker. The Queens of Egypt sometimes wielded exceptional influence, as advisers to the Pharaohs. Some queens governed Egypt for long durations. Hatshepsut, in particular, is a good example of a woman Pharaoh.

• Women could hold any position in the temple. There were priestesses of the neterw. Several of them reached the position of '**holy women**.'

Some of those '**holy women**' (similar to nowaday saints) had their own special shrines.

• As early as the fourth or early fifth Dynasty, there are records of female doctors. One had the title '**Lady director of Lady physicians**'.

• The office of scribe was not limited to males; women were known to have held the title, too.

• Women enjoyed every right pertaining to property, and had legal status which enabled them to buy, sell and take legal action.

As a Wife

• The few marriage contracts which have survived the ages show that the woman's rights were all well respected.

In a contract dating from 580 BC, but probably based on earlier contracts, the prospective husband takes oath that if he leaves his wife "***either from dislike, or preferring another***", he will return the dowry and a share of all paternal and maternal property for the children which she may bear.

• If the marriage failed, the formula for the man was to say before duly accredited witnesses, "***I have abandoned thee as wife. I am removed from thee. I have no claim on earth upon thee. I have said unto thee, 'Make for thyself a husband in any place to which thou shalt go.'***" At the same time, financial provision had to be made for the divorced wife. Similarly, a wife wishing to divorce her husband also had to pay compensation.

• It has been stated by some that the Egyptian priests were only allowed to have one wife, while the rest of the community had as many as they chose. On the contrary, the monuments depict each individual with a single consort. Mutual affection, tender-

ness and expression of endearment can be noticed by the fond manner, in which they are seated together, and with their children.

• Men and women either sat together, or separately, in a different part of the room. They were not kept in the same secluded manner as those of ancient Greece. The Egyptians treated their women very differently, as the accounts of ancient writers and the sculptures sufficiently prove. At some of the public festivals, women were expected to attend, in the company of their husbands or relations.

• The historian Diodorus reported that part of the agreement entered into at the time of marriage was, that the wife should have control over her husband, and that no objection should be made to her commands.

An instruction from the New Kingdom (c. 1500 B.C.) affirms Diodorus' account

> **Do not control your wife in her house,**
> **When you know she is efficient;**
> **Don't say to her: "Where is it? Get it!"**
> **When she has put it in the right place.**
> **Let your eye observe in silence,**
> **Then you recognize her skill:**
> **It is joy when your hand is with her,**
> **There are many who don't know this.**

• In the Osiris Legend, Isis and Osiris, the sister and brother got married. The relationship between Isis and Osiris was purely an allegorical fable. Within a larger cosmology, it can be viewed as a type of divine love. Their relationship is an image of devotion that we confuse with sexuality, and then get frightened by the act of incest.

This concept of devoted love was carried over to common people. Devoted lovers called each other brothers and sisters.

Some historians such as the Greek Diodorus never understood this concept and reported that marriages, between brothers and sisters, were owing to and inspired by the Isis/Osiris myth!
During certain periods of the ancient history, it was lawful for ancient Egyptians, Athenians and Hebrews to marry a sister by the father's side, not however, born by the same mother. Very few Egyptians married their half-sister (from the father's side), and only if she was the legal heir, so as

to inherit the throne. The Ptolemies did not observe the restrictions of the father's side, but Ptolemies were not Egyptians.

• The Wise Man, Ptah-hotep, gives the following advice to men:

> If thou art a man of note, found for thyself an household, and love thy wife at home, as it beseemeth. Fill her belly, cloth her back; unguent in the remedy for her limbs. Gladden her heart, as long as she lives; she is a goodly field for her lord.

As a Mother

Motherhood was revered in ancient Egypt. The following sage sums it up:

> Thou shalt never forget what thy mother has done for thee. ...She bore thee and nourished thee in all manner of ways. If thou forgettest her, she might blame thee, she might lift up her arms to God, and He would hear her complaint. After the appointed months she nursed thee for three years. She brought thee up, and when thou didst enter the school, and was instructed in the writings, she came daily to thy master with bread and beer from her house.

Children

• One of the characteristic traits of the ancient Egyptians was their love for their children. They displayed such a parental affection without limitation.

• As reported by Plato, education for the young was very essential. Mannerism and discipline were emphasized. They had rooted respect for old age, as well as for strangers. They required every young man to give place to his superiors in years. If seated he was supposed to rise, on the elders approach.

• The Egyptians always expected a great deal from their children, and, on the whole, their expectations were fulfilled. This was true among all classes of people.

Their tremendous love coupled with this high expectation of their children may have contributed to the long duration of the Egyptian civilization.

- There was no distinction being made between their offspring by a wife or any other woman, and they all equally enjoyed the rights of inheritance.

Cosmetics

- Ancient Egyptian cosmetics such as lipstick, rouge, and eye shadow were known to them.

- In addition to scented oils and ointments, ancient Egyptians had another way of perfuming the body. A solid mass of fat, presumably ox tallow, previously perfumed with herbs and spices, was shaped in the form of a cone and attached to the wig or placed on the crown of the head. As the heat gradually melted the fat, the wearer's body and clothes were anointed with its perfume. The practice survives till the present day, amongst certain Bedouin tribes who inhabit the deserts in Egypt.

- Some Egyptian women appear to have colored their fingernails but the nature and composition of the red coloring, used by them for this purpose, is unknown.

- Throughout the ancient world, the Egyptians were famous for their scents and perfumes.

- Cleanliness and personal appearance were matters of high priority among ancient Egyptians.

Chapter 34

Love, Egyptian Style

- The expressions and poses of married couples in Egyptian artwork, show deep feelings of love, affection and warmth. A number of poems express a notable element of romantic love. These external signs of warmth and love, particularly among married couples, are unique in the art of the ancient world.

- Egyptian love poetry left us some outstanding outpourings of emotions, by both young lovers and married people.

- In Egyptian love-songs the words *'sister'* and *'brother'* simply mean *'beloved'* and do not denote a blood relationship. It is symbolic of the ultimate love made in heaven, between the mythical brother and sister, Osiris and Isis.

The following is a bouquet of some love poems:

- **'Let her come to the lotus pond,**
My beautiful loved one,
In her transparent shift
Of fine linen.
Let her bathe herself near me
Among the flowers,
So that I may behold her
As her limbs emerge from the Water.'

My brother, it is pleasant to go to the pool
In order to bathe me in thy presence,
That I may let thee see my beauty in my tunic of finest linen
When it is wet...
I go down into the water.
And come forth again with a red fish

Which lies beautiful on my fingers.
Come and look at me....

One alone, a mistress without equal,
more beautiful than mortal man
... her excellence shines bright,
her skin gleams,
her eyes are beautiful when she gazes,
sweet her lips when she speaks.
... She steals my heart in her embrace.
She turns the head of every man, captivating him at sight.

My beloved has come, my heart exults,
My arms spread out to embrace her;
My heart bounds in its place,
Like the red fish in its pond.
O night, be mine forever,
Now that my queen has come!

- How pleasant is mine hour! Might an hour only become for me eternity, when I sleep with thee. Thou didst lift up mine heart...when it was night.

  Seamu flowers are in it! One is made great in their presence. I am thy first sister.

  I am unto thee like a garden, which I have planted with flowers and all manner of sweet-smelling herbs.

  Shedeh is it, my hearing of thy voice, and I live because I hear it.

- With Graceful step she treads the ground,
  Captures my heart by her movements.
  She causes all men's necks
  To turn about to see her;

- Seven days from yesterday I have not seen my beloved,

And sickness has crept over me,
And I have become heavy in my limbs
And am unmindful of mine own body.
If the master-physicians come to me,
My heart has no comfort of their remedies,
And the magicians, no resource is in them,
My malady is not diagnosed.

Better for me is my beloved than any remedies,
More important is she for me than the entire compendium of medicine.

My salutation is when she enters from without.
When I see her, then am I well;
Opens she her eye, my limbs are young again;
Speaks she, and I am strong;
And when I embrace her, she banishes evil,
And it passes from me for seven days.

- There are saamu-flowers in it before which we are glorified.
I am your foremost sister.
I am yours as is the acre of land which I made to flourish with flowers and all manner of sweet-scented herbs.
Pleasant is the channel in it which you dug with your own hand for our refreshment in the north wind,
a beautiful place for walking hand in hand.
My body is satisfied and my heart rejoicing at our going together.
Hearing your voice is pomegranate wine:
I live when I hear it.
If ever I see you it is better for me than eating and drinking.

- The love of the sister is upon yonder side
A stretch of water is between us,
And a crocodile waits on the sandbank.
But when I go down into the water
I tread upon the flood;
My heart is courageous upon the waters
And the water is like land to my feet.

- I shall lie down inside and feign sickness.
  My neighbors shall come in to see me
  and my girl will come and put the physicians to shame
  For she knows my disease.

- Her love it is that makes me strong;
  Yes, it makes water spell for me...
  I see my sister coming and my heart rejoices.
  My arms are opened wide to embrace her
  And my heart rejoices upon its place....
  When the mistress comes to me
  If I embrace her and her arms are opened
  It is for me as if I were the one that is from Punt...

- A passage from a poem written by a widower, to his dead wife, illustrates the kind of passions felt by spouses for each other.

> You became my wife when I was young, and I was with you. I was appointed to all manner of offices, and I was with you. I did not forsake you or cause your heart any sorrow... Behold, when I commanded the footsoldiers of Pharaoh, together with his chariot force, I did cause you to come that they might fall down before you, and they brought all manner of good things to present to you. When you were ill with the sickness which afflicted you, I went to the Chief Physician and he made you your medicine, he did everything that you said he should do. When I had to accompany Pharaoh on his journey to the south, my thoughts were with you, and I spent those eight months without caring to eat or drink. When I returned to Memphis, I besought the Pharaoh and betook myself to you, and I greatly mourned for you with the people of my house.

Chapter 35

Music and Entertainment

General

• Many writers have focused on western music as the only worthy source, implying that anything else is not eligible to be considered music.

The word *'music'* in the English language has several alternate meanings, but basically it means *'Any rhythmic sequence of pleasing sounds, such as birds, water, ... etc'.* Pleasing sounds are in the ears of the beholder just as beauty is in the eye of the beholder.

• Music and singing accompanied daily activities and religious festivals in Egypt. Workers sang simple folk songs, as they labored. Guests at dinner-parties were entertained by songs and dances while they ate and drank. Hymns to God were often sung to the accompaniment of the harp.

• There is no question that the ancient Egyptians had knowledge of music and enjoyed it. So far, we do not have any evidence to know what form of musical notations they did use. We know however, that the Greeks were using the letters of their alphabet for musical purposes by the second century B.C. Here is what some ancient travelers have informed us:

- Athenaens told us that both Greeks and the "barbarians" learned their music from Egyptian refugees.

- Pythagoras was so impressed by the Egyptian wisdom and noted that they paid particular attention to the study of music.

- Plato, who was an attentive observer of the social life in Egypt, stated that Egyptians thought that music was beneficial for youth.

• Egyptians believed that music was of divine origin, and it is possible that they used hieroglyphs (which means *sacred scripts*) as musical notes.

- The number of pictures of musicians in the sculptures and bas-reliefs, as well as the paintings, is clear evidence of the important role that music had.

Can we learn anything substantial, about music, from pictorial representations? We should remember that:

1- The temples and tombs were not meant for public displays or analysis.

2- Almost everything we see in these temples and tombs has other symbolic meanings.

Therefore, the answer to the question is still unknown. We should, however, be wary of "in-depth analyses" of some authors, and of others who declare the non-existence of certain knowledge, if they cannot find the answers that fit their western paradigm.

Harmony of the Cosmos

- The netert **Hathor** was the main divine aspect of music and entertainment. Hathor was the great provider of spiritual nourishment. She provided joy, lovemaking, music and cheerfulness. She was also the patroness of spiritual healing.

She was lovingly referred to as the '***mistress of dance***' and the '***mistress of music***'.

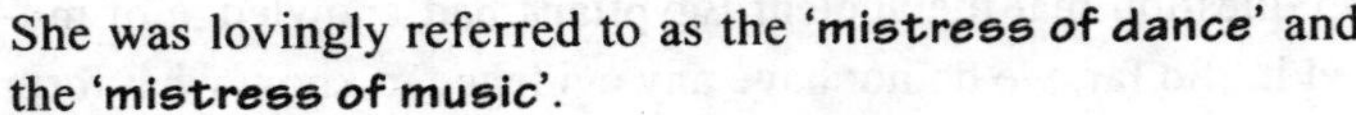

- The belief of universal harmony, in an astronomical, musical sense had ancient roots. As an example, there is a representation from the Middle Kingdom (c. 2133-1633 B.C.) showing a harpist playing a six-stringed harp. Above his head we see six red disks. A contemporary passage on the wall of another tomb refers to the owner having '**danced like the planets of the sky**'. The disks, even if they do not actually represent musical notes, at least suggest musical concepts. This idea of *'universal harmony'* in an astronomical-musical sense, was expressed more clearly in later writings.

- In a hymn to **Hathor**, at her temple in Dendara, there is another indication of the relationship between music and the cosmos:

The sky and its stars make music to you.
The sun and the moon praise you.
The neterw exalt you.
The neterw sing to you.

Instruments

• The walls of public and private monuments tell us a good deal about their musical instruments and how they developed over time. There are a good number of ancient musical instruments which have survived the ages.

• Ancient Egyptian harps can be divided into two groups: arched and angular. The angular harp became common during the New Kingdom, but the arched harp seems to have been known, from as early as the Fourth Dynasty (c. 2613-2492 B.C.).

• The harps varied in form, size, and the number of their strings; they are represented in the ancient paintings with four, six, seven, eight, nine, ten, eleven, twelve, fourteen, seventeen, twenty, twenty-one, and twenty-two strings.

• The end-blown flute changed little in appearance over the course of Egyptian history. A similar instrument, known as the **nay**, is one of the most popular instruments in Egypt and North Africa today.

• The reed instrument has generally been identified as a single-reed type, that is to say a clarinet. It is not clear from surviving examples what kind of mouthpiece it had.

• The Egyptians had several kinds of flutes, some suited to mournful, others to festive occasions, similar to the Greek's versions of flutes.

• The double pipe was as common in Egypt, as it has been in Greece. It consisted of two tubes, one played by the right, the other by the left hand, the latter giving a deep sound for the base, the right a sharp tone for the tenor.

• The trumpet was utilized for its megaphone quality.

- The drums used, were barrel-shaped and not cylindrical.

- Hand drums were used. They were of a type known, in modern Egypt, as darabukka, a clay pot open at the lower end, with a membrane glued or laced to the upper rim.

- There were many percussion instruments: they included different sizes and shapes of the tambourine, as well as the castanets, consisting of two ivory plates hung from a necklace.

Types of Music

- The ancient Egyptian music is generally classified as *'secular'*, *'sacred'* or *'military'*, and so on. These categories overlap. Military trumpets and drums were played during the processions of the neterw; sistra (cult rattles) were shaken by priestesses in religious rituals, but also on occasions associated with funerary rites.

- Egyptians were the first to utilize drums, trumpets and horns for military and processional functions. The same were later used by other civilizations, and continue to the present day. No military band nowadays would be complete without a brass section or drums to emphasize precision and supremacy.

Musicians

- Musicians achieved considerable status. They were master performers and composed their own music. Skillful performances could win a high reputation. Some musicians were able to afford important monuments of their own. Some ensembles are shown, with the players' names written next to them, and in these cases we may assume that they represented groups which actually existed. Where the participants remain anonymous, it is much more likely to be a conventional 'ideal' scene.

- The core of the ensemble generally consisted of harp, lute and double oboe, occasionally with additional instruments such as lyre, tambourine and different types of harp. The instrumentalists could be joined by people singing and clapping their hands.

• There were many combinations of various instruments. In the Bacchic festival of Ptolemy Philadelphus, described by Athenaeus, more than 600 musicians were employed in the chorus, among them were the 300 performers on the cithara.

• They had various and distinctive roles. Some of their many musical titles included *'overseer'*, *'instructor'*, *'director of musicians'* and *'teacher'*. The duties of each title is not totally clear to us.

Singing

• Singing was a very popular activity in entertaining guests. There were also many hymns, in honor of the neterw.

• A relief painted on a wall of a tomb at Saqqara, shows singers and flutists in a crouching position. The conductor is raising his hand to indicate the beats, and the singers are providing accompaniment by clapping their hands.

• There were also solo performances. Sometimes, a chorus of many people sang at a private assembly without any instrument, two or three beating time at intervals with their hands.

• No banquet music was complete without the human voice.

Dancing & Ballet

• In all civilizations, dancing has always accompanied music. During the religious ceremonies, the classical steps were always followed. The Egyptians, including the kings, danced at the temples in honor of the neterw.

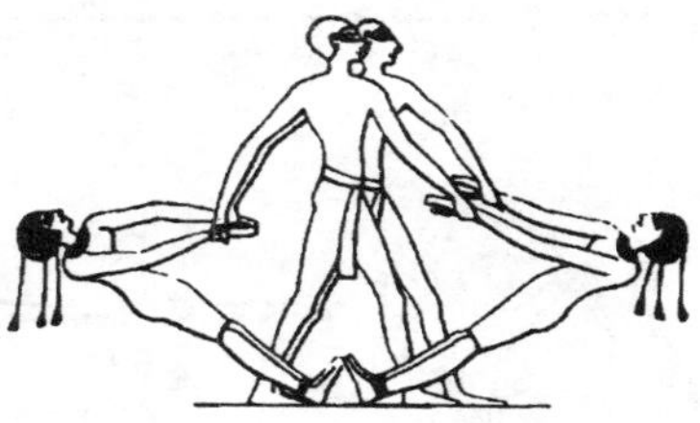

• One could dance either singly or in groups, with the sexes either together or apart. The men danced with immense vigor, accompanying their motions with rhythmic jumps. The women used slower rhythms.

- The girls and young women of Egypt were all good dancers. This activity was a favorite and regular game for them. By dancing, all of them were in fact worshipping **Hathor**, the netert of love, happiness, dancing and music.

- In the Tomb of Kagemni, at Saqqara, in the three-pillared room, five dancers are shown performing an acrobatic ballet. Ballet performances can also be seen on the western wall of the Luxor Temple.

On these wall scenes dating around 1,800 B.C., the women performed pirouettes forward and backward, cartwheels, the splits, and backward flips. Sometimes they performed these exercises in pairs, one of the female dancers standing up and the other on her back. They would do pirouettes in that position, head up and head down alternately. These were difficult exercises which could only be done with extensive training and practice.

Many of their postures do not differ from our modern ballet, and the pirouette delighted Egyptian parties, four thousand years ago.

Chapter 36

Literature in Ancient Egypt

The Cinderella Story

• There are many people who may not even want to dignify the ancient Egyptian writings by calling them *'Literature'*. However, upon a closer and more rational evaluation, perhaps it should be called 'The Literature'.

Many labels were given to the Egyptian writings to make it sound distant, weird and incoherent: Tales of Gods, Magic, Adventure. Our modern-day writings deal with the same subjects but they have fancy labels: Mythology, Biblical, Folklore, Fairy Tales, Fantasy, Miracles, Fiction, Facts and Science Fiction.

• Many aspects of ancient Egypt, including literature, found their ways prominently and permanently into our present lives. For who among us does not know the Cinderella Story.

Our present-day version of the story closely resembles a story known in ancient Egypt as **'The Girl With The Red Rose Slippers'**, where a young woman's red slipper was scooped up by an falcon (representing Horus) and dropped near the prince. Upon examining the delicacy of the slipper, the prince declared that the owner would become his bride, and went about finding the woman who fit the slipper.

• Egyptian writings are generally classified by their subject matters and according to their time period. The wealth of our available literary records came from the Middle Kingdom (c. 2160-1380 B.C.). It is this time period that we consider to be the classical writings period.

• The variety of subjects displayed in Egyptian Literature is very wide. A few subjects will be mentioned here.

Folklore, Fantasy & Fiction

Of the many stories, we shall make quick overview only to three of them (no need to mention the original Cinderella story again).

1- The most popular story ever in ancient Egypt was **'The Autobiography of Sinuhe'**. Several copies of the story were recovered. The story was taught in schools.

   Many of us know a good portion of this story but under another name, for the story of David and Goliath is a fictional story which was borrowed from the Sinuhe story (Read more about it under 'Twthomosis III, The Warrior King').

2- The ancient Egyptian story of the **'Shipwrecked Sailor'** (written on Papyrus now housed in the Leningrad Musuem) has much in common with our version of the story of Sinbad. The sole survivor of the wreck, the sailor, was cast upon an enchanted island, where he was befriended and encouraged by a serpent of fabulous appearance. Eventually, as the serpent had foretold, he was rescued by another ship and taken back to Egypt.

   There are several variations in the western literature, along the same theme as this ancient Egyptian story.

3- **'The Peasant and the Workman'** is a delightful story of an eloquent peasant who sought justice against a workman. Because he was so eloquent, the governor delayed judgment as long as possible so that he could hear the peasant's fabulous presentations. Of course the peasant was compensated fairly at the end.

Wisdom Texts

• Wisdom texts were the articulation of perfection and truth. Their truth was ethical, abstract and eternal, yet the perfection also had an aesthetic quality: truth was beauty. Thus, instructive words were also intended to entertain and give pleasure, for example:

> **Speak to me a few perfect words, choose verses, whose hearing will give my person enjoyment.**

- In the Harris Papyrus, we find the **'Song of the Harper'**, containing general advice about life:

> **Be glad therefore; forgetfulness is profitable to you.**
>
> **Follow your desire as long as you live. Put myrrh on your head, cloth yourself in fine linen....**
>
> **Do things (while) you are on earth. Do not be upset until that day of lamentation comes to you....**
>
> **Make holiday and do not weary of it. See, no-one is allowed to take his goods with him and no-one who has gone comes back again.**

- The thirty chapters of the **Teaching of Amenemope** (Amenhotep III) contain many wisdom texts which were later echoed in the Old Testament's Book of Proverbs. Numerous verbal parallels occur between this Egyptian text and the Bible, such as the opening lines of the first chapter: **"Give your ears, listen to the words which are spoken, give your mind to interpreting them. It is profitable to put them in your heart"**. (Read more about it under the chapter, 'Amenhotep III, Man of Peace').

- Practical wisdom texts are systematic instructions composed of maxims and precepts. One of the earliest examples is the **Instruction** given in 2380 B.C. to a soon-to-be high official. The **Instruction** begins with these words: **"Do not be arrogant because you are learned; do not be over-confident because you are well informed. Consult the ignorant man as well as the wise one."** This instruction is followed by more than forty maxims.

Poetry

- Love of Country

> **What do they say everyday in their hearts,**
> **those who are far from Thebes?**
> **They spend their day blinking at its name,**
> **if only we had it, they say**
> **The bread there is tastier than cakes made with goose fat,**
> **its water is sweeter than honey,**

> **one drinks of it till one gets drunk.**
> **Oh! that is how one lives at Thebes.**

- On the immortality of writers, from a Ramesside Papyrus, 1300 B.C.

> **As to those learned scribes,**
> **Of the time that came after the neterw,**
> **They who foretold the future,**
> **Their names have become everlasting,**
> **While they departed, having finished their lives,**
> **And all their kin are forgotten.**

- **'Lament of Isis and Nephthys'** is a dramatization of the Isis and Osiris story. The sister neterw, Isis and Nephthys, bewailed their brother Osiris' death and entreated him to come back to life. The text for this duet was derived from an ancient Egyptian lamentation recited three thousand years earlier, during the annual sacred mystery play in Abydos.

'Lament for Osiris' was described as having the power to stir our deepest emotions. Here are a few portions of this moving Lament:

- **Sing we Osiris dead,**
  Lament the fallen head:
  The light has left the world, the world is gray.
  Athwart the starry skies
  The web of darkness flies,
  And Isis weeps Osiris passed away.
  Your tears, ye stars, ye fires, ye rivers, shed,
  Weep, children of the Nile, weep for your lord is dead!

- **O dweller in the west,**
  Lover and lordliest,
  Thy love, thy sister Isis, calls thee home!
  Come from thy chamber dun,
  Thou master of the sun,

- **I seek thee near and far,**
  From star to wandering star,
  Free with the dead that in Amenti dwell.
  I search the height, the deep, the lands, the skies,
  Rise from the dead and live, our lord Osiris, rise!

Lyrics

• In a banqueting scene, in which the guests are entertained by dancers, a woman plays two reed-pipes and three singers beat time by clapping their hands. Part of their song reads as follows:

> **Flowers of sweet scents which Ptah sends and Geb makes to grow.**
> **His beauty is in every body.**
> **Ptah has done this with his own hands to gladden his heart.**
> **The pools are filled anew with water.**
> **The earth is flooded with his love.**

• A text celebrates the taming of the lioness at Dendara temple has an interesting song sung by the priest:

> **The King of Egypt, Pharaoh comes to dance**
> **He comes to sing.**
> **You, his Lady, see how he dances,**
> **Wife of Horus**
> **See how he springs.**

This is similar to the medieval Christmas carol in which Christ is celebrated as *"Lord of the Dance"*.

Hymns

• To Amen-Re, as the universal creator:

> **Creator are you, fashioner of your own limbs;**
> **One who brings into being, himself unborn;**
> **Unique in his qualities, traversing eternity**
> **Upon roads with millions under his guidance.**

• The Hymn to the Nile:

> **Hail O Nile, who issues forth from the earth,**
> **Who comes to give life to the people of Egypt.**
> **Secret of movement, a darkness in daylight.**

Praised by his followers whose fields you water.
Created by Re to give life to all who thirst.
Who lets the desert drink with streams descending from heaven.
Beloved of the earth-neter, controller of the corn-neter,
Who causes the workshops of Ptah to flourish.
Lord of fish who causes the water-fowl to sail upstream ...
Who makes barley and creates wheat so that temples celebrate
...
When the Nile overflows, offerings are made to you,
Cattle are slaughtered for you,
A great oblation is made to you,
Birds are fattened for you,
Desert lions are trapped for you that your goodness be repaid.

Other Texts

Theological texts, including mythical stories, were mentioned in previous chapters.

Informational texts will follow in the coming chapters under a variety of subjects such as medicine and science.

Chapter 37

Architecture

The Beauty & Power

• Goethe described architecture as *"frozen music"*. Music is an arrangement of sound waves in time. Similarily, architecture is an arrangement of building lines in space.

Oue ears can detect the sound waves in music. However, there are sound waves, such as infrasound, which can not be detected by hearing, nevertheless we are aware of its destructive powers. The ultrasound waves cannot be detected by hearing either, but are used in surgery as a knifeless scalpel.

As such, we are affected by many undetectable waves. One may wonder how and why various colors have an affect on us physically. Do colors have some type of light waves unknown to us?

• The different shapes and sizes of buildings have different effects on us, as well. The physical effect of the architectural form is evident in the case of the pyramid. A number of scientifically controlled experiments have been performed, in a scale-model pyramid, which resulted in the phenomena called **'pyramid power'.** (Read more about it under 'The Mystery of the Pyramids').

• The sound of architectural music can literally be heard at the Karnak temple where the top portion of an obelisk is lying on the ground. If one hits the obelisk with his hand, the entire enormous block resonates like a tuning fork, which can be detected by putting your ear at the angle of the top pyramidion. This phenomenon is certainly an instinctive property of granite when cut to an obelisk shape.

- Egyptian temples conform quite literally to Goethe's definition of architecture as *"frozen music"* by virtue of their geometry, proportions and measurements, as well as by the careful choice of materials employed. The emotional effect they produce upon us, are the direct results of the precision of their works, just as a musical composition is the direct result of a particular sequence of notes of different frequencies.

- The types of stone used in the pyramids and temples of Egypt were chosen with care. The choice of stone type was neither necessitated by economics, nor by practical structural consideration. It is believed that each stone type represents specific aspects of the cosmic process.
Here are the cosmic representations of some stones:

Alabaster	=	Air
Sandstone	=	Earth
Limestone	=	Water
Granite	=	Fire

- There is a general perception that Egyptian architecture and art has a serious defect which is the sense of repetitiveness. When studied in depth, however, the similarities between one temple and another disappear in the face of the differences.

One of the obvious peculiarities of Egyptian architecture is the deliberate avoidance of uniformity in the arrangement of the columns, and many of the details. As an example, the capitals of the columns in the great hall at Karnak are at different heights. Such variation can be perceived only when the eye is brought on a level, with the lower part of the capitals.

- Egyptians did not always confine themselves to the mere imitation of natural objects for ornament. Their ceilings and cornices offer numerous graceful fancy devices; among which are the guilloche, (misnamed as the Tuscan border), the chevron, and the scroll pattern. These items can be seen, in a tomb dated back to the Sixth Dynasty; i.e. they were therefore known in Egypt, many ages before they were adopted by the Greeks. The most complicated form of the guilloche covered a whole Egyptian ceiling, more than a thousand years before it was represented on those comparatively late objects, found at Nineveh.

Arches

• The arch was employed in Egypt at a very early period. Crude brick arches were commonly used in roofing tombs, at least as far back as 1600 B.C., in Thebes.

• Stone arches were found from the time of Psammitichus (c. 700 B.C.). Other stone arches, of the same time period, were found at Giza.

• An arch being of stone is no stronger proof of its existence than are those of brick at Thebes. The principle of the arch is the same, regardless of the material used. Basically, the brick arch (like the stone) radiates to a common center. It is not necessary that an arch should be of any particular material; nor does the arch have to have a keystone to be qualified as an "arch". Arches, both round and pointed, are found at all eras, without a keystone. The same was the case in Egypt.

Architectural Sites

Many twentieth-century architects, eager to break free of the Victorian clutter and other demoralized European architectural forms, went back to Egypt for inspiration. Saqqara and the equally clean-lined temple of Hatshepsut at Luxor, particularly suited emerging contemporary styles.

Saqqara

• It had always been assumed that the Egyptians began using the mighty blocks in Giza, after successive pyramid experiments in the Step Pyramid, the Collapsed Pyramid of Meidum, and Snefru's two pyramids of Dahshur. The enclosure wall at Saqqara was built several centuries prior to the large pyramids. It is a major achievement by itself, and it invalidates this assumed progression theory of the pyramids.

The Enclosure Wall

The wall was uncovered by archaelogical excavation in 1926.

This wall may not look Egyptian, only because its neat architecture has been copied, in many modern western cities.

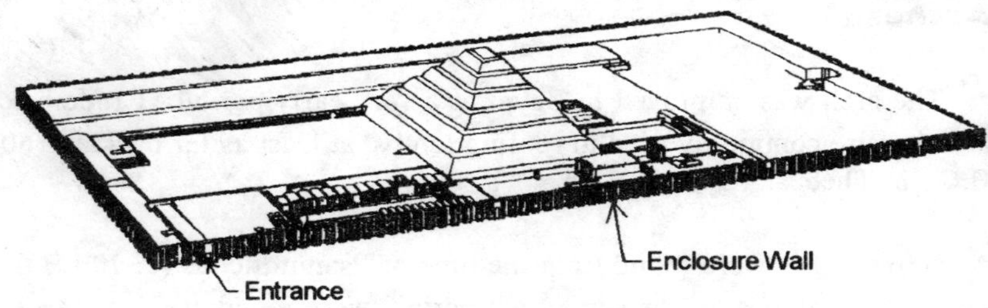

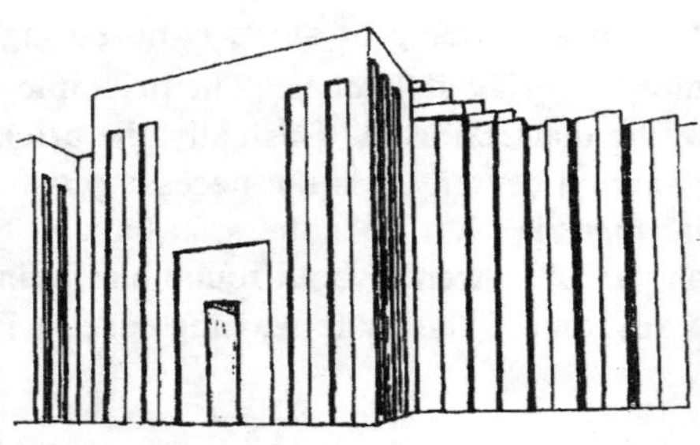

Its style of recessed paneling is taken from the earlier mastabas (the above ground superstructure of older tombs). More than a square mile of desert is enclosed within the wall. When complete, the enclosure wall was nearly 600 yards (549 m) long and 300 yards (274 m) wide and rose to a height of over 30 feet (9.1m). As such, the enclosure wall was by itself an impressive project. Its successive recesses and projections required more than triples the amount of both stone and labor, of a similar simple wall. The craftsmanship is superb. The strange, inverse external corners are unique and worthy of attention.

Entrance Passage

The axis of this passage is different from the axis of the colonnade behind. The different axes can only be deliberate, though their purpose is unclear. This cannot be an oversight, given the razor-edged perfection of the massive enclosure wall.

The ceiling of the entrance passage simulates a roof of split logs. Similar imitations, of organic originals, are present in many Egyptian buildings.

False Doors

The purpose of the false stone doors and windows, in Egyptian buildings, is still a mystery. The minute details of the false doors become evident, to the left and the right, as one emerges from the entrance passage.

Colonnade

Read about it in the chapter, 'The Mastery of Columns'.

Temple of Hatshepsut

The mortuary temple built by Queen Hatshepsut is called in Egyptian **"The Most Splendid of All"**. Many scholars, architects, and visitors consider this temple the finest in Egypt, and one of the great architectural masterpieces of the world.

Along with Saqqara, this temple has exercised considerable direct and indirect influence on contemporary architectural thinking all over the world.

Karnak

- Here, in this Hypostyle Hall, all aspects of creation - religion, philosophy, science and art - are realized in the stones. The result, aesthetically, is overpowering.

- In Egyptian cosmology, the initial act of creation was represented as a hill (matter) rising out of the formless chaos. This is the teaching at Heliopolis, which represents metaphysical rather than physical creation.

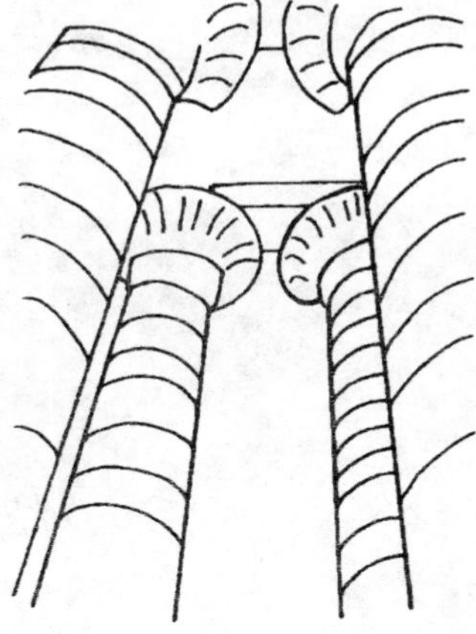

- The massive crowded columns of the hall effectively recreate the thicket quality, of the actual papyrus swamp. There are seven rows of nine columns, on each side of the double row of the six higher columns in the center. This emphasis upon six, seven, and nine is found nowhere else in Egypt. Seven, the number of process and growth, multiplied by nine.

Nine, the Ennead, is a reiterated theme of ancient Egypt. The Great Ennead is held responsible for bringing the Universe into being, and sustaining it.

- Nowhere in the world is there a more eminent or nobler architectural conception, or one carried out with such superior effectiveness than the Hypostyle Hall, at the Karnak Temple.

Chapter 38

Life in Masonry Buildings

Masonic Symphony

• The masons claim that their rites, knowledge and traditions are rooted in Egypt and there are many indications that this may be so.

There are (and were) many people who are members of a widespread secret fraternal society called 'Free and Accepted Masons' (popularly known as Freemasonry). There is a natural, instinctive fellowship and sympathy between their members.

• Modern masons claim their deep roots from the ancient Egyptians. It is interesting that the obelisk and the pyramid were an important symbolic form for them, long before Egyptology and archeology began. The Founding Fathers of America (many of whom were masons), put the un-American pyramid on the dollar bill, and chose the shape of an obelisk for the design of a monument for George Washington, also a mason.

• Napoleon, like so many eminent men of his era, was a Freemason. His campaign to conquer Egypt was part of his imperial military plan, but it was coupled with an intense desire to unlock the secrets of Egypt, which Napoleon believed to be the source of Masonic knowledge. Accordingly, in 1798, along with his 25,000 soldiers, he brought several hundred of the leading experts of his day, including the best draftsmen and artists in France.

• In Mozart's Masonic Opera, 'The Magic Flute', the free spirit Papageno is trapping wild birds. This is purely Egyptian symbolism, because for the ancient Egyptians, birds such as the falcon, vulture, stork, phoe-

nix, goose, etc., symbolized various spiritual qualities. Each species of bird represented a wild spiritual aspect that must be trapped, caged, sometimes tamed and other times offered to the neterw in sacrifice.

• These ancient stones of Egypt speak with resonant, clear voices. But it is a mistake to think they speak in a familiar twentieth-century language. We must try to capture the spirit of the past as we listen, through our modern ears, and as we attempt to understand what everything means.

Masonic Powers

Here are but a few examples of such powers.

The Great Pyramid of Giza

- On the Giza plateau, Egypt was at the very height of its powers, producing a monument of grandeur, with perfection of craftsmanship, and purity of line. The stoneworking techniques are very remarkable and worth examining.

> Scholars involved in Masonic, Rosicrucian, Theosophist, and other societies that claim a heritage in Egypt, have long maintained that the system of passages and chambers in the Great Pyramid served as centers for initiation ceremonies. Madame Blavatsky, the founder of Theosophy, theorized that, externally, the pyramid *"symbolized the creative principle of Nature and illustrated also the principles of geometry, mathematics, astronomy and astrology,"* that the interior of the pyramid was *"a temple of initiation where men rose toward the gods* (neterw) *and the gods* (neterw) *descended toward man."* Blavatsky considered the granite coffer in the so-called "King's Chamber", as a holy vessel in which the person was placed to emerge as a supernaturalist. Many other writers have attempted to specify the functions of the various corridors and chambers.

The Valley Temple of Chephren at Giza

This very ancient temple provides us with two interesting observations:

1- Many of the stones are set at different angles. This practice which was common in Egyptian buildings, has no structural advantage, over regular coursing. The additional calculations and labor involved in this type of jointing is considerable. The purpose or function of such a technique is unknown.

We are then left to guess and theorize. The famed Egyptologist De Lubicz believed that the joints and courses are carefully calculated, to coincide with the symbolic intent of the friezes on the walls, so as to form a kind of invisible nervous system, in this organic and very alive building.

2- The stone corners are not regular, interlocking dovetails, but rather alternate inverse quoins. The joints go around the corners. To form such corners, the entire face of the stone has been carved away, in some cases dramatically, for over a foot; in other cases, barely creating a return of only an inch or so. This strange method of creating corners was commonly used throughout Egyptian history.

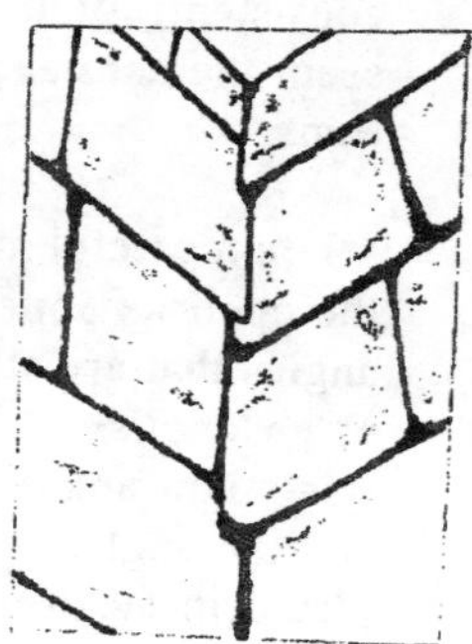

If the temple is a living structure which embodies specific relevant cosmic laws, it could be that, creating these types of continuous corners would allow the temple's "energies" to flow unimpeded, as opposed to the broken right angle joints. This may sound far-fetched, but there are many other similar pieces of corroborative symbolic thinking, throughout Egypt.

The Obelisks

- The obelisk is made of one piece of pink granite. Like all the pink granite of Egypt, it was quarried several hundred miles to the south, at Aswan, transported several miles to the river, loaded onto a cargo ship, floated down to Thebes, and then set up on its pedestal with perfect accuracy.

- Many of these obelisks found their way to Europe and America.

- Ritual reliefs show the Pharaoh single-handedly raising an obelisk by means of a single rope, tied to its upper extremity. This is of course symbolic. According to the famed Egyptologist Franqois Daumas, the erection of the obelisk was a symbolic reproduction of the djed pillar, the familiar Osirian symbol standing for the backbone (i.e., support) of the physical world and the channel through which the divine spirit might rise through matter to rejoin its source.

- But did the obelisk just have a symbolic function or did it serve a scientific function?.

  - Having two obelisks at the entrance to the temples and having them consistently of different height and dimensions (where symmetry would seem the natural procedure) have suggested possible scientific functions.

  - Upon careful measurements and analysis, it was found that although the obelisks appear perfectly square, they are not. Their edges form angles that are slightly out of square, and in a device cut as precisely as an obelisk, this cannot be accidental. According to Lucie Lamy, this slight angle variation, along with the dimensions of the obelisk, and the angles of the pyramidion (the pyramid-shaped top, originally plated in electrum, an alloy of gold and silver), is all calculated according to geodetic data pertaining to the exact longitude and latitude where the obelisk was originally set. This will make the obelisk much more than a simple sundial.

  - The shadows cast by the pair of unequal obelisks, at the entrance to a temple, would enable the astronomer/priests to obtain precise calendrical and astronomical data, relevant to this given location. Egyptians were then able to coordinate such data with similar readings from other key sites which are also furnished with their peculiar obelisks.

Chapter 39

The Mastery of Columns

General

• The ancient Egyptians were the masters of the vertical principle as well as the horizontal line. They mastered the vertical principle by means of the long lines of their lofty pyramidal towers, their obelisks and the lengthy columns that extended up the whole front of their houses.

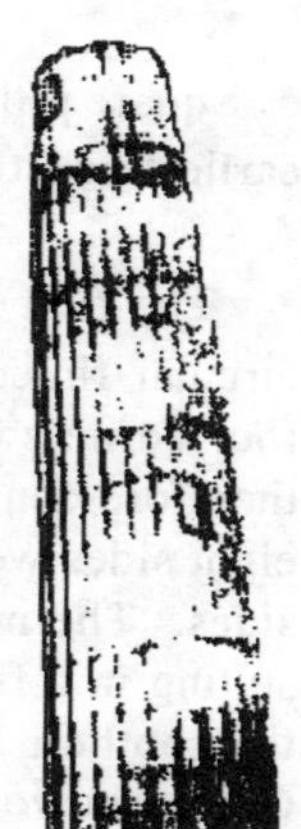

This vertical principle was adopted afterwards by the Greeks and the Romans, as evident in their arches and columns.

The slender Egyptian columns, known as reeded columns, found their way into the houses of Rome.

Other vertical lines were introduced much later in the form of towers, minarets and other edifices.

• The oldest monuments of Greece have the predominant Egyptian sloping and/or pyramidal lines.

• The columns in the oldest Greek forms are almost purely Egyptian. The wrongly-called Greek Doric columns were actually fashioned in Egypt, at least two thousand years before they were copied by the Greeks.

Hatshepsut Temple
(1490-1468 B.C.)

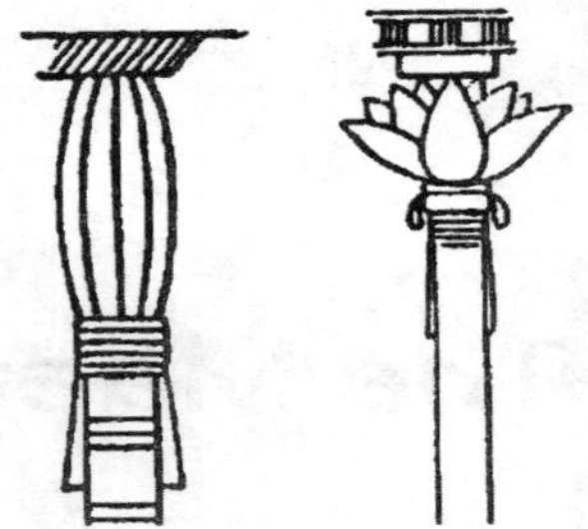

• Egyptian architecture derived much of its design elements from the beauty of nature itself, such as palm trees, and other various plants of the country.

Their love of flowers showed up in their columns, where they fashioned their pillars to resemble flowers - individual, bunches, full blossoms or buds.

Their Individual Types

• Square pillars were used initially. This type can be found in some of the earliest constructed porticoes, and in the peristyles of the old temples.

• The first stage in the formation of the polygonal and circular fluted column came as a result of cutting off the four corners of the square pillar. The square shape was therefore converted into an octagonal shaft. The resulted eight sides were again subdivided, into 12, 16, 20, and 32 sides. The multiple flat facets were thereafter hollowed into grooves resulting in a fluted column. The Egyptian Doric columns can be found at the southern buildings, in Saqqara. It was doubtless from this that the Greeks borrowed their Doric shaft.

• Another totally different style of column was also developed by the Egyptians. It was a round shaft which was topped by a palm-tree capital, or by a blossom, or the bud of the papyrus. Such shapes were painted earlier, or represented in relief, upon the flat surfaces of a square pillar.

• The water-plant capital with the blossom and bud for both the lotus and the papyrus plants, as well as the palm-tree column, were all in use, at least as early as the Sixth Dynasty (2323-2150 B.C.).

• The Doric capital is a slight modification of the Egyptian water-plant column. As the illustration shows, once the upper part, of the Egyptian water-plant, is removed and the top slab is brought down, the result is the shape of

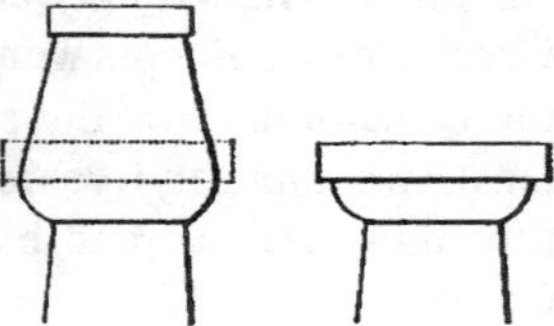

the Doric capital.

Also, the circlet around the neck of the early Greek column is very similar to the Egyptian bands tied round the cluster of water-plants; which are an anomaly in a single shaft, where there is nothing to bind.

- Reeded columns were apparently in imitation of columns, made of bound bunches of reeds.

- The Egyptian column, like that of Greece, was constructed of several pieces; except that it consisted of half (not of whole) cylinders. The joint between the halves was placed alternately one way and the other. Each set of joints was placed at right angles, with those below and above them. The joints were sometimes secured by dovetailed cramps. For reasons unknown to us, whole cylinders were never used, except in a few small granite shafts.

The Colonnades

1- At Saqqara

- At the Pyramid Complex of Zoser, past the Enclosure Wall, this exceptional colonnade, was reconstructed by fitting bits and pieces, found buried in the sand in the area.

There are forty columns in the colonnade. Originally, the colonnade was roofed in. The roof over the shorter end columns formed a long T-shaped gallery.

- The columns of the colonnade are popularly called fluted, which is technically incorrect. They are reeded.

These columns are peculiar in that they are attached to the main wall by connecting masonry. To suggest that the connecting walls were needed because the Egyptians lacked the technical capability, to design free-standing columns, is incomprehensible. It is difficult to imagine that the Egyptians, with their innumerable innovations at Saqqara, would be incapable of designing a rather elementary freestanding column, if they wanted to.

The purpose of this peculiar style, at this location is still a mystery.

As the colonnade progresses west, the distance between the columns also narrows. With the superb Egyptian knowledge of harmony and proportion, there must be a deeper purpose to this narrowing than sheer artistry.

2- At the Karnak Temple

a- Grand Hypostyle Hall

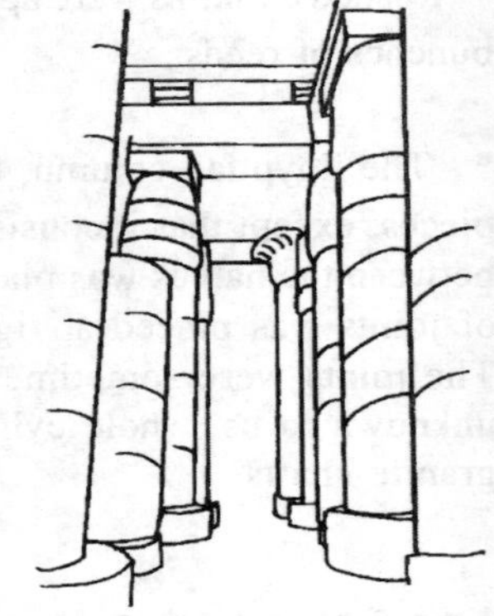

- The grand Hypostyle Hall is the structure that, along with the Great Pyramid and the Sphinx, has won universal recognition as one of the world's greatest architectural masterpieces.

The chapter, 'Architecture', covers this in more detail.

b- The Festival Temple of Twthomosis III

The columns here are tapered in reverse, i.e. narrower at the bottom than at the top. The style of these columns together with their capitals are shaped in reversed calyxes, gives this temple a special tent-like effect.

3- At the Luxor Temple

a- **The Colonnade of Amenhotep III** consists of a double row of seven smooth papyrus columns. Seven is the number symbolizing 'process'. The tall graceful columns represent clustered papyrus stalks with budded capitals.

b- **The Hypostyle Hall** consists of thirty-two densely packed columns. The paving stone of the floor at the base of the columns, show the chiseled successive phases of the moon. The moon is new at the southernmost row of columns. The second row shows the crescent moon. The third and fourth rows show the growing size of the moon,, up to a full size.

Chapter 40

The Egyptian Calendar

The ancient Egyptians knew, a long time before their dynastic history, how to keep track of time, with great accuracy. Their calendar was superior to the Julian and Gregorian calendars, which would not come until much later.

When Julius Caesar came to Egypt in 48 B.C., he was impressed by the Egyptian calendar and he commissioned the astronomer Sosigenes (from Alexandria) to introduce a calendar into the Roman Empire. This resulted in the Julian calendar of 365 days a year and 366 days every leap year.

The Julian calendar, however, did not take into account that the year is a bit longer than 365 1/4 days. In 1582 A.D., the Gregorian calendar attempted to fix this error, however it was still off by about one full day every 3000 years.

In their attempts to have a different looking calendar than the Egyptian system, both the Julian and the Gregorian calendars fell short of the exact system, as developed by the Egyptians.

- The ancient Egyptians knew that the year was slightly over 365 1/4 days. The earth takes 365.25636 days to complete one revolution around the sun. The ancient Egyptians were completely aware of this fact, as evidenced at the Abu Simbel

Temple of Ramses II. Located at the back of its sanctuary, 180 feet away from the only opening to the Abu Simbel Temple, is a statue of Ramses II, among other statues. The rays of the sun have illuminated his statue, next to Amon's statue, on February 22 (his coronation day) of each year for more than 3,200 years. The difference, between 365.25 days and 365.25636 days, over a span of 3,200 years, is 20 days. If such a minute difference of 0.00636 days per year was not accounted for, the date of illumination of the statue would have changed, from its original date, many years ago. The illumination of the Ramses II statue has been perfect for all these 3,200 years, because they knew the exact length of the year to a level of accuracy as high, if not higher, than we do nowadays. Moreover, they were able to construct a monument with a perfect precision, to match their perfect calculations.

• When the Aswan Dam was being built in the 1960's, the Abu Simbel Temple was in direct line of the High Dam Lake, and would have been submerged. The best engineers in the west arrived in Egypt, to move the Abu Simbel Temple, to a higher ground. In spite of careful planning and calculations, these engineers moved the temple, but caused the illumination to occur a day later, i.e. February 23. Who knows, if the illumination will continue to fall on this new date for another 3,200 years, now that the temple has been moved by modern day engineers.

• Having a perfect calendar requires knowledge of astronomy, of which the ancient Egyptians had superior skills. This should not come as a surprise, because everything in their lives, no matter how mundane, was related to cosmography.

The assigning of numbers to anything in ancient Egypt was based on specific cosmological reasons. Anything to do with time keeping was based on the number six or its multiples. The day is 24 (6 x 4) hours. The hour is 60 minutes (6 x 10), and the minute is 60 seconds. The month was 30 days (6 x 5). The year was 12 months (6 x 2), plus a fraction. The fraction is equivalent to a bit over 5 1/4 days.

• An embodiment of their knowledge of the calendar is evident in one of their oldest mythological fables. After establishing that each year contains twelve months, and each month contains thirty days, Mercury played dice with the Moon. Mercury won from her 'the five days of epact', which were added to complete the 365 days of the year. This fable originated thousands of years before the history of dynastic Egypt.

Isis

• Also during these very remote periods, Isis was associated with the star Sirius (the brightest star in heaven), whose annual rising ushered in the Nile's inundation and the Egyptian New Year. This fact is clearly acknowledged in the Webster dictionary which defines the **Sothic year** as:

- *"of having to do with Sirius, the Dog Star"*
- *"Designating or of an ancient Egyptian cycle or period of time based on fixed year of 365 1/4 days (Sothic Year) and equal to 1,460 such years."*

The length of each year was computed from one rising of the Dog Star (Sirius) to another. It was therefore called the "Sothic year". But the annual rising of Sirius was not made the beginning of the year because Sirius appears to move in a spiral orbit, from one year to another. The Sothic period was fixed when Sirius was visible again at the same spot, at the beginning of the period (1460 Sothic years equal 1461 solar years).

• Adopting the Sothic year meant an adjustment for the slightly shorter solar year (1460 Sothic years equals 1461 solar years). Surviving records show that the Sothic year was fixed in the year 1322 B.C., but we don't know if this was the first time, or if such adjustments occurred in prior Sothic periods.

• As the Sothic period was fixed in 1322 B.C., the observation and calculation of the differences between the solar and Sothic cycles must have started at a very remote age.

The shown writing is a memorandum from the Overseer of the temple to the Lector-priest notifying him that Sirius would rise on the sixteenth day of the fourth month, so as to take note of its exact location and time.

• The first direct notice of the five days of epact is evidenced on a box at Turin of the time of Amunoph III. Egyptologist M. de Rouge has shown that the five days of epact were used in the Twelfth Dynasty (1991-1783 B.C.), and that <u>the Festival of Sothic was celebrated at that time, as well.</u>

• Having a perfect calendar should not surprise anyone, because a year of exactly 365 days is inadequate for people who rely on agriculture for their livelihood. The most careless observation would show that a whole month would be lost every 120 years. The rise of the Nile, the time of sowing and reaping, and all other time-related agricultural activities, would no longer coincide with the same month. As such, adding a 1/4 of a day to the year (an additional full day every four years), began before the history of dynastic Egypt, to remedy the defect. Additional adjustments were also implemented to fix the Sothic period every 1461 years, and thus having a perfect calendar, as evidenced at Abu Simbel Temple.

For ordinary purposes, such as the dates of their kings and other events, ancient Egyptians continued to use the vague year of 365 days. Every calculation could thus be corrected, by comparing the time of the list with that of the Sothic or sidereal year.

• Modern day Egyptians, unofficially, still follow the Coptic calendar, which is the same as the ancient Egyptian calendar, for agricultural, weather, and other matters. It is by far the most practical and accurate calendar in use in the world, for even the dates of the four seasons, of the Julian or the Gregorian calendars, do not coincide with the actual weather patterns.

Chapter 41

The High Seas

General

• Columbus Day is an annual national holiday in the U.S.A. celebrating the idea that Christopher Columbus allegedly discovered North America. Scandanavian countries claim that the Vikings had been to North America, many years before Columbus.

• It was a Scandanavian adventurer who some decades ago wanted to prove the possibility that ancient Egyptians may have reached the New World before any European sailor. He was intrigued by the **pyramids in Mexico** and wanted to prove the possibility that they were the influence, if not the actual work, of ancient Egyptians. He made a simple boat out of papyrus reeds and set sail from the west coast of Africa to the Americas. He assumed that ancient Egyptians were primitive in their knowledge of boats' construction and navigation. Nevertheless, the trip was successful, and he proved his theory.

A few years after that successful sail, the Cheops boat was found next to the great pyramid. That boat, housed now in a musuem next to the Great Pyramid, is superior and much more seaworthy than Columbus' Mayflower or the Vikings' ships. The physical evidence is clear that the Egyptians had the means to go on the high seas. Sizes of even larger ships than Cheops' will be detailed later.

• Cosmography was the basis of all aspects of life in ancient Egypt. As such they were very aware and knowledgeable of astronomy since the earliest times. It was this type of knowledge which facilitated many aspects of their life such as traveling.

This may sound far-fetched in an age where it seems that computers do almost everything for us. But we should remember that when the U.S. spacecraft Apollo 13's computer system failed, the astronauts were able to come back safely to earth and on target, using their knowledge in astronomy and simple science.

- Travel in ancient days was much more extensive and common, than is generally imagined.

- The needs of a civilized society, such as the ancient Egyptians, were not fully satisfied by the produce of the homeland, and trade routes were developed to far away places. The Nile was navigable throughout the length of Egypt. The Red Sea gave access to Africa and the Far East. The Mediterranian Sea gave them access to countries in and around the area, and, dare we say, even to northern Europe and the Americas.

- Timber suitable for large scale carpentry and for boat building was imported from **Syria** and **Lebanon**. Arsenic copper was imported for the most part from **Cyprus**. Tin was imported from **Asia** and/or **Europe**. Lapis Lazuli came from **Afghanistan**. The natural volcanic glass, obsidian, was from **Abyssinian** origin. Trade routes were developed with **Crete**, the **Greek Islands** and **Greece**.

- Egypt had a strong and formidable navy to protect its shores and its overseas trade routes. More about the navy later.

- Where else did the Egyptians go? Here are some possibilities.

1- Stonehenge in **England** resembles stumpy Heliopoloitan obelisks. Stonehenge is believed to be an ancient astronomical observatory, located in an ancient religious center. The same thing can be said of the obelisks at Egyptian temples. The structures at Stonehenge are possible imitations of the much older Egyptian obelisks.

   In the graves and burial plots clustered around the Stonehenge area, blue Egyptian faince beads (known as mummy beads) had been discovered. How did they get there?

   Was there a direct Egyptian contact? Or perhaps, was it the Egyptians' seafaring and mercantile neighbors from Crete and Mycenaean Greece who may have gone to pre-Roman Britain, taking Egyptian beads and stones with them?

   Egypt had to import tin. Did it come from **Britain**? The Phoenicians first visited the British coasts in search of tin, about 400-450 B.C. Tin was used many centuries previously, in making bronze vessels and implements, at Thebes and other parts of Egypt. Were the Phoenicians following the Egyptians, in search of tin from Britain?

2- There is not much dispute that Egypt had reached the shores of **western Africa**, the **Arabian Sea**, the **Indian Ocean** and **India**.

Since they had the knowledge and vessels to travel that distance, why do some want to dismiss the possibility that they went further?!

3- Among the many bottles found in the tombs of Thebes, and other places, there was a considerable number of Chinese manufactured bottles bearing inscriptions in that language.

Chinese bottles found in the Egyptian tombs.

There is no evidence whatsoever, as some suggested, that these Chinese bottles were deposited, all over numerous ancient Egyptian tombs, by later Moslem population. And besides, why would they do it?!
It is also worth noting that the older statues of Buddha bear a striking resemblance to those of Amon's. Were there contacts between ancient Egypt and **China**?

4- In **Mexico**, we hear about a civilization which came from nowhere and in a very short time it disappeared abruptly into thin air. They left behind some pyramids and other ruins.

Later we shall see that Cheops boat, which is at least 4500 years old, is more seaworthy than Columbus' Mayflower or the best Viking ships, which means that ancient Egyptians were capable of traveling great distances.

If a simple boat made of papyrus reeds can cross the Atlantic Ocean, a boat similar to Cheops boat could have made it to Mexico with no problem whatsoever.

Maybe Egyptians wrote about their adventures and the records were destroyed by Arab invaders. Maybe it was not a big deal and there was no need to brag about it. They have never bragged about anything anyway unlike the current trend of labeling everything we do as a *'New frontier'*, *'breakthrough'* or *'invention'*, ...etc.

Their Ships

- Since navigation was the principal means of transport, the Egyptians built a whole range of practical boats, well adapted to different uses and to the geography and climate.

- Ships varied enormously in size. Some of them were huge. Diodorus mentions one, made of cedar, built during Sesostris' reign, which measured about 450 feet. Another boat, this time a military vessel, built on the orders of Ptolemy Philopator, was of the same length, but was 75 feet wide and 100 feet high. According to Diodorus it could carry four hundred sailors, four thousand oarsmen and three thousand soldiers. This certainly seems a heavy load, besides which the passengers must have been very cramped!

- There were some very large freighters, used for transporting grain, stone, bricks and even the gigantic obelisks, which were hewn out of a single block in the quarries of Aswan, and then carried on the river to the site of the temple, where they were triumphantly erected.

- There was also a naval fleet, the size of which varied according to the defense needs of the country, at a given period. The sailors of the Royal Navy "King's Ships" were specially trained for the sea.

Herodotus and Diodorus both mentioned the fleet of long vessels, or ships of war, fitted out by Sesostris on the Arabian Sea. There were four hundred ships. As such, the trade, and the means of protecting it by ships of war, existed there, at least as early as the 12th Dynasty, about two thousand years B.C.

- These commercial and naval ships were served with several ports, guiding landmarks, water markers, loading and unloading facilities. Several roads, along with supply stations were provided between the seaports and the populated centers along the Nile.

- **Cheops Boat**

  It is at least 4500 years old, and is presently housed in a musuem next to the great pyramid at Giza.

  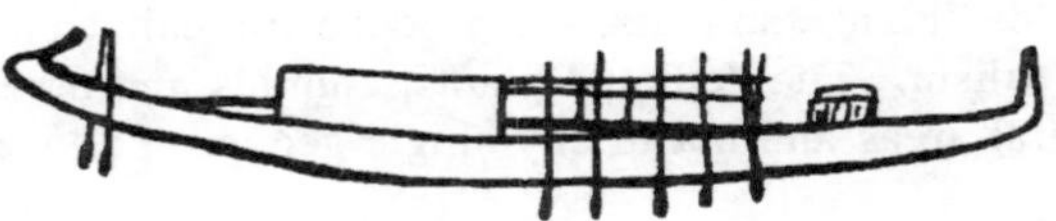

  The Cheops boat is one of the largest ancient boats found to date. For instance, the extreme length of Viking boats found in Europe was not more than 98.5 ft. (30 m), while the Cheops boat is 142.5 ft. (43.4 m) long. It is about 19.4 ft. (5.9 m) wide and 5.75 ft. (1.75 m) deep and has a displacement of over 40 tons. The prow, formed in the shape of a papyrus-bundle, is about 20 ft. (6 m) tall. Its stern rises to 23 ft. (7 m). Its rudder consists of two massive oars. The boat has several cabins on its deck.

  The ropes were used to bind together the various parts of the boat in a most peculiar manner, and no metal nails were used in its building.

  There is some evidence that the Cheops boat was actually used in water. Marks caused by abrasion between the ropes, which shrink when wet, and the wood of the vessel, which expands in water, are still clearly visible in many places.

  The exact function of the boat is unknown. In any case it is a remarkable piece of evidence that ancient civilizations were <u>thoroughly familiar with the surface of the entire globe</u>.

The Punt Question

- Erroneous statements have been repeated again and again about the Punt Expedition, as portrayed in the Hatshepsut Temple on the west bank of Thebes. There are those who insist on giving answers where there are no answers and as a result, they have publicized that Punt is Ethiopia or Somaliland. There is not a single piece of evidence to support their supposed geographic location of Punt.

- Punt was always referred to in the Egyptian texts as a Holy Land, and that some neterw were born in Punt. All indications lead to the conclusion that Punt was a mythical and not a geographical location.

- While the setting of the scene, in Hatshepsut's temple, is unmistakably African, there are numerous geological, racial, and botanical un-African matters, in these supposedly realistic friezes. Semitic and African races are shown together, or in adjacent scenes where they never lived side by side. Plants, animals, and produce are realized in the carvings with graphic realism. The depicted plants, animals and other items are native to several areas and not to any single geographic location.

- There is no agreement on the geographic location of the mysterious Punt, or the purpose of the expedition, or why it was given such prominence in the Hatshepsut temple colonnade.

- Hatshepsut was not the only Pharaoh who recorded non-historical events, as if they were historical. The walls of temples built by other Pharaohs of the New Kingdom are typically covered with battle scenes which have symbolic significance, and a suspect historical content. These battle scenes are actually symbolic representations of the battle between the forces of Inner Light and Inner Darkness. In the same light, we may be reasonably safe in assuming that these seemingly realistic Punt friezes serve some analogous purpose. Accordingly, Hatshepsut journeyed peaceably to the Holy Land of Punt with its foreign (i.e., barbarous) races with exotic merchandise and animals. She also extended the civilizing influence of Egypt by setting up statues of the neterw. As such, she accomplished by peaceful symbolic interaction, what the other Pharaohs accomplished by symbolic conquest.

Chapter 42

Magic and Evolution

• Magic, in its various forms, enters into a very large body of Egyptian texts. In our modern age, magic is often equated with superstition or illusion trickery. When we review the meanings of the word *magic* in the dictionary, we find that one of its meanings is very close to the ancient Egyptian understanding.

Magic = *"Any mysterious, seemingly inexplicable or extraordinary power or influence."*

Magic is the mysterious or unknown factor in a process, of any kind.

• We may shy away from using the word magic, but we use its meaning in various shapes and forms. If something works against all known scientific reasonings, we explain it by saying *"By the grace of God"*. We may also use the expressions *"miracle"*, *"power of the mind"*, *"supernatural"*, *"mind over matter"*, ...etc.

In short we have only substituted the word magic with other phrases and words, but the meaning does not change a bit.

• There are people who can captivate their audience not so much by what they say, but how they say it. Faith healers and some preachers claim great accomplishments with their followers. This type of power exists and its influence and results are evident.

• Magic for ancient Egyptians was the profound understanding of cosmic resonances.

The location of the sun and the moon affects the tides of the waters of the earth (approx. 4/5 of its surface is water) on a daily, monthly and seasonal basis. Water tides are the result of cosmic resonances. We, as human beings, are made mostly of water and therefore we must be subject to the same influence, of the stars in the cosmos. This is called astrology.

- Magic, for the ancient Egyptians, was the principle underlying the transformation of the world. Upon God's command, his Word created the flesh of man. Magic is what caused the Word to be transformed into flesh. Many things in our lives go through the process of transformation from one form to another, such as transforming matter (food) to energy. We may be able to explain the process. However, the force that caused the processes to occur remains a mystery. This unknown force was called "magic" by Egyptians and it has a new name in our modern times: Evolution.

Evolution, in the dictionary is defined generally as:

> *"A process of change in a certain direction."*

- Most of the Egyptian incantation/spells were derived from religious texts. They were very similar to our modern day praying. They were meant to set the healing process into motion, so that the person becomes whole again, victorious over the invaders of his/her body and soul.

- One can also equate the magical spells (even if the spell is the proper interpretation of the Egyptian word) with exorcism. In many cases, it may not be the meaning of the words of the "spell" which are important but rather the vibration and rhythm of its delivery, which have influence on specific energies in the person.

Egyptian magic must have been based on vibrations that we don't understand, because it's important that one use the correct tone of voice when uttering the spell. This is consistent with how a speaker can captivate an audience, how hypnotism works and why faith healers are successful with their patients.

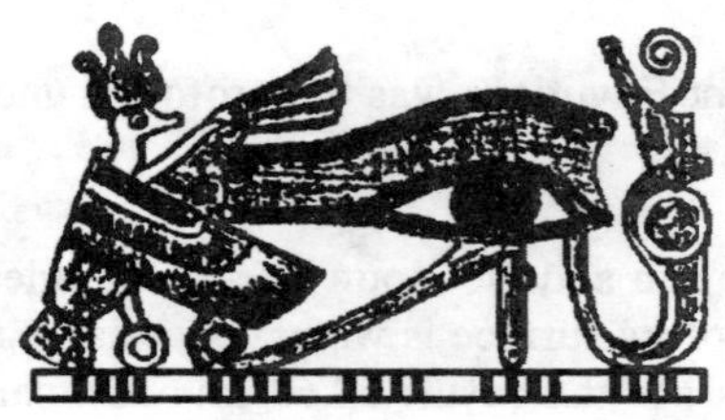

Chapter 43

Health and Medicine

General

• We continuously hear of *'western medicine'*, *'modern medicine'*, *'scientific medicine'*, ... etc. All these terms infer that medicine from other regions and other ages do not count. So we seek the definitions of the words *Health* and *Medicine*, in the Webster dictionary.

Health: *"Physical and mental well-being; freedom from disease, pain or defect; normality of physical and mental functions, soundness."*

Medicine: *"The science and art of diagnosing, treating, curing and preventing disease, relieving pain, and improving and preserving health."*

• The practice of health and medicine in ancient Egypt is closer to the above definitions than *'modern medicine'*.

Good health, to Egyptians, meant wholeness, integration and preservation. Healing, for them, was the search for wholeness, not just for our bodies, but for our souls, our minds, our spirits, our relationships, and for the environment around us.

• As modern studies progress into such areas as the psychological aspects of healing, and effects of sound waves upon the body (ultrasound is commonly used in advanced surgery; infrasound is known to have powerful disruptive capacities), ancient Egyptian magic and the incantation may come in for serious consideration.

• Surgical operations were performed by the ancient Egyptians, even in pre-Dynastic times. Mummies were found which have very neatly cut parts of the skull, indicating a highly advanced level of brain surgery. A number of skulls have been found indicating the nature of the operations; and that the patient sometimes survived, as is proved by the fact that the severed section of the skull had knit to the parent bone.

- When the first Egyptian medical papyri were deciphered, the German scholars responsible were shocked. They called Egyptian medicine *"sewage pharmacology"* because Egyptians treated various inflammations, infections and wounds by applying dung and similar substances.

The later invention of penicillin and antibiotics in recent decades, has made us realize that the ancient Egyptians were applying rudimental and organic versions of these remedies. What the Germans described as "sewage pharmacology" was recently ratified as "modern medicine". Moreover, Egyptians knew of the different types of antibiotics. The Egyptian prescriptions called for specific types of antibiotics to correspond to specific maladies.

- Scholars, studying the ancient Egyptian techniques of furnishing statues with inlaid eyes, concluded that the Egyptians must have understood not only the anatomy of the eye but also its refractive properties. The Egyptians approximated those properties by using combinations of stones and crystals (up to four different kinds, in a single eye). When photographs are taken of these Egyptian statues, the eyes actually look real.

- Today's familiar sign for presciption, Rx, originated in ancient Egypt. In the second Century, Galen used mystic symbols to impress patients. Accordingly, he borrowed from the Egyptian myth: the eye of Horus. The myth tells how Horus attacked his uncle to avenge his father's murder. In the fight, Horus' eye was torn into fragments, whereupon Thoth restored it completely. The complete eye had come to mean whole, unharmed and was used in hieroglyphic writing to represent wholesomeness and unity.

The eye symbol has gradually evolved into today's familiar sign for 'prescription', Rx, which is used throughout the world no matter which language is used.

International Reputations

- Many of the Egyptian remedies and prescriptions have been passed on to Europe via the writings of Pliny, Dioscorides, Galen and other Greek writers.

- Warren R. Dawson, in The Legacy of Egypt, writes:

> *The works of the classical writers are...often merely the stepping-stones by which much of the ancient medical lore reached Europe, apart from direct borrowings...From Egypt we have the earliest medical books, the first observations in anatomy, the first experiments in surgery and pharmacy, the first use of splints, bandages, compresses and other appliances, and the first anatomical and medical vocabulary...*

- It is evident that the medical science of the Egyptians was sought and appreciated in foreign countries. Herodotus told us that Cyrus and Darius both sent to Egypt for medical men. In later times too, they continued to be celebrated for their skill: Ammianus says it was enough for a doctor to say he had studied in Egypt, to recommend him. Pliny also mentioned medical men going from Egypt to Rome.

- The care which the Egyptians took of their health was a source of astonishment for foreign observers, particularly Greeks and Romans. Pliny thought that the large number of doctors meant that the population of Egypt suffered from a great number of diseases—a paradoxical piece of logic. Herodotus, on the other hand, thought that there were no healthier people than the Egyptians.

Medical Profession

The Physicians

- The names and titles of more than a hundred doctors were determined from archaelogical findings, with sufficient detail to uncover an overall picture of the medical practice. The name of Imhotep has become forever linked with Egyptian medicine. He was vizier, architect and chief physician to the Pharaoh Djoser (Third Dynasty). During the Greek Period he was deified and identified with Asklepios, the Greek god of healing.

• As far back as the Old Kingdom, the medical profession was highly organized, with doctors holding a variety of ranks and specialities. The ordinary doctor was outranked by the *'overseer of doctors'* the *'chief of doctors'*, the *'eldest of doctors'* and the *'inspector of doctors'*. Above all these practitioners, was the *'overseer of doctors of Upper and Lower Egypt'*. A distinction was made between physicians and surgeons, the latter being known as the *'priests of the netert Sekhmet'*.

• Pliny reported that the Egyptians examined the bodies after death, to ascertain the nature of the diseases of which they had died. This was definitely an effective method of acquiring knowledge and experience.

• In an earlier chapter 'Neterw, The Angels of God', the term angels was defined by the Metaphysical Bible Dictionary as those who *"guard and guide and direct the natural forces of mind and body, which have in them the future of the whole man".*

Ancient Egyptian medicine had a similar concept to the above definition. The human body was divided, according to ancient Egyptians, into 36 parts and each came under the protection of a certain neter/netert (patron saint) such as:

Isis for the liver
Nephthys for the lungs
Hathor for childbirth

Each physician was well trained, and practiced only in his area of specialization.

• There were eye doctors, bowel specialists *'Guardians of the Anus'*, physicians who specialized in internal diseases *'who know the secret and specialize in the body fluids'*, nose doctors, *'sickness of the upper air passages'*, doctor of the abdomen, and dentists.

Childbirth was basically the province of the midwives. Herodotus saw in that a sign of scientific advancement, and the result of truly profound knowledge.

• There were also female doctors. Doctor Peseshet (Fourth or early Fifth Dynasty) had the title of *'Lady Director of Lady Physicians'*.

The Conduct & Practice

- Egyptian doctors were highly specialized. Herodotus points out that *"they could practice no branch other than their own"*.

- Egyptian doctors had a special status. Physicians administered their treatments in accordance with a written law, which was composed in ancient times by many famous physicians. After being authorized to practice their art, on completion of certain prescribed studies, they were officially approved and drew their salary, like any other civil servant, from public funds. They could be summoned at any moment and had to provide care for the needy, free of charge. They were under State supervision. If their patients failed to get better, or died, the State could inquire into the reasons for such a failure, and make sure that the doctor had followed the rules of his art. Diodorus thought that these rules were based on the belief that tradition and past experience were the safest guarantee of any therapy. A doctor who was proved negligent was subject to punishments, in accordance with the applicable laws.

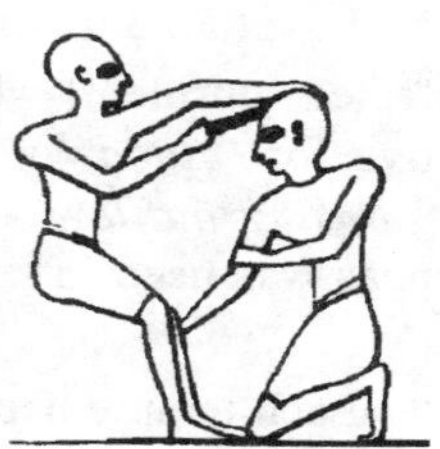

- Some surgical tools and instruments are depicted in tombs and temples, such as:

  - The Tomb of Ankh-mahor, at Saqqara contained several unique medical and surgical reliefs. Among them was a flint knife which some considered as evidence of its remote origin. The most recent surgical research however, is vindicating the flint instruments of antiquity. It has been found that for certain neurological and optical operations, obsidian possesses qualities that cannot be matched by the finest steel, and an updated version of the old flint knife is coming back into use.

  - On the outer corridor wall of the temple at Kom Ombo, a box of surgical instruments is carved in relief. The box includes metal shears, surgical knives, saws, probes, spatulas, small hooks and forceps.

- Although no surgical scars have been reported in mummies (apart from embalmers' incisions), there are thirteen references in the Smith Papyrus to 'stitching'. The Papyrus also mentions wounds being brought together with adhesive tape which was made of linen. Linen was also available for bandages, ligatures and sutures. Needles were probably of copper.

• Egyptian doctors distinguished between sterile (clean) wounds and infected (purulent) wounds. The former were written using the determinative for *'blood'* or *'phlegm'* and the latter, using the determinative for *'stinking outflow'* or *'feces'*. A mixture of ibex fat, fir oil and crushed peas was used in an ointment to clean an infected wound.

• Each temple had a full-scale laboratory, where medications were made and stocked.

The Medical Library

• Some time ago in pre-Dynastic Egypt, there were six books on medicine which were attributed/inspired by or dedicated to Thoth. He is the personification of divine intellect, the patron of Learning and Literature. The first of these medical books was related to anatomy.

Another book on anatomy was written during the reign of Athothis (c. 3000 B.C.).

• According to a Christian writer, Alexandrinus Clemens, living in Alexandria in about AD 200, the priests of Early Dynastic Egypt had written the sum total of their knowledge in forty two (42) sacred books which were kept in the temples and were carried in religious processions. Six of these books were concerned totally with medicine, and dealt with anatomy, diseases in general, surgery, remedies, diseases of the eye and diseases of women. No examples of these books survived, nor of the anatomy books, said to have been written during Athothis' reign.

• Several medical papyri have survived the ages. They contain prescriptions for treating diseases of the lungs, liver, stomach, bladder and for various afflictions of the head and scalp (including recipes for preventing the hair falling out or turning grey). They also contain prescriptions for rheumatic and arthritic complaints and for woman's diseases. The following is a summary of the major medical papyri:

Edwin Smith Papyrus

- It has been dated to about 1600 B.C. The presence of Old Kingdom words in the text, suggest that the Papyrus was copied from earlier work around 2500 B.C. when the pyramids were built.

  This is the earliest book of surgery in the world. It contains a total of forty-eight surgical cases, of traumatic nature, methodically arranged from the head and generally going down the body to the lower limbs.

- Each case is preceded by a brief caption expressing a summary diagnosis, followed by another detailed diagnosis, a brief but clearly formulated prognosis and sometimes the therapy.

- The diagnosis was established, after extraordinarily precise observations had been made. In its conclusion it proposed three possibilities: a doctor could act with full success, he could try, with some chances of success, or he stood no chance at all, in which case he should do nothing.

  The techniques were numerous and varied. Fractures were properly set, splints were applied, and wounds were sutured. There was a sort of adhesive plaster which worked wonders with broken bones. Perfectly healed fractures can be seen in numerous mummies.

- The most exciting sentences are to be found right at the beginning of this papyrus:

  > ***The counting of anything with the fingers [is done] to recognize the way the heart goes. There are vessels in it leading to every part of the body ... When a Sekhmet priest, any doctor ... puts his fingers to the head ... to the two hands, to the place of the heart ... it speaks ... in every vessel, every part of the body.***

  The medical papyrus proves that the Egyptians understood the relationship of the heart to the circulation of the blood, and that they believed the heart to be the source of life within the body, and they felt the pulse and measured it, by comparison with their own pulses.

- The Egyptians also believed that all the 'inner juices of the body' flowed through vessels radiating from the heart and collected at the anus, whence they could again be redistributed to various parts of the body. Air, blood, urine, mucus, semen and feces flowed around the system, usually in harmony, but occasionally getting out of hand and thence causing an illness.

- The Smith Papyrus contains what is probably the first documented description of the human brain:

  When you examine a man with a ... wound on his head, which goes to the bone; his skull is broken; broken open is the brain of his skull ... these windings which arise in poured metal. Something is there ... that quivers (and) flutters under your fingers like the weak spot in the head of a child which has not yet grown hard ... Blood flows from his two nostrils.

- Advances in modern neurology prove that the Egyptians understood, in detail, the workings of the nervous system, and the relationship between the areas of the brain and the manner in which these areas controlled the bodily functions.

Ebers Medical Papyrus

- The date of its origin is about 1555 B.C. It is considered to be a manual for the teaching of anatomy and pharmacy.

- It contains 876 remedies and mentions 500 different substances used in medical treatments.

- The Ebers Papyrus describes treatment of and prescriptions for stomach complaints, coughs, colds, bites, head ailments and diseases; liver complaints, burns and other kinds of wounds; itching, boils, cysts and the like, complaints in fingers and toes; salves for wounds and pains in the veins, muscles and nerves; diseases of the tongue, toothache, ear pains, women's diseases; beauty preparations, household remedies against vermin, two books about the heart and veins, and diagnosis for tumors.

Kahum Medical Papyrus

- It has been dated between 2100 and 1900 B.C.

- It is devoted to diseases of women and pregnancy.

Berlin Papyrus

- It has been dated between 1350 and 1200 B.C.

- It deals with childbirth and infants.

- It contains a test for pregnancy which recognized that urine carried the pregnancy factor. It calls for steeping some wheat and some barley in her urine. If the wheat sprouts, it will be a boy, if the barley sprouts, it will be a girl.

- In 1963 Ghalioungui found that, whilst urine from non-pregnant women prevented the growth of (modern) barley and wheat, it proved impossible to detect the sex of an unborn child from the rate of growth of either grain, possibly because the grains and the soils were both different in ancient Egypt. Nevertheless, the fact that the Egyptians recognized that urine carried the pregnancy factor was remarkable. The standardization of reliable urine tests for pregnancy did not occur until 1929.

  It is astounding to know that this Egyptian recipe found its way to Europe, for in an ingenious book of the seventeenth century, Peter Boyer wrote: *"Make two holes in the ground, throw barley into the one and wheat into the other, then pour into both the water of the pregnant woman, and cover them up again with earth. If the wheat shoots up before the barley, it will be a boy, but if the barley comes up first, thou must expect a daughter."*

  There is also a little English book, called 'The Experienced Midwife', in which this recipe appears, in a somewhat modified form.

The Hearst Papyrus

- It has been dated to about 1550 B.C. and it appears to be the guideline for a practicing physician.

- It contains over 250 prescriptions and spells, and has a section on bones and bites, afflictions of fingers, tumors, burns, diseases of women, ears, eyes and teeth.

The Chester Beatty Papyrus

- It has been dated around 1200 B.C.

- It deals with the diseases of the anus and rectum and gives appropriate presciptions and remedies.

Cures & Prescriptions

• Homer, in the Odyssey, describes the many valuable medicines given by Polydamna, the wife of Thonis, to Helen while in Egypt, *"a country whose fertile soil produces an infinity of drugs, some salutary and some pernicious; where each physician possesses knowledge above all other men."*

Pliny frequently mentioned the Egyptian products, and their use in medicine.

• The ancient Egyptians had full knowledge of the uses of herbs and natural therapies, to the extent that they perfected the procedure of embalming the corpses of their dead, a feat which modern man is yet unable to conquer.

• The various prescriptions in the Ebers and Hearst papyri, as well as other medical papyri, seem to be quite rational and natural applications, for the alleviation of symptoms. These prescriptions are the product of knowledge of general physiological properties and actions of plants, animals and minerals as well as the human body.

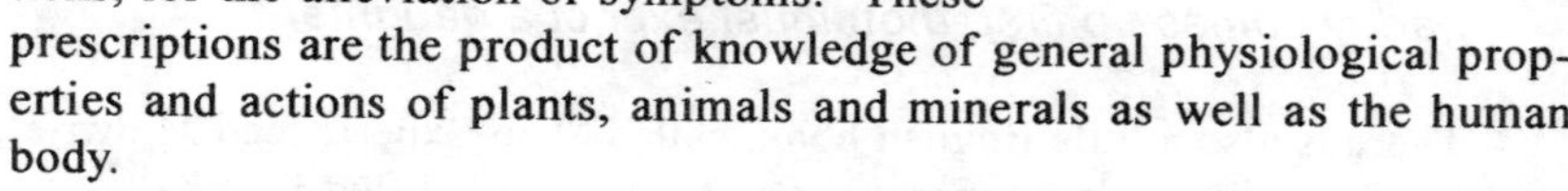

• The Ebers Papyrus, alone, contains 876 remedies and mentions 500 substances, used in medical treatment. It gives recipes for many remedies, such as plasters, balms and ointments, of vegetable, mineral and also animal origin.

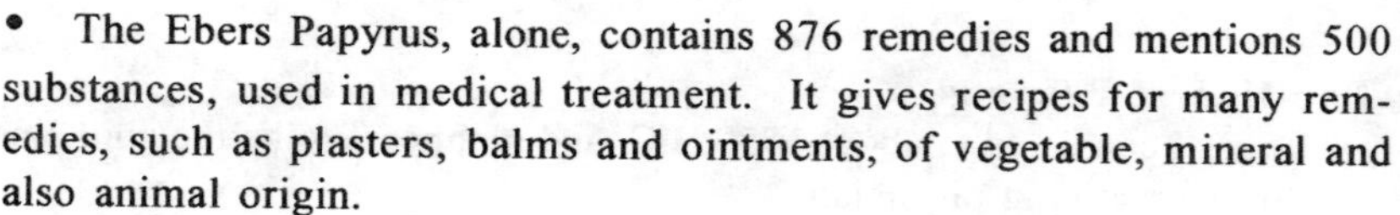

The ingredients were sometimes crushed, and sometimes boiled or blended. They may be sifted through a piece of fabric. They may be diluted with clear water, beer, wine, oil, or milk.

• From the Ebers Papyrus we learn that a single prescription may include as many as 35 substances.

- Presciptions were given in different forms, either as a drink or in the form of pills or as a rubbing oil or fomentation. Some prescriptions were inhaled.

- They weighed and measured their prescriptions very carefully.

- Dosages of medicine varied according to the age, weight and sex of the patient.

- Incantations (magical spells) were spoken over various remedies in order to endow them, with the right power. (Read about the meaning of magic in ancient Egypt, in the previous chapter).

Incantations varied from one medical papyrus to another. For example, the Ebers papyrus contains very few of them, compared to other papyri, which may mean that the doctor who compiled this particular book of recipes, from older sources, had a lower opinion than others, of the importance of incantations.

- Medical plants were well known. Dozens of them were used as ingredients for medicine, such as those in castor oil.

Medical plants not native to Egypt were introduced during the Dynastic Period and continue to flourish to the present time.

- Many important raw materials, used in the manufacture of medicines, came from outside Egypt. From Syria and Asia Minor came fir (Abies cilicia Carr.), its pungent resin, invaluable as an antiseptic and an embalming material. Oil of fir was used as an anthelmintic, and to clean infected wounds. From eastern Africa came aloe, used to 'expel catarrh from the nose', and cinnamon (Cinnamonium zeylanicum Nees), an essential ingredient in an unguent for ulcerated gums and in incense.

- An important constituent in most remedies was honey. Honey is highly resistant to bacterial growth. It also has an antibiotic action due to the presence of a bactericidal enzyme called inhibine. In modern studies honey has proven to be effective against staphylococcus, salmonella and candida bacteria. It is also used to treat surgical wounds, burns and ulcers, having more rapid healing qualities than conventional treatment.

- Another bee product called propolis (bee glue) is a hard, resinous material derived by bees from plant juices, and is used by bees to seal cracks in their hives. Propolis also has antibiotic as well as preservative properties. A small mouse, which crept into an ancient Egyptian hive three thousand years ago, was found perfectly preserved, covered with propolis, and with no sign of decomposition.

- Beer is also mentioned as an agent by which many drugs were administered, and beer was a popular and healthy drink.

- They knew and used the benefits of yeast, applying it raw to boils and ulcers, and swallowing it to clear digestive disorders. Yeast contains vitamin B as well as antibiotic agents.

- Earlier we mentioned the use of antibiotics in ancient Egypt, to treat wounds or open sores.

Dental

- The Ancient Egyptians had few dental troubles. Nevertheless they were treated by skilled dental surgeons, as evident in a tomb from the pyramid period, where a skull was found showing clear evidence of a successful operation, for the drainage of an abcess at the root of the first molar. Another skull showed two teeth skillfully tied together with gold wire, evidently to fasten a loose tooth to its more stable neighbor, to prevent it from falling out.

- Their dentists also adopted a method, which was recently implemented, in our times, of capping teeth with gold, as evident from some mummies of Thebes.

Chapter 44

Science and Technology

General

• It is the common belief of the modern world that our society is the most advanced that ever existed, and that all science prior to our era was undeveloped.

Despite the prejudices against ancient Egypt by the modern religions and the derision of the western rationalists, there has never been a match for the Egyptian doctrine in which science, theology, philosophy and art were fused into a grand synthesis.

The entire Egyptian doctrine was based on how the spiritual is generated and how it interacts with the physical aspect. In our modern times, we tend to separate the study of the physical aspects (we call it science) from the study of the spiritual aspects (we call it religion). For the Egyptian, the physical and the spiritual are intertwined and interrelated.

It is this fusion that left the world with unmatched accomplishments. Our modern science remains piecemeal and unable to handle the non-quantifying factors of life such as the spiritual, emotional and psychological aspects. As our modern science solves some problems, they are causing problems on other fronts. Nobody can deny that social and family matters are getting worse and worse.

• Science in ancient Egypt intertwines with other aspects of life and cannot be easily carved out as a separate subject. Our attempt here is to try to reach the minds of our modern societies, and in carving the subject of science and technology out of the whole synthesis we shall lose many aspects of the subject. I apologize to the ancient Egyptians.

• Egyptian writings always showed an enthusiastic reverence for learning. A father tells his son:

"Give thy heart to learning and love her like a mother for there is nothing that is so precious as learning."

And about the importance of learning to the individual, he tells him:

"Behold there is no profession which is not governed. It is only the learned man who rules himself."

- Science, as defined in Webster's dictionary, is:

"Systemized knowledge derived from observation carried on in order to determine the nature of what is being studied."

Technology is defined as:

"Technical method of achieving practical purposes."

The ancient Egyptians have met these definitions and a lot more.

Astronomy

- A few decades ago, those who suggested that astronomy had reached an advanced state, long before the invention of the telescope, were generally ridiculed or ignored. But in the past few decades, the evidence has mounted overwhelmingly. Many scholars now accept that the precession of the equinoxes (supposedly discovered by the Greeks) was actually known, in pre-Dynastic times.

- Astronomers studying Egypt have long argued that Egyptian astronomy was highly advanced, that the precession of the equinoxes was known to them, as was the heliocentric system, and many other phenomena supposedly only recently discovered.

- Egyptian mythology, which is much older than the dynastic Egyptian history, is fully based on cosmology and cosmogony. As such, astronomy was known to them, long before the recorded history of dynastic Egypt.

- Astronomy in ancient Egypt was closely related to their agricultural civilization. Observations, measurements and calculations were made for the rising Nile: seasons, and the period of the annual return of the inundation. Astronomical knowledge was the only way to organize their agricultural activities.

• A systematic kind of astronomical observation began in very early times. The most ancient astronomical texts, presently known, are found on the lids of wooden coffins dating from the Ninth Dynasty (c. 2150 BC). These texts are called **'diagonal calendars'** or **'diagonal star clocks'**. They give the names of the decans (stars which rose at ten-day intervals at the same time as the sun), of which there were thirty-six. More elaborate star charts were found in the New Kingdom on the ceiling of the tomb of Senenmut, Queen Hatshepsut's architect, and on the ceiling at the temple of Abydos. In the tombs of Ramesses IV, VII, and IX, inscriptions which relate to the first and the sixteenth day of each month, give the position occupied by a star at each of the twelve hours of the night in relation to a seated figure: **'over the left ear'**, **'over the right ear'**, etc.

• Numerous monuments can be found throughout ancient Egypt attesting to their full awareness and knowledge of cosmology and astronomy.

Mathematics

• The numerous monuments of ancient Egypt, with their perfect construction, attest to their superior knowledge, among other things, of mathematics and geometry.

• No documents were ever recovered that show the design and calculations of any of their monuments.

• The famed Egyptologist, Sir J. Gardiner Wilkinson in his book, The Ancient Egyptians, Their Life and Customs, wrote:

> *"... Herodotus, and others, ascribe the origin of geometry to the Egyptians; but the period when it commenced is uncertain. Anticlides pretends that Moaris was the first to lay down the elements of that science, which he says was perfected by Pythagoras; but the latter observation is merely the result of the vanity of the Greeks, which claimed for their countrymen (as in the case of Thales, and other instances) the credit of enlightening a people on the very subjects which they had visited Egypt for the purpose of studying."*

- R. W. Sloley, in The Legacy Of Egypt, writes:

"The Egyptians developed a practical system of numeration and could carry out arithmetical calculations (involving the manipulation of complicated fractional expressions) with ease and accuracy.... He could solve problems involving two unknown quantities and had elementary notions of arithmetical progression using fractions, as well as of geometrical progression. He was familiar with the elementary properties of rectangles, circles and pyramids. Thus he could deal successfully with mathematical problems encountered in his daily life."

- The study of mathematics began long before the found mathematical papyri were written. These found papyri do not set mathematical rules, but they list problems and their solutions. The Rhind Mathematical Papyrus begins with a long table of the division of 2, by odd numbers from 3 to 101, and continues with eighty-four problems of an arithmetical kind which include mensuration, the calculation of areas, and the measurement of angles of slopes. The purpose of writing this papyrus is not known.

- The Egyptians adopted a decimal notation since the earliest times and employed units as high as 1,000,000. Addition and subtraction were used by them. Multiplication, except for the most simple cases in which a number had either to be doubled or to be multiplied by ten, involved a process of doubling and adding, which is, by the way, how the computer process works. Our multiplication tables rely totally on memorization and nothing more and can by no means be considered a human achievement. The computer process is easier, more accurate and faster, as we all know.

- Geometry, to the modern rationalist, is describing the properties of plane, curved or solid figures. In short, it is merely descriptive.

Geometry for the ancients was the means by which humanity could understand the mysteries of the divine order. Geometry was therefore a sacred science to the Egyptians and to the Greeks such as Plato.

- Ancient Egyptians were aware of the functions of diagonals. Even though we consider diagonals to be transcendental numbers, they are not. Only that which can be enumerated is a number. The diagonals symbolize the functions, of creation itself.

The ancient Egyptians knew the transcendental numbers Pi and Phi, by their consistent use of measures, derived from the diagonal of certain squares or rectangles.

• Their knowledge and use of the transcendental number Pi is evident in the design of many monuments. A good example can be found at the Great Pyramid of Giza, where its apex represents the pole and the perimeter represents the equator. This is the reason that the ratio of the perimeter to the height is equal to (2 x Pi).

• The mathematical proportion known as the golden section, expressed mathematically as (1+ square root of 5)/2, was known and used by Egyptians thousands of years before the Greeks. This simply expressed but mysterious proportion (known to us, now as the transcendental number 'Phi') has fascinated architects, artists, philosophers, and scientists of the ancient Greeks and Romans, the Neoplatonic era and of the Renaissance era, especially Leonardo. It continues to fascinate our minds, to the present time.

• The proportions of the Great Pyramid expressed the transcendental number (Phi) with considerable precision.

The floor plan of the so-called "King's Chamber" is a 2 x 1 rectangle, 34' 4" x 17' 2" (10.5 x 5.2 m; 20 x 10 Egyptian cubits). The height of the King's Chamber is 19' 2" (5.8 m). This measure is arrived at by taking one half the length of the diagonal of the floor. This seemingly simple operation is nevertheless mathematically significant. The diagonal of the 2 x 1 rectangle is the square root of five. The modern formula for the proportion called the golden section or Phi is (1 + square root of 5)/2.

• The diagonal of the 2:1 rectangle is very significant. In a religious sense, when the one became two, the result (diagonal) is the universe. The diagonal symbolizes the functions of creation itself.

Earth Science

• In a country which relies on agriculture, geodesy (the science of earth measurement) was developed, long before the time of Menes. Measurement of the superficial area as well as the various elevations of the country were very important, because this information were needed in order to distribute the water to the farmlands, Geodesic data were also needed in the design, construction and operation of canals and dikes.

• The pavilion of Sesostris I (1971-1926 B.C.), at Karnak Temple, incorporates geodesic knowledge in its design, and it also provides a wealth of geodesic information. Its platform acts as a measuring rod set in several simultaneous measurements, like our rulers calibrated in both meters and feet and various other subunits. It has a list of all the provinces of Egypt with their respective land surface areas, proving that actual surveys were made. Major towns are listed, the total length of Egypt is given, and the normal height of the Nile flood noted at three principal points along the length of the river. Much more other useful information is also provided.

Physics

• The Big Bang theory which was described in the ancient Egyptian myths, is now recognized by almost all scientists.

It is ironic that our modern findings lead us to respect and appreciate the ancient Egyptian traditions. Scholars can now find a coherent and consistent system behind the ancient Egyptian cosmology and cosmogony.

• New generations of Egyptologists are now able to communicate the ancient Egyptian myths in modern terms. The modern frontier sciences of high energy physics and molecular biology and genetics can now be related to the ancient Egyptian creation myths.

The more we know, the more we appreciate their knowledge.

• The power of the form of an object cannot yet be defined and quantified by our modern science. The mysterious impact of the pyramid on us, and the well documented pyramid power, signify unknown physical phenomena, yet to be discovered by modern science.

• Optics was a developed science in ancient Egypt. We cannot fully perceive the artistic details of the feathers of birds and other details, as depicted on the walls of temples and tombs, without a magnifying glass.

The art of glass making reached a very high level by the ancient Egyptians. (More about it later this chapter and in the next chapter.)

• Their higher knowledge of sound waves and frequencies and their powers, is evidenced in the delivery of magical phrases, for various purposes.

• The Egyptians had superior knowledge of mechanics. This is evident in the moving and transporting of immense weights, to considerable heights and manipulating them into position with the utmost precision.

They understood and utilized techniques of mechanical balance unknown to us. What would be magic to us was a method to them. They used simple tools but with a highly sophisticated understanding of the principles involved.

No insight was given into the secrets of their mechanical knowledge. Our simplistic explanation of their construction techniques, reflects our ignorance.

• It is amazing that Pliny attributed the invention of the potter's wheel to Coroebus the Athenian. A long time before the recorded history of dynastic Egypt, the neter Khnum's divine function was to fashion men on the potter's wheel. Khnum working at the wheel is shown in many places all over ancient Egypt.

Additionally, workmen making pottery on the wheel, as shown in the illustration, is depicted throughout ancient Egyptian tombs.

• Egyptians were knowledgeable of the pulley as evident by the one found, and now displayed in the Leyden Museum. This pulley was probably intended for drawing water from a well, canal or the Nile.

Chemistry

• The Egyptians possessed considerable knowledge of chemistry and the use of metallic oxides. This is evident from the nature of the colors applied to their glass and porcelain. They were acquainted with the influence of acids upon color. In the process of dyeing or staining cloth, they were able to bring about certain changes in the hues, by the same means adopted in modern times.

• The beautiful colors they obtained from copper, and the composition of various metals, attest to their knowledge in this subject.

Metallurgy

• Metallurgy is the science and technology of metals. Properties of the different materials were known to them, as evidenced by their ability to use the right metallic tool to work on other bodies or surfaces.

• Their knowledge of metal ductibility is evident in their ability to manufacture wires. Silver wires were found in the tomb of Twthomosis III, and gold wires were found, attached to rings bearing the name of Osirtasen I, who lived 600 years before Twthomosis III.

Gold thread and wire were the result of wire-drawing, and there is no instance of them being flattened.

Wire-drawing was first attempted, by them, with the most ductile metals such as gold and silver before brass and iron.

• The Egyptians perfected the art of making the thread from metals. It was sufficiently fine for weaving into cloth, and for ornamentation; as evident in some of Amasis delicate linen, on which numerous figures of animals were worked in gold threads, which required a great degree of fineness.

• Cutting glass and hard stone is a very precise work, which requires extensive knowledge of the properties of the material of the cutter, and the material to be cut or carved.

Pliny reported that Egyptians engraved emeralds and other hard stones. Although we do not know the precise method adopted by the Egyptians for cutting glass and hard stones, we may reasonably conclude that they were acquainted with the diamond, and adopted it for engraving purposes.

Emery powder and the lapidary's wheel were also used in Egypt; and there is little doubt that the Israelites learned the art of cutting and engraving stones in Egypt.

The art of cutting glass was known, to the ancient Egyptians, at the most remote periods as proven from the hieroglyphics and other inscriptions, being frequently engraved upon vases and beads. The specimens of ancient glass, cut, engraved, and ground, which were discovered in Egypt, suffice to prove the art was practiced there long before its supposed re-invention in the 17th century when Gaspar Lehmann, at Prague, obtained the patent from the Emperor Rodolph II.

Technology

Technology is by definition the technical method of achieving practical purposes. Most historians and scholars agree on the pragmatic and practical characteristics of the ancient Egyptian. Here are just glances, of some technological achievements.

- **The Yale Lock** In 1848 Linus Yale supposedly invented the compact cylinder pin-tumbler lock and his name became a generic term for this kind of lock. Yale's invention was a reinvention of the ancient Egyptian's pin-tumbler mechanism, commonly employed in the locks of their houses, thousands of years ago.

- The Egyptians invented the **bellow**, one of which is represented in the tomb of Twthomosis III. It consisted of a leather bag; secured and fitted into a frame, from which a long pipe extended for carrying the wind to the fire. Bellows were worked by the feet. From the painting, it was observed that when the man left the bellows unattended, they did not deflate; and, this would imply a **knowledge of the valve**.

• The **siphons** were also invented in Egypt, at least during the reign of Amunoph II (c. 1500 B.C.).

In a tomb at Thebes, bearing the name of Amunoph, one observes a priest pouring a liquid into some vases, and another priest drawing it off, by applying the siphon to his mouth, and then to a large vase. Similar scenes are shown again in the paintings in Ramses III's tomb.

Heron of Alexandria, a notable early writer, mentioned the Egyptian siphons. He lived under Ptolemy Euergetes II. Heron reported that siphons were employed as hydraulic machines on a grand scale, for draining lands, or conveying water over a hill from one valley to another.

The name, *siphon*, is derived from the word siph or sif, to *'ingest'*, or *'draw up with the breath'*, analogous to, and perhaps the origin of, the English *'to sip'*.

• They had also invented **syringes**, used for injecting liquids into the head and body of mummies, during the embalming process. There is also a similar instrument which is often represented in the sculptures of early times, and which has the appearance of a **portable pump**.

• Dikes were followed by, or accompanied by, the invention of **sluices, and all their operating mechanisms**. Sluices were essential in the regulation of the supply of water, to the fields. Much scientific skill was required to operate the sluice so as to release the prescribed quantity of water to the designated land.

They had to make precisee observations of the increase of the Nile elevation during the inundation season. Nilometers, for measuring the gradual rise and fall of the Nile, were constructed in various parts of Egypt, and water surface fluctuations were recorded and reported. The elevations at the Nilometers throughout Egypt were all tied to a single common datum. The mouths of the canals were closed until the river rose to a specific height, before opening the sluice to a determined height and duration.

Woodwork

- The technical skill of the Egyptian woodworker is evident in their boat-building and chariot-making. Both objects consist of small pieces built to withstand many internal and external stresses and strains in their use. As such, they must have been knowledgeable of the design properties of different woods, which led to the manufacture of durable and stable moving parts of the joinery.

- More than 4000 years ago, Egyptians had already invented and commonly used a form of **pole** to make chariots. This type of pole was first introduced into Europe in the early 1800s. Refer to Ahmed Osman's book, <u>Stranger in the Valley of the Kings</u>, to dispel previous views that the Hyksos introduced chariots to Egypt.

- Practically the only modern carpenter's tool which the Ancient Egyptian did not possess was the plane, but he could do such fine work with the adze, that he did not need the plane. Many examples of their carpenter tools have been found in Egyptian tombs: squares, levels, chisels, drills, horn of oil, nails, mallets, and saws which differ very little from their modern counterparts.

- Using glue in woodwork was a very early Egyptian invention. Several wooden boxes and coffins have been found, in which glue was employed to fasten the joints.

- A scribe wrote of a woodcarver:

Each artist who works with the chisel
Tires himself more than he who hoes [a field]
The wood is his field, of metal are his tools.
In the night—is he free?
He works more than his arms are able,
In the night—he lights a light.

Fabrics

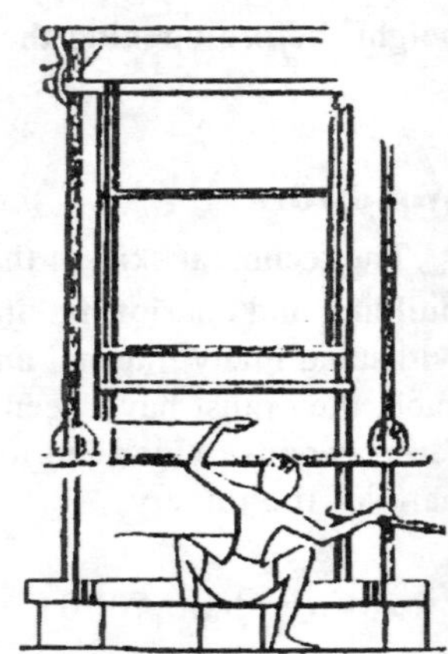

- There are some interesting examples of Egyptian weaver's looms and shuttles in the British Museum which are basically the same design as those used today, except that they were manually operated.

- The Egyptians were always celebrated for their manufacture of linen and other cloths, and the produce of their looms was exported to, and eagerly purchased by, foreign nations.

- The dye was unknown to Herodotus, for he made no mention of it. It was Pliny who noted the Egyptians' use of the dye. He did not know of its true nature, nor the history of its production. He, however, correctly described the most characteristic of its properties, which was the emission of a beautiful purple vapor when exposed to heat.

- The Egyptians were capable of dyeing their old clothes, to extend their use and beauty.

- The Egyptians had carpets, which were a very early invention. Homer, who mentioned them, gave them the same name which they are still known by, Tapeta, hence tapis and tapestry.

- The threads used for nets were remarkable for their fineness; and Pliny stated *"some of them were so delicate that they would pass through a man's ring, and a single person could carry a sufficient number of them to surround a whole [forest]."*

- Flax was used for making ropes, string, and various kinds of twine. The Egyptians excelled in rope making (necessary for the hauling of huge monuments). Specimens exist of rope made from palm fiber, five inches thick. These ropes are as strong and well made as any manufactured today.

Paper

- Paper making of papyrus has survived the ages (the true test). The preserved papyri in the less arid climate of Lower Egypt, still maintain their pliability; and as such they may be bent, and even twisted in any way, without breaking, or without being more injured than a piece of our common paper.

- The secret art of making this parchment was never revealed. In all the records and drawings found, not a single word or drawing discloses the method of the papyrus making process.

The Egyptian material was exported to all the surrounding areas. Indeed, today the records found of the Greek and Roman Empires, were preserved on Egyptian made paper.

The Egyptian word was **'Pa-pe-ra'**. The Greeks called it *'Papyrus'*. One can easily see that the English word *'paper'* came from the Egyptian **'pa-pe-ra'**.

Your dictionary will also confirm that the word *'Bible'* is of an Egyptian origin. The *'Bible'*, or book, was derived from *'byblos'*, which is the Egyptian hieratic word for papyrus.

Glass

- Ancient Egyptians were using glass, at least as early as the reign of the first Osirtasen, more than 4000 years ago; where the process of glass-blowing is represented in the paintings of his tomb, at Beni Hassan. Similar scenes are shown on later monuments throughout Egypt.

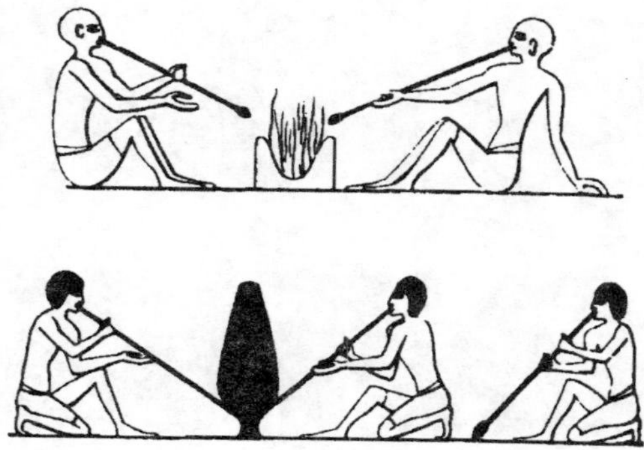

More about glass and glazing in the next chapter.

Leather

- The tanning and preparation of leather was also a branch of art in which the Egyptians showed considerable skill.

The process of curing and dyeing the skins, as well as stretching and bending leather over a form, are frequently represented at Thebes. The semicircular knife, similar to that of our modern times, was commonly used by the ancient Egyptians.

Shoes, or low boots, were common in Egypt. Many of them have been found at Thebes.

Chapter 45

Metals and Industry

General

• Metallurgy was defined earlier as the science and technology of metals.

At an early period, the Egyptians learned how to work metals, and by the beginning of the Dynastic Age they had developed the techniques of mining and refining; and went outside Egypt to acquire additional sources of supply.

• The tombs revealed many copper objects and tools, and an immense quantity of wonderfully crafted stone vessels, some of which were made from the hardest stone known. The walls show the process of working, melting, forging, soldering and chasing of metal.

• The skill of the Egyptians in compounding metals is abundantly proven by the vases, mirrors, and implements of bronze, discovered at Thebes, and other parts of Egypt. They adopted numerous methods for varying the composition of bronze, by a judicious mixture of alloys. They also had the secret of giving to bronze, or brass blades, a certain degree of elasticity; as evident in the dagger now housed in the Berlin Museum.

The science and technology to manufacture metallic products and goods were known and perfected in ancient Egypt. The industrial revolution was nothing more than mass production of previously invented and produced goods.

The upper pin, on which the door turned.

Lower pin.

• One of the interesting findings of ancient Egypt includes several vessels with bulbous bodies and long slender necks. The bodies have been hollowed out, leaving a uniform, very thin shell. The process or tool used to create these jars is still unknown.

- Gold, silver, copper, lead, iron, sulfur, emerald and other quartz mines have been discovered, in the desert near the Red Sea.

Glass & Glazing

- Some people have argued that glazing and many of the other crafts attributed to Egypt were not invented there, but naturally in Europe; and that they were brought over to Egypt over the course of the Hittite invasions!

For example, the burial chamber at the Step Pyramid of Saqqara is lined with beautiful blue tiles. Some decided that glazing of this type was unknown in Egypt, when the Step Pyramid was built during the Third Dynasty. In order to explain the presence of the tiles at the Step Pyramid, it was suggested, without any supporting evidence, that the tiles were set much later, during the Saite Dynasties (800-600 B.C.) when renovations were carried out.

It does not make sense that the Saites randomly chose this one location, in the whole of Egypt, to set the beautiful blue tiles.

Furthermore, the authors of the European origin theory chose to ignore or did not know about the contrary evidence to such an unfounded theory. The contrary evidence is located in the **Southern Tomb** (only 700 feet from the Step Pyramid) which was discovered at Saqqara by Lauer and Firth in 1924-26. It consists of several chambers lined with blue tiles exactly like the burial chambers of the Step Pyramid. It was apparently intended to hold the canopic jars, containing the viscera.

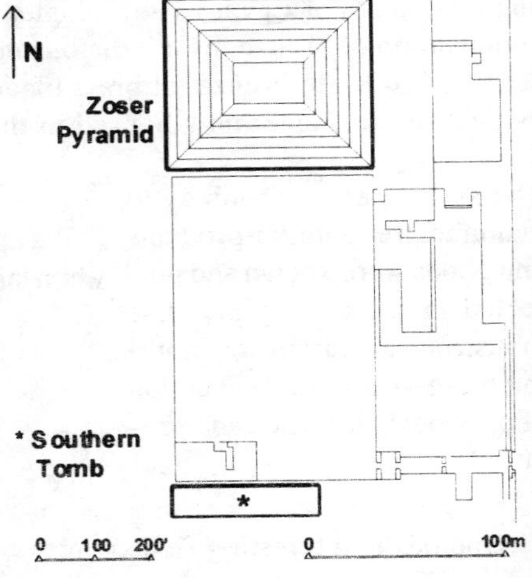

The **Southern Tomb** was found unmolested, by Lauer and Firth, and there is no evidence of later restorations or Saite intrusion!

- Glass bottles are shown on monuments of the Fourth Dynasty, more than 4000 years ago. The transparent substance shows the red wine they contained. Egyptian glass bottles, of various colors, were exported into other countries such as Greece, Etruria, and Rome.

- More than 3000 years ago, the Egyptians manufactured common glass items, such as beads and bottles of ordinary quality. They also developed the art of staining glass with diverse colors, as evident from the fragments found in the tombs of Thebes. Their skill in this complicated process, enabled them to imitate the rich brilliancy of precious stones. Some mock pearls have been so well counterfeited, that even now it is difficult with a strong lens to differentiate them from real pearls.
Pliny confirmed that they succeeded so completely in the imitation so as to render it *"difficult to distinguish false from real stones."*

- Glass-blowing is shown at the tombs of Ti (2465-2323 B.C.) at Saqqara, Beni Hassan (more than 4000 years ago) and other later tombs.

- Since glaze contains the same ingredients fused in the same manner as glass; glass making may therefore be attributed to the Egyptians even at a much earlier date. The hard glossy glaze is of the same quality as glass. The technique which was applied to the making of glass vessels was a natural development in the technique of glazing.

- Glazed articles appeared as early as the Pre-Dynastic Period. Glazed objects from this early time are mostly beads, with solid quartz or steatite being used as a core. Glazed solid quartz was in use until the end of the Middle Kingdom, mostly for beads, small amulets, and pendants and a few larger articles. Steatite was used for carving small objects like amulets and small figures of neterw, and it proved an ideal base for glazing. It does not disintegrate under heat. Glazed steatite objects are found throughout the Dynastic Period and it is by far the most common material for scarabs.

The same technique was used to mass-produce funerary equipment (amulets, shabti-figures) and house decoration (tiles, inlays of floral patterns).

• The precise method of glazing is uncertain, but the probability is that the glaze was applied, as a viscous fluid coating the object. Glaze and body material were then fused together by heating, giving the manufactured object its strength and coherence.

• The most common color of the glaze was blue, green, or greenish-blue. The color is the result of adding a copper compound.

• The ancient glass was formed by strongly heating quartz sand and natron with a small mixture of coloring agents such as a copper compound, or malachite to produce both green and blue glass. Cobalt, which would have been imported, was also used. After the ingredients were fused into a molten mass, the heating ceased when the mass reached the desired properties. As the mass cooled, it was poured into molds, rolled out into thin rods or canes, or other desired forms.

• Many glass ornaments, such as beads, have been found in tombs all over Egypt. It is interesting to know that a bead bearing the name of a Pharaoh who lived about 1450 B.C. was found to have the same specific gravity as the British crown glass. This is yet more evidence of the Egyptian knowledge of glass making.

• Glass mosaics were made of various parts, made at different times, and afterwards united by heat by means of a flux applied to them. Their glass mosaics have wonderful, brilliant colors.

• Glass is frequently found in what is commonly called Egyptian cloisonné-work, a term used to describe an inlay consisting of pieces of glass, faience, or stone set in metal cells - the cloisons - and fixed with cement. The process consisted of putting powdered glass in the cloison and applying enough heat to melt the powder until it became a compact mass. In the past, it was generally maintained that the Egyptians never produced true cloisonné-work, but recently this view has been contested based on found evidence.

Metal Working

A scribe wrote of a metal worker:

> ***I have never seen the smith as an ambassador,***

Or the goldsmith carry tidings;
Yet I have seen the smith at his work
At the mouth of his furnace,
His fingers were like crocodile [hide]
He stank more than the roe of fish....

Gold

- At the Middle Kingdom tombs of Beni Hassan, the scenes give a general indication of the goldsmith's trade. The process of washing the ore, smelting or fusing the metal with the help of the blow-pipe, and fashioning it for ornamental purposes, weighing it, recording of materials inventory, and other vocations of the goldsmith, are all represented, in these tombs.

- When the gold was not cast solid, it was flattened into a sheet of even thickness. Gold in sheet form was used to decorate wooden furniture. Thicker gold sheets were hammered directly on to the wood and fixed by small gold rivets. Thinner sheets were attached by an adhesive, probably glue, on a prepared base of plaster. Very fine sheets were used as a coating for statues, mummy masks, coffins, and other items. It was applied over a layer of plaster, but the nature of the adhesive used by the Egyptian craftsman has not been identified.

- The ability to work large masses of the material is shown in the 300 lb. gold coffin of Twtankhamen, at the Cairo Museum.

- Gold and silver were cast to make small statues in the same manner as copper and bronze.

Bronze

- Copper does not occur in its metallic state in Egypt. It was extracted from ores as early as the Pre-Dynastic Period, and was used for small articles like needles. A number of areas show traces of ancient mining and smelting both in the Eastern Desert and in Sinai.

- Before the introduction of tin, Egyptian copper was hardened by the addition of arsenic, which had to be imported. Arsenical copper was employed from the Early Dynastic Period right up to and including the Middle Kingdom, after which it was largely replaced by bronze.

• The addition of a small proportion of tin to copper produces bronze, and results in a lower melting-point, an increased hardness, and a greater ease in casting. The date of the introduction of bronze into Egypt is uncertain. The alloy was regularly used for tools and weapons until it was replaced by iron. Tin does not exist in Egypt and had to be imported.

• Many bronzes of a very early period have been found. A cylinder bearing the name of Papi, of the 6th Dynasty, showing clean cut lines as well as other bronze articles of the same period, indicates that the molding of bronze items dates to earlier than 2000 B.C.

• Copper, and later bronze, provided material for a wide range of tools and weapons. The personal weapons of the Egyptian soldiers included daggers, swords, and axes. The main weapon of the Egyptian infantryman was the battle-axe. In the Old and Middle Kingdoms, rounded and semicircular forms, of battle-axes, predominated.

• It is not known at what period they began to form statues and other objects in bronze, or how long the use of beaten copper preceded the art of casting in that metal.

• Finding figure subjects made of metal is relatively rare, before the Late Dynastic Period. The Palermo Stone records the making of a copper statue of Khasekhemwy of the Second Dynasty. A copper statue of Pepi I, of the Sixth Dynasty, is the earliest surviving example of metal sculpture, and is presently in the Cairo Museum. The precious nature of all metals in Egypt no doubt explains the rarity of early pieces, since much of the metal would eventually have been melted down and re-used several times.

The majority of discovered bronzes are reproduced figures of neterw, sacred animals, and emblems. They date, for the most part, from the Saite and Ptolemaic Periods.

• The color of their bronze depended on the utilized alloys. Yellow brass was a compound of zinc and copper. A white and finer kind had a mixture of silver, which was used for mirrors, and is also known as "Corinthian brass." Adding copper to the compound produced a yellow, almost gold, appearance.

Iron

• Iron and copper mines are found in the Egyptian desert, which were utilized in ancient times. Herodotus mentions iron tools being used by the builders of the pyramids. Herodotus' account is confirmed by the presence of found pieces of iron tools in various places embedded in old masonry from the Old Kingdom era. Also, the monuments of Thebes, and even the tombs around Memphis, dating more than 4000 years ago, represent butchers sharpening their knives on a round bar of metal attached to their apron, which from its blue color can only be steel. The distinction between the bronze and iron weapons in the tomb of Rameses III, one painted red, the other blue, leaves no doubt of both having been used at the same periods.

- The argument that because no iron instruments, or arms, bearing the names of early monarchs of a Pharaonic age were found, therefore only bronze was alone used, is incorrect. Iron tools can easily decompose especially when buried for ages in the nitrous soil of Egypt. The Greeks and Romans continued to make bronze articles of various kinds such as swords, daggers, spear-heads, other offensive weapons, and defensive armor, long after iron was known and used by them. Nothing should have stopped the Egyptians from using both metals, as the Greeks and Romans did.

- The discovery of Greek and Romans arms and tools, made of bronze, was never used to claim their ignorance of iron.

The Mysterious Tools

- The ancient Egyptians were able to sculpt and engrave many granite monuments, with a superb minuteness and finish which is impressive, to this day. To carve stone as hard as granite requires an extremely strong tool.

One wonders what type of tools were used, to sculpt the Statue of Chephren (at Cairo Museum) from diorite, the hardest known type of granite.

The beautifully executed hieroglyphics, carved several inches deep into the granite obelisks is another wonderment. How did they do it?

- There are many who insist that Egyptians were ignorant of steel and only knew of bronze. We presently do not know of a method to temper copper or unite it with other alloys, so as to provide the bronze that can sculpture or engrave the granite. The addition of tin or other metals to harden the bronze, if it exceeds a certain proportion, will make it too brittle for use.

- Even if we go along with bronze tools and nothing else, then we are confessing that their skill in metallurgy was far beyond our own knowledge and indirectly confess that they had devised a method of sculpturing stone of which we remain ignorant.

- Some claim that new granite being somewhat softer will require less labor. A somewhat softer granite is still very hard to handle with bronze tools. This opinion also ignores the fact that new sculptures were frequently added, 100-150 years after the erection of an obelisk. The new added lines of hieroglyphics on obelisks were found more deeply cut and more beautifully executed than those previously sculptured on the "softer" granite.

Jewelry

- To many people all over the world, gems possess magical qualities. Since magic is the profound understanding of cosmic resonances, it is therefore possible that each gem has a resonant physical property that we respond to. As an example, turquoise represented celestial joy. The neterw were called The Turquoise Ones, and mining turquoise was an elaborate and sacred task.

Jewelry had a profound and immensely complex symbolism, behind its decorative facade. Each stone, each metal, had its specific power, and the combinations of stones and metals as well as the shapes of the numerous rings, pendants, anklets, pectorals, all had their definite cosmological meanings.

Chapter 46

Art

General

• The Egyptian sculptures, friezes, and paintings are very carefully planned according to harmonic, geometric, and proportional laws. They are all testament to their knowledge, and to the mastery of their individual artists.

• The symbolic meanings of their work is totally lost to us. Their art was not meant to be seen by living eyes. This may seem to be useless and selfish art. Yet when we compare the artistic activities now and then, we find that a larger number of the citizens of ancient Egypt spent their lives utilizing and perfecting their human creative talents, as compared to our societies nowadays. In short, we just talk about creativity, whereas they delivered it.

• The artist is basically the main beneficiary of his/her art. The modern artist may share some of his private experiences in public, but most of his creative experience and satisfaction remains within. A true artist never seeks the glory, and he will be the first to be surprised by it, if it happens.

It may seem a total waste, in our modern eyes, to bury the results of art work in tombs. But from the point of view of the Egyptian artist, his reward was the exercise of his own talent. Self-fullfilment is the most important thing to an artist.

The Character of Egyptian Art

• Art, like anything in Egyptian life, was a part of the Master Plan of man and the universe. The Egyptians were able to reduce their universal environment into a rational and finite system. Accordingly, the art had a canon of proportion, to which it should conform. As a result, the ground plan and elevations of an Egyptian building reflected a particular and a meaningful mathematical order.

• The Egyptian art has its unique quality and charm. Its dominant feature is its humanity. The main subject is man and his many activities. The few colossal figures only magnify the heroic and beneficial qualities of divinities and kings, and not the horrific power of tyrants and demons. The seduction of sinister and hostile forces are reduced to intellectual and symbolic concepts.

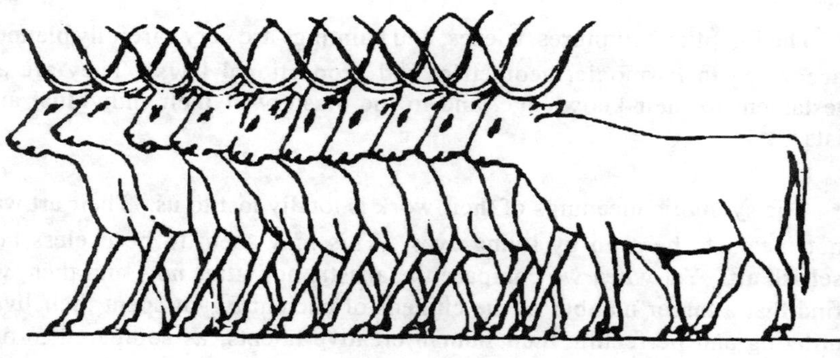

• Because religious and symbolic considerations were the primary objectives, the similarities between Egyptian sculptures and paintings are far more conspicuous than the differences. Nevertheless, art historians find many subtle differences, both in the attitude of individual artists and in their techniques.

• The Egyptian was highly conscious of the box-like structure, which is the model of the earth or the material world. Since the Middle Kingdom, the form of statuary, called the *"cube statue"* was initiated. The subject was integrated into the cubic form of the stone. In some of these cube statues, there is a powerful sense of the subject emerging from the prison of the cube. Its symbolic significance could possibly be that the spiritual principle is emerging from the material world.

The king is often shown sitting on a cubic throne or seat signifying the spiritual principle domination and triumph over the material.
Other tradifions, such as the Platonic and Pythagorean, adopted the same concept of the Egyptian cubic representation of the material world.

• The careful definition of the separate planes of this cubic universe is revealed, in an art which is essentially two dimensional. In order to represent three-dimensional objects on a plane surface, the Egyptians avoided the perspectival solution of the problem. That resulted in a two-dimensional profile with the exception of a few parts of the body, like the eyes and sometimes the horns. The Greek's vision of the natural world, as an image frozen at a certain moment in time, seems presumptuous, and concerned only with illusion, a mere distortion of reality, as far as the Egyptians are concerned. Many will agree with their view.

• The Egyptian artist presented, in his work, the idea of objects rather than their exact realization in a spatial context. Their creative artistic concept is similar to God's creative actions. As a result of God's Word (utterance), the world was created.

Similarly, every creative work of art, even a statue, has inscriptions describing the action or defining its purpose as well as the names of the actors.
Additionally each statue, painting, relief or building had to undergo on its completion the ritual of the **Opening of the Mouth** to ensure that it was transformed from an inanimate product of man's hands into a vibrant part of the divine order charged with numinous power.

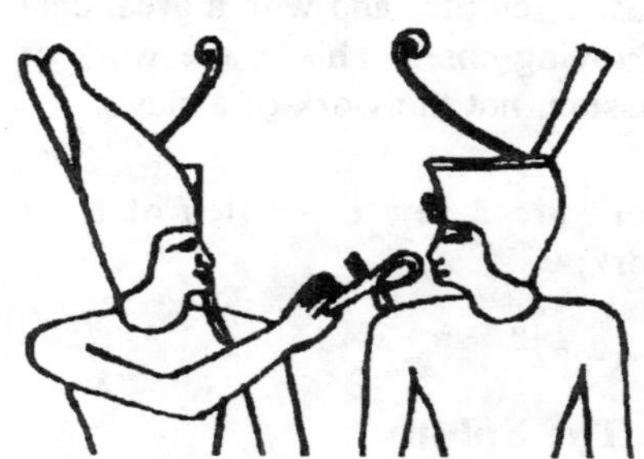

The Artists

• Names of some artists are shown on various art work. The ruins of some artists' studios have been recovered from archaeological excavations.

• In the workshops pictured in the Old Kingdom reliefs and the New

Kingdom wall paintings, craftsmen of different trades, from sculptors and metalworkers to joiners and jewelers, are shown working side by side.

- The chief designers, in earlier times, were the High Priests of Ptah of Memphis. They were taught the sacred art of ancient Egypt.

Sculpture

From the tomb of a sculptor (Twelfth Dynasty):

> **'I was an artist skilled in my art, pre-eminent in my learning....I knew [how to represent] the movements of the image of a man and the carriage of a woman...the poising of the arm to bring the hippopotamus low and the movements of the runner....'**

The ancient Egyptian sculptors achieved perfection in their work, and the shapes wrought were the complex, subtle forms of the human anatomy. The huge sculptures could only have been brought to life through the sensitive hand and watchful eye of a master sculptor and with a great deal of loving care. This is the work of passion, not the work of a slave.

Here are a few examples of their work:

- **The Sphinx**

If you happen to be among those who are "struck" by the Sphinx, this was the intention of its sculptors.

As an artistic synthesis, the Sphinx is a work of mastery, without parallel anywhere on earth. So perfect is the fusion of lion and human that it seems organic.

Read more about it under the chapter 'Sphinx - Older Than History'.

• The Statue of Chephren

This statue is generally acknowledged as one of the great masterpieces of world sculpture. In terms of technique and expressiveness, it would be a wonderous sculpture even if it were carved from some easily managed stone. But it is carved from diorite, the hardest known granite.

It is located at the Cairo Musuem.

• The Cross-Legged Seated Scribe Statue

One of these statues, with its lifelike eyes, gazing into eternity, is housed in the Cairo Musuem. The inlaid eyes of the statue, have excited the admiration of many, including scholars, sculptors, and physicians.

When photographs are taken, of this and other similar statues, the eyes actually look real. The Egyptologist Mariette recorded that when his workmen dug up the famous Seated Scribe, now in the Louvre, the eyes frightened them; they thought the statue was actually alive.

• The Fallen Colossus of Ramses II

The fallen colossus lies broken in several gigantic pieces, at the Mortuary Temple of Ramses II. It was originally carved out of a single block of granite weighing 1,000 tons (907 metric tons). The seated colossus was originally 60 feet (18 m) high, which was the largest statue in Egypt. The Sphinx is much bigger but it was carved, in-situ, out of the living rock.

The gigantic monolith was quarried in Aswan, where all the granite came from, transported several miles from the quarry to the river, lifted onto a boat or boats, then ferried to Thebes, offloaded, transported several miles to the temple, and, finally erected on the site.

The colossus was brought down, possibly as a result of the earthquake that shook Egypt in 27 B.C.

In pieces on the ground, the colossus is still an awesome scene, the ear is

3 1/2 feet (1.2 m) long, the circumference of the arm at the elbow is 17 1/2 feet (5.3 m), the index finger is 3 1/4 feet (1 m) long. The workmanship is superb.

- **The Colossi Of Memnon**

The Colossi stand over 60 feet (18m) high in the western bank of Thebes, and originally both had crowns and so were even taller.

They were carved from monoliths of a pebbly, quartzose sandstone. The sandstone is extremely difficult to work and at the same time highly porous and subject to relatively quick decay. In addition, it is not local to the area, but comes from Edfu, a hundred miles to the south.

Wall Reliefs

- Relief was of two kinds:

1- **raised relief** (bas-relief), in which the entire background was lowered, leaving the figures and inscriptions raised from the field.

In general, raised relief was used in work of high quality, and is usually found, on the interior walls, where the lighting is diffused.

Raised relief also exists in hard stones, particularly in the royal stelae of the Archaic Period.

2- **sunken relief** (relief en creux) in which the outlines are deeply engraved into the background, and the subject modeled within these contours.

Sunken relief was usually used on exterior walls, in strong sunlight. It also appears frequently on monuments, in granite, alabaster, quartzite and other hard stones in which the entire sinking of the background would have been difficult.

A development of sunken relief was the sinking of the background for a distance around the contours of subjects, and the tapering of it gradually to the surface of the stone. As such, less stone was removed from the field.

• Temples early in the New Kingdom have very shallow reliefs such as those of Hatshepsut's temple in Deir el Bahari. Later reliefs become increasingly more definite.

The reliefs at Abydos Temple, completed during the reign of Seti I are noticeably finer than those done by his son Ramesses II as he completed the temple.

The quality of work reached its peak in the last great temple of the age, the Temple of Medinet Habu built by Ramesses III, where some of the hieroglyphs are hammered ten inches deep into the stone.

Furniture

The best line of furniture can be seen at the Hetepheres room, at the Cairo Musuem. In the long history of the world, there is very little to match this furniture.
The contemporary feel of the Hetepheres furniture combines simplicity with sophistication.

Caricature

Egyptians were addicted to caricature. An idle moment was often occupied by making rough sketches on a piece of stone or on some other common material, frequently papyrus. Some papyri in the British and other museums show that even religious subjects were not exempt from caricature.

Jewelry

• Apart from gold and semi-precious stones, the materials used most often in Egyptian jewelry were glass and faience.

Their jewelry comprises a treasury of pieces, all beautiful, many breathtaking.

Read more about jewelry in the previous chapter.

The Overrated Amarna Art

It has been repeated that Akhenaten broke with tradition and initiated a new era of artistic realism and freedom. There is nothing realistic about his famous exaggerated colossi, located in the Cairo Museum. This is not realism as much as a form of high caricature.

The Amarna style was imposed throughout the land, and was followed by the artists and sculptors of the nation. As such, the new Amarna style was not free at all.

Epilogue

Chapter 47

Influence in Daily Life in the USA

Throughout this book, you may have noticed how ancient Egypt has achieved eternity by leaving lasting impressions on the daily life in the USA and the rest of the world.

The U.S. Dollar

The father of the USA, namely George Washington, was a mason. The masons of the world have always claimed that their rites, knowledge and traditions are rooted in Egypt. The U.S. reflects the masonic regard for the pyramid by displaying its picture on the back of the dollar bill. The pyramid is shown topped with the eye which is the sign of the neter (god) Re, representing the principle of light and vision.

The back of the U.S. Dollar bill

The Washington Monument

The capital city of the USA is mostly recognized by the Washington monument which is the shape of an Egyptian obelisk, the Egyptian solar symbol.

Obelisks can also be found as tombstones in U.S. cemeteries.

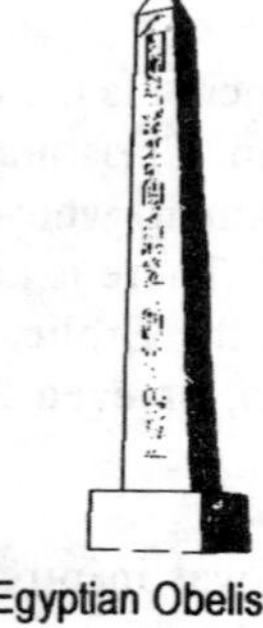

Egyptian Obelisk

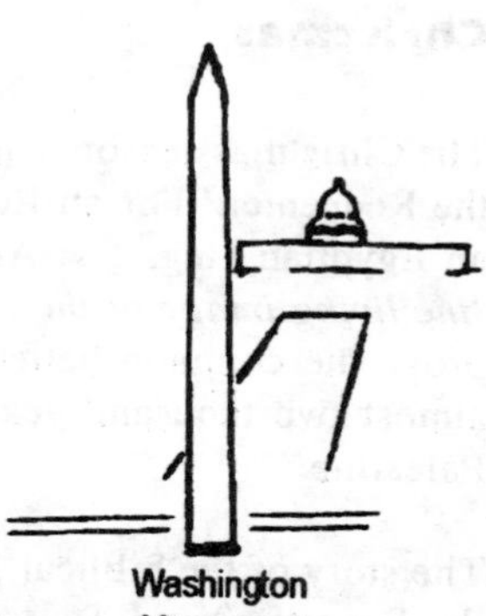

Washington Monument

U.S. Halls of Justice

Hatshepsut Temple
(1490-1468 B.C.)

1.) Both Federal and county court houses have the same features on the exteriors. They all have the "Doric" fluted style columns, which are purely Egyptian design, and were used in Egypt, at least 2000 years before Greece ever used them. Examples of this column design still stand in Saqqara, and other places throughout Egypt.

2.) The symbol of modern-day justice is a blind-folded lady, carrying a scale. The ancient Egyptian's symbol of justice was also a blind-folded lady, however the Egyptian lady is holding the emblem of truth, to emphasize the main concept of Justice: *'Search for the truth'*.
Next to the scale of Justice, she is shown in double form, representing the two opposing sides of the Litigation.

Christmas

The Christmas season's main theme is the celebration of the birth of Christ the Redeemer. For an Egyptian, Christmas is the birthday celebration, of an Egyptian king, Twt Ankh Amen, whose birth name, translated, means *'the living image of the Lord.'* There is no credible historical evidence to prove the common belief that the Biblical Jesus was born in Bethlehem almost two thousand years ago, or even that he lived and died in Israel/ Palestine.

The story of the biblical Jesus was inspired by the actual life and death of the Egyptian King Twt Ankh Amen.

Easter

Easter is the happiest day in the Christian calendar. Easter is and has been celebrated in Egypt for over five thousand years, and was initiated to celebrate the death, burial and disappearance of Osiris on Friday, and to celebrate his resurrection the following Sunday. The Christian Easter is a mirror image of the ancient Egyptian Easter in timing, details, theme, and objectives.

Amen

In the three religions of Judaism, Christianity and Islam, whenever the faithful pray, regardless of language, they always end their prayer by saying **Amen**. There is no linguistic translation for Amen, because it is a name and not a word. The dictionary, mistakenly indicated that the origin of this word (Amen) is from the Hebrew language. The origin of Amen is Egyptian, for Amen was the name of God. The Jews have learned about Amen during their sojourn in Egypt, which lasted for four generations. The name of Amen, which means *'the Hidden One'*, in ancient Egypt, has never died.

Words and Names

<u>Sir</u>: This word is pronounced as *s-a-r* and it means a *'man of rank or position'*. The exact same word, and its meaning, was used in Ancient Egypt as well as by the Hebrews.

<u>Sarah</u>: The feminine form of the word *s-a-r* is achieved, in the ancient Egyptian language, and other old languages in the region, by adding *'ah'* at the end of the word. Sarah means princess, or even queen, in ancient Egypt.

<u>Mary & Merry</u>: The consonant letters in this word are *'m'* and *'r'* and the sound of vowels vary slightly. The origin of the two words is Egyptian for they meant, in the ancient language, *beloved*. The name Miriam is a composite word (Meri-am) which in ancient Egypt meant *Beloved Mother*, the same as it means in Hebrew.

The Hebrews' sojourn in Egypt was greatly influenced by their host country, in all matters such as religions, names, languages, customs, etc.

The Cross, Christianity and Judaism

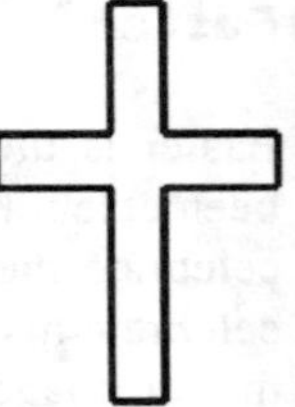

The cross is seen everywhere in Christian countries such as the USA. The shape of the cross is a slight modification of the Egyptian Ankh. The ankh is the emblem of eternal life.

The cross, as a representation of the alleged biblical crucification of the Messiah by the Romans, has absolutely no supporting historical facts.

The Egyptian ankh emblem was the symbol of early Christians in Egypt. It was later changed slightly, so as to disassociate themselves from the origin of their theology.

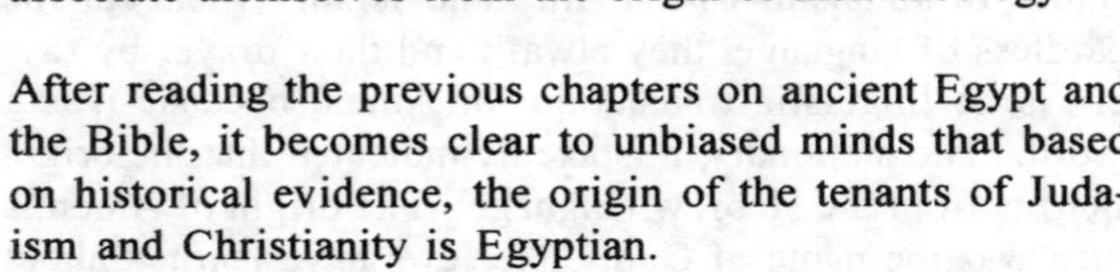

After reading the previous chapters on ancient Egypt and the Bible, it becomes clear to unbiased minds that based on historical evidence, the origin of the tenants of Judaism and Christianity is Egyptian.

Ballet

Ballet and many other fine arts were practiced in Egypt thousands of years ago, as shown on the walls of the various temples. Ballet, for example, is shown on the walls of the Luxor Temple and the tombs at Saqqara.

Medical Prescription

The origin of the Rx abbreviation, that doctors use all over the world, and in all languages, originated from the eye symbol of Horus. (Read more about it under the chapter, 'Health & Medicine').

"There Is No New Thing Under the Sun"

This phrase is attributed to Solomon, who was known for his wisdom. The story of the biblical Solomon is basically the story of the historical Pharaoh Amenhotep III. This wise phrase is echoed in our common saying: *'The more things change, the more they stay the same'*, and this is the truth.

BIBLIOGRAPHY

Aldred, Cyril. *Egyptian Art*. London, 1990.

Budge, Sir E.A. Wallis. *Egyptian Language, Easy Lessons in Egyptian Hieroglyphics*. New York, 1983.

Carter, Howard and A.C. Mace. *The Discovery of the Tomb of Tutankhamen*. New York, 1977.

Carter, Howard. *The Tomb of Tutankhamen*. Cassell, London, 1933.

Conder, C.R. *The Tell Amarna Tablets*. London, 1893.

Cottrell, Leonard. *Life Under the Pharaohs*. London, 1957.

Edwards, I.E.S. *Tutankhamun's Jewelry*. New York, 1976.

Erman, Adolf. *Life in Ancient Egypt*. New York, 1971.

Freud, Sigmund. *Moses and Monotheism*. London, 1951.

Gardiner, Alan. *Egypt of the Pharaohs*. Oxford, 1961.

Green, Roger L. *Tales of Ancient Egypt*. London, 1970.

H.M.N. *The Egyptian Prescription*. Cairo, 1988.

Herodotus. *The Histories*, tr. A. de Selincourt. New York and Harmondsworth, 1954.

James, T.G.H. *An Introduction to Ancient Egypt*. London, 1979.

Josephus, Flavius. *Against Apion*, tr. H. St J. Thackeray. London, 1926.

Kenyon, Kathleen M. *The Bible and Recent Archaeology*, rev. ed. by P.R.S. Moorey. London, 1987.

Lambelet, Edouard. *Gods and Goddesses in Ancient Egypt*. Cairo, 1986.

Lambelet, K. *How to Read Hieroglyphics*. Cairo, 1974.

Malek, Jaromir. *In the Shadow of the Pyramids, Egypt During the Old Kingdom*. Oklahoma, 1986.

Manniche, Lise. *Music and Musicians in Ancient Egypt*. London, 1991.

Massey, Gerald. *Ancient Egypt*. New York, 1970.

Montet, Pierre. *Eternal Egypt*, tr. Doreen Weightman. New York, 1964.

Murray, Margaret. *The Splendor That Was Egypt*. New York, 1972.

Museum of Cheops Boat. at Giza, Cairo, 1993.

Neubert, Otto. *Tutankhamun and the Valley of the Kings*. New York, 1977.

Osman, Ahmed. *The House of the Messiah*. London, 1994.

Osman, Ahmed. *Moses, Pharaoh of Egypt*. London, 1991.

Osman, Ahmed. *Stranger in the Valley of the Kings*. London, 1989.

Parkinson, R.B. *Voices From Ancient Egypt, An Anthology of Middle Kingdom Writings*. London, 1991.

Polano, H. *Selections from the Talmud*. London, 1894

Reeves, Carole. *Egyptian Medicine*. Great Britain, 1992.

Romant, Bernard. *Life in Egypt in Ancient Times*. Italy, 1986.

Silverman, David P. *Language and Writing in Ancient Egypt*. Pittsburgh, 1990.

Stewart, Desmond. *The Pyramids and Sphinx, Egypt Under the Pharaohs*. New York, 1977.

Wagner, N.E. *Abraham and David*. Toronto, 1972.

Wagner, N.E. *Studies on the Ancient Palestinian World*. Toronto, 1972.

West, John A. *The Travelers Key to Ancient Egypt*. New York, 1989.

Wilkinson, Sir J. Gardner. *The Ancient Egyptians, Their Life and Customs*. London, 1988.

Yadin, Yigael. *Hazor*. London, 1975.

————. *The Egyptian Book of the Dead*. New York, 1967.

————. *Jewish Encyclopedia*, managing editor Isidore Singer. New York and London, 1904.

INDEX

About the Author

Moustafa Gadalla was born in Cairo in 1944. He graduated from Cairo University with a Bachelor of Science in civil engineering in 1967. He immigrated to the U.S.A. in 1971 and continued to practice engineering as a Licensed Professional Engineer and land surveyor. He is an independent Egyptologist who spent most of his adult life studying, researching scores of books about Egyptology, mythology, religions, the Bible, languages, etc. He often lectures and writes articles about ancient Egypt. He spends a few months of every year in Egypt visiting and studying sites of antiquities.

As an engineer by training and practice, he approaches the issue analytically, logically and writes the findings and conclusions in a rational and clear manner.

Ordering Information

Ordering information may be obtained from Bastet Publishing:

Head Office:

P.O. Box 7234
Erie, PA 16510
U.S.A.
Tel: 814 - 899 - 0346
Fax: 814 - 898 - 1827
email: ushorus@aol.com

Egypt Office:

c/o Hani Mansi
2 Street 261
New Maadi 11742
Cairo
Tel : 352 1255
Fax : same